THE
ICE CREAM BLONDE

The Whirlwind Life and Mysterious Death of Screwball Comedienne **Thelma Todd**

Michelle Morgan

CHICAGO REVIEW PRESS

An A Cappella Book

Published by Chicago Review Press Incorporated
814 North Franklin Street
Chicago, Illinois 60610
ISBN 978-1-61373-038-6

Library of Congress Cataloging-in-Publication Data
Morgan, Michelle, 1970–
  The ice cream blonde : the whirlwind life and mysterious death of screwball comedienne
Thelma Todd / Michelle Morgan.
      pages cm
  Summary: "This authoritative biography traces the life of beloved film comedienne
Thelma Todd, who worked alongside the Marx Brothers, Laurel and Hardy, and dozens
of others, and offers fresh evidence regarding Todd's mysterious death at age twenty-nine,
arguing what many people have long suspected: that Thelma was murdered"— Provided by
publisher.
  Includes bibliographical references and index.
  ISBN 978-1-61373-038-6 (hardback)
  1. Todd, Thelma, 1905–1935. 2. Actors—United States—Biography. I. Title.

  PN2287.T575M68 2015
  791.4302'8092—dc23
  [B]
                          2015029269

Interior design: Jonathan Hahn

Printed in the United States of America
5 4 3 2 1

For my husband, Richard.
He has been there since the very beginning of my
writing journey and has always believed in me,
even when I didn't believe in myself.

And to the memory of Joyce and James Brubaker,
who inspired me so much at the beginning of this project.

CONTENTS

ACKNOWLEDGMENTS

This biography has taken nearly five years to research and write, and during that time I have been helped by a great many people who have provided information, given advice, and generally kept my spirits up. I would like to thank each and every person who has been involved in the project—particularly the following:

Christina Rice, a wonderful author and dear friend. She provided me with a great many articles and has continued to be a source of help and inspiration. This book could not have been written without her.

The staff of the following have all been wonderful: the Santa Monica Public Library (Kathy Lo), the Glasgow Library (Olga MacGregor), the Boston Library (Diane Parks), the Lawrence Library (Louise Sandberg), the Lawrence History Center (Amita Kiley and Jenn Williams), the Academy of Motion Picture Arts and Sciences (Faye Thompson), Arizona State University, and the Library of Congress (Arlene Balkansky). Arlene, it should be said, has been absolutely incredible. I am very grateful for the research she carried out for me.

Leland Petty provided me with some interesting television programs about Thelma. Mortician Katy King answered some questions about Thelma's death. Bruce McAlpine allowed me the use of his excellent Thelma Todd home movie. Benny Drinnon provided me with some very important papers from the FBI files and allowed me access to his private correspondence with Rudy Schafer Jr. Michael G. Ankerich provided me with some fantastic photos and shared an interview he did with Lee Heidorn. Phil S. Dockter sent me some beautiful photos and newspaper articles. Adam Tunney shared his memories of touring the Sidewalk Café building.

Thanks must also go to Tegan Summer, Ellen Poulsen, Laurie Jacobson, Marvin Wolf, Katherine Mader, Michael Williams, Martin Turnbull, Dave Stevenson, and Craig Calman, who either answered some specific questions or provided information.

Joyce and Jim Brubaker were supportive of this project from the very beginning and graciously shared some photographs from their collection, along with thoughts on Thelma's death. I am so sad that they are not here to see the fruits of my labor. Don Gallery and his lovely wife, Patricia, were very gracious and gave me a long, thoughtful interview. The family of Mae Whitehead gave me some very interesting pieces of information about Thelma and Mae. Jill and Kip Adams were extremely kind and trekked up the hillside to the garage where Thelma passed away. They and their family provided me with photos for my research and answered many questions.

Paulist Productions has been wonderful and very patient with my questions. I would like to particularly thank Joseph Kim and Mark Ortiz for their generosity and time.

My agent, Robert Smith, never gave up on this project, even when the going got tough. Thanks also to Lisa Reardon and Devon Freeny, my editors at Chicago Review Press, and copyeditor Cathy Bernardy Jones.

I would like to thank my friends and family—especially Mum, Dad, Paul, Wendy, and Angelina—for always being there for me.

Finally, my husband, Richard, and daughter, Daisy, have been (as always) fantastic. Without their love and support, I would never be able to do the job I do. I am forever grateful and lucky to have them both in my life.

THE BODY IN THE GARAGE

*I*t had been a cold weekend in Los Angeles, with temperatures dipping to twenty-five degrees Fahrenheit and winds sweeping across the region. Weathermen warned of possible early morning frost the following Monday, December 16, 1935. By 10 AM that day the gales had calmed, but as Mae Whitehead left her home on West Thirty-Sixth Place, there was still a nip in the air.

Mae had been Thelma Todd's maid and right-hand woman since 1931. She would always insist that the world-famous actress was wonderful to work for. Mae had seen her employer go through some turbulent times, including the breakup of her marriage and various other dramas. The past year, in particular, had brought a long string of stressful events, and as Mae drove across town toward the Pacific Ocean, she was well aware that 1935 was one year Thelma would be anxious to put behind her.

The housekeeper turned onto the quiet residential streets that led to number 17531 Posetano Road, where Thelma's garage was located. Actually, although the actress had full access to the building, it belonged not to her but to her business partner, film director Roland West, and his estranged wife, Jewel Carmen. The couple owned the home nestled in the hill above the garage, though in recent times part of the sprawling mansion was occupied by café manager Rudy Schafer and his wife, Alberta (Jewel Carmen's sister). Jewel was now living elsewhere, and Roland spent more than the odd night in the apartment above the Sidewalk Café—the business he and Thelma operated down the hill.

The official reason for West staying above the café was simple: he worked late, and by the time the venue closed, it was just simpler for him to spend the night in the room upstairs. This was all well and good, except that in recent months Thelma had also moved in, and their bedrooms were separated only by a sliding wooden door. Some raised their eyebrows on hearing of this arrangement, but as far as Mae Whitehead was concerned, it was none of her business.

It was Mae's habit to drive her own car to the garage where Thelma's 1932 Lincoln phaeton was located. Once there she would take Thelma's car out of the stall, leave her own vehicle inside, and then drive down the hill to the café in the phaeton, parking it at the front of the building so that Thelma had access to it during the day. This was a ritual developed because of Thelma's distaste for walking and especially for trudging up and down the 271 hillside steps that went from the café to the garage. In fact she loathed it so much that on most evenings she would ask Bob Anderson, one of her young café employees, to take the car back up to the garage for her when she was done using it for the day. Anderson later explained his job to the coroner.

By the time the housekeeper arrived at the garage that Monday, it was 10:30 AM and all was quiet, except for the distant lapping of the Pacific Ocean two blocks away. The garage doors were unlocked, as they always were, a lapse of security that mystified most people. In fact, both Thelma's Lincoln and West's Hupmobile coupe were always, without exception, left with their keys in the ignition.

Mae slid open the door and made her way to Thelma's car on the right side of the garage (the left was reserved for West's vehicle). She approached on the passenger side so that she could load in the bundles of clothing and various other items she was bringing to her employer that day. At that point she noticed nothing out of the ordinary: no smell, no heat, no noise. In fact nothing at all prepared her for the sight that was about to greet her.

When Mae opened the passenger door, there was beautiful Thelma Todd, her eyes closed, still wearing the blue dress she had worn two evenings before, when she left for a party at the Trocadero nightclub.

"She was slumped in the front seat of her car," Mae later told detectives. "Just bent over, her head to the left."

Mae could see that Thelma's hair was still styled in tight curls and her clothing immaculate. She was wearing a fur coat, and on the seat next to her was a white evening bag. Everything appeared eerily calm, and no evidence of foul play was anywhere around. Even though Mae had never found her employer asleep at the wheel before, in those first shocking moments she believed that this must be the case. "I went around to the left side of the car—the driver's side—and I thought I could awaken her, that she was asleep," she later said.

At that point, Mae noticed the driver's door was open. She took a good look at Thelma and noticed a small amount of blood around her nose. With her head slumped onto her chest, she was not lying down exactly but certainly not upright. Her arms were placed in her lap, and her feet hung down toward the floor.

From where Mae stood, it now became frightfully apparent that Thelma was not asleep as she had first thought, and no amount of prompting was ever going to wake her up. She left immediately for the café to raise the alarm.

Roland West was asleep in his quarters above the Sidewalk Café. It had been a long, sleepless night, and at five or six in the morning, his body had finally succumbed to exhaustion. Now, shortly after 10:30 AM, the phone was ringing incessantly.

Shaking himself awake, West lifted the heavy receiver to his ear. He listened for a few moments to the voice of café treasurer Charles Harry Smith, who told him that Mae Whitehead had come down from the garage and reported something was terribly wrong with Miss Todd.

"What's wrong with her?" asked West.

"Mae thinks she is dead," came the reply.

The words must have hung in the air like thick fog, as West pulled on his trousers, shirt, and coat. Hurrying downstairs, he was met by Mae, who quickly blurted out what she had seen. The pair dove into her car and roared up the hill toward the garage.

Distraught, the maid missed the road she was supposed to go down and was forced to turn back. At this point, one of the café employees was coming down the hill and noticed the car and the state of the occupants inside. "He thought [Mae] was taking me to the doctor, because I was as white as a sheet," West later explained. Eventually Mae and Roland arrived at the garage, and the director went to see for himself what had happened inside. He instructed Mae to go up to his main house to alert Rudy and Alberta Schafer.

When West entered the garage, he saw the actress lying silently in the car. Instinctively he reached out to touch her face, and as he did so, he noticed what he later described as several drops of blood near her nose. Moments later the Schafers arrived at the garage, flushed and in an obvious state of disbelief. Both approached the Lincoln phaeton, where Rudy Schafer touched Thelma's cheek and confirmed that she had most certainly passed away. He too noticed blood, only his recollection would be that it was all over her mouth and ran down onto the seat where she was slumped. Some of it was wiped off with a handkerchief.

Did he notice anything that would indicate she had been sick? "Well, I tell you," he explained to the coroner, "at that time it was hard to determine, because the blood was all over her mouth. Any other evidence, there was none."

Schafer left to telephone both the police and a doctor. However, rather than phone from his house just up the hill from the garage, Schafer decided to drive into town instead, using Roland West's car. "I thought I would go into West Los Angeles in order to eliminate any publicity right away, until we found out what it was all about," he explained to the coroner. However, he ended up stopping slightly closer to home. "While I was going into Santa Monica I stopped in the printing shop up there and went into their private office and made the call—called West Los Angeles."

Left in the garage with Alberta Schafer, West got into the car and looked around. He examined the ignition switch, noted that it was in the on position, got out, walked up and down, went back to the car, and looked at Thelma once again. Later he told the coroner's inquest that at that point he became certain she had been trying to get out of the car when she died. "I know that, because otherwise she would not have been turned in the way she did, and the door would not have been open," he said.

Once Rudy Schafer made his phone call, he returned to the café and waited for the police to show up. When officers arrived, he then led them up the hill, and a short while later the once-quiet garage on Posetano was surrounded by police, photographers, reporters, and hangers-on. They were all present by the time Thelma's friend Harvey Priester arrived with Todd's mother in tow. He had heard the news while in a bank in Hollywood and rushed to Alice Todd's house immediately—just beating Mae Whitehead, who had been sent there by West. In a state of shock and despair, Alice made her way toward the garage to see Thelma for herself. As she reached the door of the building she turned to those present. "My daughter was murdered," she said firmly, and then disappeared inside.

1

LAWRENCE'S LUCKY GIRL

Thelma Todd would never have been born were it not for two families deciding to pull up stakes and move all their worldly possessions to America. John Todd had moved to the city of Lawrence, Massachusetts, from Ireland with his parents and brothers and sisters in 1883, when he was merely a child. Alice Edwards had been born in Canada before immigrating to the United States in 1895, when she was nineteen years old.

Several years after moving to America, Alice met John, who was by that time working for the Thomas O'Callaghan & Co. carpet store in Boston, which specialized in fine carpets, oil cloths, rugs, and mattings. It was a good job with a well-respected company, and the young man spent his time learning the arts of carpet renovating and upholstery. After they dated for a while, John proposed. The young woman said yes.

On the evening of June 20, 1900, the couple stood in the front parlor of the groom's father's house in Lawrence, almost thirty miles from Boston, and exchanged vows before family and friends. The pastor of the city's South Congregational Church looked on as the bride, dressed in a white silk gown with satin trim, clutched a bouquet of roses and promised to love her husband until death parted them.

After returning from their honeymoon, they settled into a house in Boston, where John resumed working at Thomas O'Callaghan's and

Alice set about making their new abode into a home. They did not stay in Boston long, however, soon moving to Lawrence to be near John's family. There, the young man went into business as a carpet restorer, and he and Alice became active members of the church. John also joined the Lawrence Elks Lodge, and together the couple became valued members of the local community.

On July 27, 1903, they welcomed their first child, a son named William, and then three years later, on July 29, 1906, came a much-loved daughter, Thelma Alice. Her uncle Alex later described Thelma as "always a very happy, healthy child. She managed to evade the various illnesses that most children have." Alice was a broad, almost matronly woman, but Thelma seemed to be the opposite, skinny with blonde, curly hair that quickly grew down her back. As she toddled around the house, relatives would comment frequently on the likeness between her and John, and she seemed to bring fun and laughter wherever she went.

The family wasn't particularly rich, but the children didn't want for anything. They had friends to play with, were surrounded by a mixture of uncles, aunts, and cousins, and had a stay-at-home mother to look after them both. Later, during one of the few times Thelma ever spoke about her early family life, she told friend and reporter Catherine Hunter, "I was fortunate in having a mother and father who were genuinely in love."

In the summer of 1910, Alice took the children to Randolph, Vermont, to visit family there. It was a fun trip, and they were due to return to Lawrence on August 26, in time for the start of school. During the vacation, seven-year-old William became fascinated by the machinery at the local creamery. On most days the workmen were there to shoo him away or make sure he came to no harm. But the day before the family was due to leave, he found himself at the establishment again, only this time without the presence of staff.

With no adults present to tell him that he was acting recklessly, William decided to investigate the creamery machine, standing too close with his coat dangling dangerously into the equipment. Within a matter of seconds his clothing got tangled in the shafting, pulling him into the machinery. The young boy was whirled around and mangled. As soon as the family learned what had happened, a doctor was called, but with a fractured skull and neck, there was no way to save him. William Todd passed away on August 25, 1910, less than a month after his seventh birthday.

From Vermont, Alice sent a telegram to her husband, and the shocked man left Lawrence immediately. Reporters descended on the homes of various Todd family members, who told them that the boy had been "bright and winsome" and always seemed to radiate sunshine. Staff at the Saunders School, where William attended, told reporters that he had been a favorite student at the school and they would miss him greatly. The body of Alice and John's son was brought back to Lawrence. His funeral procession left from John's parents' home at 22 Bowdoin Street, and the boy was buried at the Bellevue Cemetery on August 28, 1910.

Tragically, while no mention was made of it in the death record or in the newspapers at the time, four-year-old Thelma had actually been with William at the time of the accident, and it was most likely she who had run to get help. Her presence was confirmed in 1932 during an interview with her friend Catherine Hunter, after which the reporter wrote that William "was crushed beyond recognition before [Thelma's] very eyes." The young girl had adored her older brother, and the two went everywhere together. She later described this close bond to reporter Gladys Hall: "I can remember William saying to my mother, 'Ma, dress Thelma up pretty so I can take her out and show her off to the boys. . . .' I had long golden curls and things."

After the death of her brother, Thelma's once carefree existence was now darkened by her parents' grief over the loss of their firstborn child. Childhood friend Edna Hamel recalled that certain people in Lawrence actually blamed John Todd for his son's death, even though he was back in Massachusetts when it happened. Perhaps the mere fact that he had let his wife and children travel alone was enough for some observers to assign blame. Such finger-pointing must have been devastating; Thelma later told Hall that there were many times when she could hear her dad crying out in despair, "Why did it have to be him?"

The young girl quickly made up her mind that perhaps if she were more like William, her parents would not be in so much pain. From that moment on, Thelma attempted to play the role of both son and daughter. She started going out wearing what one observer described as "bloomers and middies," while other young girls in the neighborhood were dressed in frilly gowns and lace bonnets. Picnics were abandoned in favor of making mud pies, jump ropes gave way to hiking boots, and pushing a doll's baby carriage was nothing compared to the thrill she felt when racing around on a boy's bicycle. She joined a baseball team at age eight, walked for miles with her male companions, and would think nothing of jumping into a pond to test her swimming skills. Of course all of these rough-and-tumble activities ensured that she frequently had scuffed knees and other injuries, but the young girl didn't care. If she could see a smile on her father's otherwise desperate face, she was happy, bruises and all.

By 1912, John Todd had garnered enough positive regard in Lawrence that he was elected as an alderman. He was then assigned to the Department of Public Health and Charities and acted as superintendent of the city home, a poorhouse of sorts, and worked tirelessly for the community for the next two years. When he failed to be reelected in 1914, Todd became the superintendent of streets.

During his time in office, John Todd was required to do public speaking and attend many meetings. This ability to speak for and care about people rubbed off on his daughter, and around this time Thelma, who previously had toyed with the idea of becoming a teacher, told her family she would like to be a lawyer or an engineer.

Just like her brother, Thelma attended the Saunders School; she later moved on to Packard Grammar School. She continued her determination to be more "boylike" but refused to cut her hair. As a result, it grew down to her waist in soft, golden curls that made her mother so proud that she invented her own hair-care regimen for it from two beaten eggs.

Before long, the girl who wanted desperately to be one of the boys was now becoming popular with them for other reasons—chiefly because she possessed a charm and grace that never failed to win them over. By the age of twelve Thelma was never without a young man desperate to carry her books to school or accompany her to a local dance. The boys' romantic requests, however, fell on deaf ears, and she was often overhead telling the young lotharios that despite their feelings, she thought of them as friends and brothers, certainly not boyfriends.

By the time Thelma entered Lawrence High School, she was not only a popular pupil but a very outspoken one too. She prided herself on the fact that she wasn't easily taken in by people and always stood up for what she believed in. Several years later during one of her first press interviews, Thelma described her attitude as follows: "I hate people who are not natural, I hate people who are stuck up, and I hate hypocrites. Aside from that I get along with everybody." The young woman was popular with teachers too and did well in nearly all her classes. She excelled in playing piano, and because of her confident nature, she became known as a good leader and a school role model.

Fellow students described her as modest, if ever so slightly old-fashioned. Years later, high school friend Grace Fallon told the *Boston Post*, "She was a regular girl and a perfect companion." She went on to describe Thelma as forever jolly and of a good temperament. This observation seems to have been shared by just about anyone who met Thelma throughout her life.

She did still have a reputation for putting barriers between herself and potential boyfriends—so much so that she would wait until the age of eighteen before she'd let a boy kiss her. (She reinforced this attitude as an adult when she said, "I'd kill a man who started to neck with me.") The stance proved to be fine with her father, who was extremely strict about who Thelma should be seen with. Any potential suitors brave enough to knock on the Todd door would be met by the stern John Todd, who made a point of being thoroughly introduced before they were allowed anywhere near his daughter.

That didn't mean Thelma stayed totally out of trouble. Once, Thelma and a male friend decided to enter a car race at the county fair. With her friend driving and Thelma by his side, they arrived at the track and took a few practice runs. The experience went no further when they came face to face with their parents standing on the sidelines. Alice and John were so angry, the story goes, that they spanked the teenager right there on the track.

But most of Thelma's ventures were tamer. She, Grace Fallon, and other friends created a school social club. On the school newspaper, she contributed small items to the gossip column. When the members of the staff were photographed, the boys all dressed similarly, in shirts, ties, and jackets, while the girls wore plain uniforms. The only girl who stood out from the crowd was Thelma, wearing a gingham dress, hair piled on top of her head, and smiling broadly for the camera.

Thelma took an interest in almost everything Lawrence High had to offer, including dance classes, public speaking, and singing, of which John Todd was particularly proud. "It was her father's greatest pleasure to have his daughter sing for him," her uncle Alex later said. His favorite songs included "Roses of Picardy" and "Love's Old Sweet Song."

Thelma was interested in acting too, and she took part in various school productions. On May 4, 1923, she acted in a play at Lawrence City Hall called *Lavender and Old Lace*, under the direction of her dance teacher, Teresa Sheridan. Away from school, she enjoyed going to the cinema and often headed to the Broadway Theatre, where manager Jim Carney would greet her, take her nickel, and allow her inside. Once seated, Thelma would become besotted with what was taking place on the screen.

Although the silent movie industry had had its fair share of doubters in the beginning, by 1923 it was in full flourish, and the kinds of films Thelma would have watched at the theater included *Adam's Rib*, directed by the legendary Cecil B. DeMille; *The Hunchback of Notre Dame*, starring Lon Chaney; and *Three Wise Fools*, directed by King Vidor. Stars included such heavyweights as Harold Lloyd, Buster Keaton, Charlie Chaplin, and Mabel Normand. Years later during a trip back home to Lawrence, Thelma would stand on the Broadway Theatre stage and tell the audience that in all the times she had visited the cinema, she never dreamed that her own movie would play there one day.

After she became famous, several friends came forward to say that even though Thelma was a keen cinemagoer, she had never harbored any ambitions to become a professional actress. In fact, classmate Helen Pierce remembered that Thelma was actually quite scornful of movie stars. This attitude probably came about because of several highly publicized scandals buzzing around Hollywood at the time Thelma frequented the Broadway Theatre. This included the 1921–22 manslaughter trials of funnyman Roscoe "Fatty" Arbuckle, who was accused of raping and killing actress Virginia Rappe during a party in San Francisco. After two hung juries, he was finally acquitted, but by then his entire life had been ripped to shreds by the media and his career had been ruined. Around the same time, director William Desmond Taylor was found shot to death in his Los Angeles home, with actresses Mabel Normand and Mary Miles Minter seen by some as suspects in his death. With scandals such as these going on, it is little wonder that she openly complained, as Helen Pierce recalled, that no amount of fame could ever bring happiness.

In spite of Thelma's own protestations, it must have been clear to others that she enjoyed performing, at least as an amateur, and some saw professional success in her future. In a Lawrence High School yearbook section titled "Prophecy of the Class of 1923," a classmate of Thelma's predicted that they would one day see Thelma on the screen at the Empire Theatre, "her blonde beauty outstanding, with her dashing leading man." Another student did not mention any such ambition but did note her strengths: "Thelma Todd leaves to the class of 1923, her beauty and her independence," she wrote.

After graduating from high school, Thelma took various modeling and dancing jobs. In October 1923, she was sitting at home on a rainy evening, bored and looking for something to do. Dressed in her red gingham dress, the young woman decided on the spur of the moment to head out for a drink at the local drugstore. While she was quietly drinking her soda, she became aware that two people nearby were talking about her. The couple in question were a Mr. and Mrs. Fredericks, who were about to put on a fashion revue at a local theater.

"There's just the girl to lead our revue," exclaimed Mr. Fredericks, loud enough that she could hear. His fawning did not impress Thelma, as she had no idea what he was talking about. She finished her drink and left.

"Mrs. Fredericks followed me up the street and asked me if I would be in the show," Thelma later recalled. "I said maybe, and I was wishing that I didn't have on such a funny looking gingham dress!" But, funny dress or no, Mrs. Fredericks wanted Thelma, so the young woman ran home and got permission from her parents to take part. When she eventually took to the stage, she was a big success, and the work netted her $20 in gold, a pair of shoes from the Twentieth Century Store, and a three-month free membership at the theater.

In April 1924, Thelma took part in another event, this time as part of a vaudeville show at the Empire Theatre, during which she modeled a variety of jackets, neck pieces, and wraps as part of the "Fur Fashion Review of 1924." Other entertainers on hand during the evening included dancers, acrobats, successful comedian Tommy Levene, and singer Arthur Huskins. The show ended with a screening of the movie *In Search of a Thrill*, starring Viola Dana.

The same year, Thelma reportedly won a small role in her first film, a local production called *The Life of St. Genevieve*. It was produced by Rosario and Peter Contarino, brothers who had bought an old movie camera, borrowed some cash, and created Aurora Film Inc. Together they ran amateur nights in Lawrence, which enabled them to spot talent for their movies, and it was because she attended one of these events that Thelma was ultimately given a role in *The Life of St. Genevieve*. It seems she did well enough in the part that she was cast in their next film, *Tangled Hearts*, too. Unfortunately, no prints of either film are known to exist, so it is hard to determine just how big her roles were in either production. They are believed to be minimal; when *The Life of St. Genevieve* was advertised in the local press, the ads failed to mention her at all.

Modeling and acting were an exciting way to earn money, but Thelma sought out more traditional employment as well. She obtained a job in a local drugstore but soon got bored and moved on to another position, this time as a salesgirl in a department store. This job was apparently even more troublesome; when she was assigned to work at the Christmas counter, she became mobbed by admirers on the first day. This would have been fine if not for the fact that they were all eager to admire Thelma but not so keen to spend money on the products she was selling. A grossly exaggerated version of events appeared later in a 1926 *American*

Weekly article, which explained that she was so popular with the young men that the manager had no option but to transfer her to the basement. There, the article claims, she was given the job of filling stockings with candy, but she was mobbed again, this time by young sales assistants desperate to discover what her beauty routine consisted of.

While the media may have embellished the story, it does seem to be true that she was eventually let go by the manager and went home in tears. So upset was Thelma that her father stormed to the shop to find out exactly why his daughter had been fired and was told that she was just too beautiful for the job. This was not the only time her beauty got in the way of an opportunity. Shortly after Thelma's death, a man named George W. Ashton told the story of how Thelma once had come into his shoe store to interview for a part-time job in the hosiery department. "I didn't hire her," he said. "But I didn't tell her why . . . she was just too beautiful."

Going on one year out of high school, Thelma started to think more carefully about her future. She enjoyed modeling and acting, but she was a sensible girl who doubted that she could make a career for herself in show business. It also seemed that her father was beginning to tire of the stream of entertainment jobs coming her way and wondered if she had any intention of settling down. Things came to a head when she was asked to work full time in a vaudeville show, similar to the one she had recently appeared in at the Empire. John Todd forbade his daughter to do it.

It was around this time, childhood friend Edna Hamel remembered, that Thelma's father became rather short-tempered with her—and at times even physically abusive. Indeed, photos taken at the time show her posing wildly for the camera while John Todd looks on, a grimace on his face registering his apparent disapproval. He was soon buoyed, however, when Thelma suddenly turned her attention to an idea she had flirted with several times during her childhood: that of becoming a respectable schoolteacher.

There is some disagreement as to when Thelma began her teacher training at Lowell Normal School, but it was most likely in the fall of 1924. Thelma settled into her studies in the same way she had at

Lawrence High, becoming a popular and valued member of the team. Over the years it has been said that Thelma became a full-fledged teacher during her time there, but this is not the case. As part of her studies, she student-taught history and English classes to six- and eight-year-olds, but she was never an accredited teacher.

That said, Thelma enjoyed the experience and thought caring for children in that age range was tremendously important. She later explained to author Frederick Russell, "They are the most interesting. Boys and girls at that age are just beginning to mold their characters. So much can be done for them with the right sort of influence and inspiration." When Thelma later began her acting career, she would often receive letters from the children she had taught, and she would happily write back, telling them about her experiences in Hollywood.

In addition to teaching, Thelma threw herself into various extracurricular activities, such as playing on the hockey team, becoming chairwoman of the social committee, and appearing in the odd school play. She still considered herself a "tomboy" and freely admitted that she had always gotten along much better with males than she did with females.

Keen to add to her list of daring activities, she decided to take up horseback riding—and this newfound interest almost cost her life. One day Thelma wanted to go riding in the countryside with some friends, so she took out a stallion from the local stables. At some point in the ride, Thelma accidentally slackened the reins and the horse bolted. Her friends were horrified, but there was nothing they could do, and before anyone knew it, both Thelma and the horse were galloping over the countryside.

"I wasn't scared a bit," she later explained. "But I did lose my stirrups and then I had to hold him around the neck." The horse kept on running and finally turned toward a hay bale, into which Thelma managed to throw herself. The experience didn't put her off, however, and she rode the horse all the way back to the stables.

The eighteen-year-old's nerves of steel were useful when it was announced that the Normal School would be implementing new rules that would make the allocation of teaching assignments more complicated. The student teachers were not happy about this and put together a committee to fight the new policies. As the most outspoken of all the young women, Thelma was elected spokesperson. In a meeting with a handful of the school's senior staff, Thelma argued that her fellow students should not have to take part in the new plans, because they had all been present in the school long before the new rule came into force. Surely it should only apply to *new* student teachers, she argued, and despite efforts to make her change her views, she stood firm.

Her attempts were, in the end, fruitless, and the rules were implemented across the board. But Thelma's efforts had earned her the respect of her opponents in the senior staff; they later said that she had the discussion technique of a lawyer and applauded her for not compromising her principles. This episode won her even more respect from her fellow student teachers, but soon they would have to fight their own battles, as a change for Thelma was just around the corner.

2

BRIGHT YOUNG THINGS

*A*fter a short break in April 1925, Thelma returned to Lowell Normal School to continue her studies and teaching. Then, thanks to her father's involvement with the Elks Lodge, she became aware that a beauty contest was being held to crown a local lady as Miss Lawrence. When she jokingly told her friends about it, she was shocked to discover they all thought she should enter. The idea was ludicrous in Thelma's eyes; though she'd worked as a model, competing with other women over their looks was a different matter—one that didn't interest her at all. "She would just laugh at people when they told her how beautiful she was," explained fellow classmate Helen Pierce, "and she would say, 'There are hundreds of girls just as pretty as I am.'"

Later she complained about the perils of beauty while talking to reporter Alice L. Tildesley: "[It's] all very well," she said, "but I think it would be good if someone would write a book on how to keep your sense of humor while you're struggling to be beautiful." But if Thelma was determined not to flaunt her looks, her friends were adamant that she must—after all, they said, she was bound to win the competition hands down. She tried to laugh it off, but then her family became involved in the lectures too. Even her father, who had dissuaded her from pursuing her modeling and acting, seemed keen for Thelma to take part. The seed was planted, and finally, just four days before the competition, Thelma filled out an application form.

It was to Thelma's advantage that she had previous theatrical experience, and as she took to the Roseland Ballroom stage on June 1, 1925, the judges were impressed with her natural confidence. It did not take long for them to vote her the winner. Her family was delighted, her friends ecstatic, and the young woman was thrilled and somewhat amused that she of all people had actually won a beauty competition.

At the time, she looked forward to moving on to the Miss Massachusetts pageant. However, in later years Thelma would become increasingly frustrated (and at times furious) when columnists and reporters claimed that she had gotten into the movies by winning a beauty contest. "Beauty alone cannot achieve victories," she wrote. "It has to be backed up by a certain amount of intelligence and a tremendous amount of real hard work." She was correct; ultimately, winning the contest had little to do with the start of her film career.

In fact, Thelma's path to the silver screen began several months before the Miss Lawrence contest. In April 1925, Jesse Lasky, the first vice president of the Famous Players–Lasky Corporation, announced his intention to create a school for future movie actors and actresses. Lasky told reporters they would search the entire country for twenty young men and women and bring them together at the Long Island studio as the first class of the Paramount Pictures School Inc.

The idea was to send representatives to various parts of the United States, gathering applications from wannabe actresses age sixteen to twenty-five and actors age eighteen to thirty. The representatives would then whittle down the applicants until eventually a lucky fifty would be interviewed by Lasky himself.

In the end, some thirty thousand applications came flooding in to the various representatives, and thanks to an eager friend, one of the photographs was of a young woman by the name of Thelma Todd. Napoleon L. Demara, who operated a club at the Empire Theatre, had seen an article on the school and approached Thelma about applying. He told her that she was sure to get in, and in turn the young woman laughed, pretended to be flattered, and then went on with her day. However, Mr. Demara was adamant that she had star potential, so he gathered up some photographs and sent them in to the local Paramount School representative.

Just as Thelma was taking part in the beauty contests, an exciting telegram arrived at the Todd house from the school. The young woman had been invited for an interview, but although she was intrigued, she was also unsure whether to do anything about it. Ultimately, she decided to give it a go, not so much because she wanted to be an actress but because she felt it would be something interesting to tell her schoolchildren about when she got back to Lowell.

Her trip to the Famous Players–Lasky studio did not get off to an auspicious start. With her mother as chaperone, she was met by a studio rep who was more than a little bored of shepherding around new recruits. But when it came time for her interview, Jesse Lasky must have been impressed. He told her that he was interested in signing her as a studio player, but at that point he had no suitable production for her. "The studio told me they were putting me into the Paramount School," she said. "They needed a group of youngsters and I hadn't been cast for a production, so they thought I might as well go to school."

Thelma agreed with the decision and signed up for the course. But before it started, she first attended the finals of the Miss Massachusetts contest on June 15, 1925, in Swampscott, during the annual business section of a three-day Elks Association convention. Miss Lawrence paraded before the judges. "There was more noise and cheering than at any football game I ever attended," Thelma later said. "But I couldn't tell whether they were cheering me or someone else."

The crowd was indeed shouting in her direction. The judges described her as "a golden dream of beauty" and took great pleasure in crowning her their new Miss Massachusetts. The accolade, reporters decided, was the "highest honor paid a woman," and Thelma lost no time in giving interviews to talk about the competition, her film contract, and her teaching studies. The last of those, she said, was coming to an end the very next day.

Saying good-bye to the Lowell Normal School was never going to be particularly easy, but Thelma was comforted by the thought that it might not be a permanent separation. If she didn't like the Paramount School, she thought, she would return home on the next train. On her last day as a student teacher, the young woman bade farewell to her classmates and wrote in their autograph books. To one fellow student, she clutched her pen, pursed her lips, and thought about something witty to say. Finally she began to scribble: "Live a gay life, die young, and make a beautiful corpse." How prophetic these seemingly joking words would become.

On June 22, 1925, the students of the Normal School held a surprise party for the future actress. Then on July 8 Thelma traveled to Whalom Park in Fitchburg, Massachusetts, where she was scheduled to appear at a dance hall. Ads for the event called her "A charming bit of Golden Femininity" and encouraged the public to see her for the last time before she joined the Paramount School. The result of this advance publicity was that when Thelma showed up at the dance hall, she was greeted by fifteen hundred fans and spectators, all eager to catch a glimpse of Miss Massachusetts in the flesh.

As she walked onto the stage, the young woman was introduced by the mayor of Fitchburg, who presented her with a key to the city and congratulated the judges on choosing her. Thelma took the honor in stride; she spoke highly of Whalom Park and Fitchburg, thanked everyone for turning out to see her, and expressed how they were "unusually fair and open-minded in greeting the winners of beauty contests." She ended her appearance by singing several songs, which drew particular praise from local reporters.

Later that week, Thelma traveled to Boston, where she was to model shoes for the Haverhill Shoe Manufacturers' Association. She was joined not only by pageant rival Miss Lowell, Anna Galloway, but also by Agnes Butler, who had the dubious honor of being known as Miss Slipper City. After the event, it was time to make serious plans for the future, which would not include any more beauty contests.

Childhood friend Edna Hamel remembered that John Todd objected mightily to his daughter moving to New York to take her place at the

Paramount School. According to Edna, Thelma had to "run off," with Alice's help. The idea of the young woman sneaking out of the house with her mother's assistance, behind the back of her father, is perhaps a little far-fetched. But John Todd was certainly less than thrilled that his daughter would be taking this path in life. The actress herself alluded to this in a short but revealing interview with the *Daily News* in 1929: "It was a long time before I overcame family prejudice against my adopting a screen career. . . . Hollywood as it is painted by newspaper people presented an aspect of life that was very distasteful to my family." Hence Edna's claim that Thelma had been forced to run away from home.

Shortly before she said good-bye to her old friends and neighbors, Thelma told them she was very happy to have been given the opportunity to get into the movies. "I think I'm going to like it more than I would have enjoyed teaching school," she said.

3

THE PARAMOUNT SCHOOL

*S*ince plans were announced in the spring of 1925, various critics had questioned the value of the Paramount School. They claimed that extras who hung around the studio gates would have a better chance of making it in the business than the new school's students. After all, extras were working alongside actual movie stars on the sets of real movies, whereas the students were merely, in the words of the *Boston Globe*, "petted and chaperoned boys and girls." Thelma would come to agree, later telling several reporters, including one from *Film Weekly* magazine, that she was sure she'd have learned a lot more by working as an extra. "She is on the spot. She can soak herself in the atmosphere of the studios," she said.

To its founders, however, the Paramount School was a place where talented young people could be nurtured and grow into mainstream actors. With that in mind, they designed an intense course load that included classes in makeup, costumes, character study, etiquette, improvisation, and loss of self-consciousness, as well as a series of lectures by prominent industry names.

Thelma and her fellow students gathered on July 20, 1925, for the first day of school. The men and women chattered nervously among themselves, wondering what the future might bring. At the front of the hall stood members of the school board—Sidney R. Kent, Walter

Wanger, and Tom Terriss—who all gave welcome speeches and shared words of advice from Jesse Lasky, all the way from Hollywood. Then it was time for the real work to begin.

From the very start, Thelma found it hard to take things seriously and wondered if she would be able to settle in. "I suppose I was young and foolish, but I couldn't help looking on the whole thing as a joke," she later wrote. It would be easy to see why she felt this way: one minute she was dressed up as a beautiful maiden and the next as a Zulu, complete with a huge putty nose. Young actresses would be made to look like old ladies, while the boys would become old men with fake beards and moustaches. Thelma thought the entire thing was a gigantic waste of time—what was the point of dressing them up for old parts when they had no chance of being cast in such roles while still young?

Never one for worrying about the color of her lipstick, Thelma also balked when forced to undertake intensive classes on the art of good camera makeup. She later confessed that when she tried out the techniques she learned, she found the results ludicrous.

Her reluctance to take part in such activities, along with her quips that the whole school experience was "unreal," quickly made her the black sheep of the school. She was berated for not taking things seriously in pantomime class, when she was asked to recite "Mary Had a Little Lamb" with appropriate expressions and gestures. Though such visual cues were essential during the silent film era, Thelma couldn't keep a straight face. In costume class, she complained about being too old to play dress-up. Low grades soon followed, and the teachers started to despair. "They thought me quite terrible, and I agreed with them," she said later, telling reporters that she was proud to have been both the student with the most difficult reputation and the only actress in the class who successfully made a name for herself. "And I'm not relying on beauty to keep me here," she added.

Her uninterested attitude also irritated some of her fellow students, who found her aloof and unfriendly. But other classmates soon became her friends, including Jeanne Morgan (a.k.a. Harriet Krauth) and Dorothy Nourse. The three young actresses complemented each other perfectly: Thelma was the one who spoke her mind, Jeanne was calm and demure, and Dorothy was the joker of the pack, always getting into trouble for organizing practical jokes in the hotel where the school put them up. One trick involved filling Jeanne's bed with apple cores, hairbrushes, and an assortment of rubbish—but when bedtime came, the girl failed to notice there was anything strange about her bed and went on to have a good night's sleep. This caused a great deal of hilarity when the girls woke up the next morning.

Thelma also became friends with actor Robert Andrews, though interactions with her male classmates were made more difficult by the fact that they were housed in a different hotel than the girls. Every day the two groups would meet up on the subway and travel to class together, but in the off-hours they had to contend with a chaperone. Mrs. J. Walter Taylor was a no-nonsense, unsmiling woman, sensibly dressed and ready to keep all her charges in line.

This was the first time Thelma had ever ventured to New York. She was excited to go out and have fun, but their matronly overseer would have none of that. Instead of dancing in nightclubs all night long, Thelma and her new friends were bundled off to bed by 10 PM, which drove them all to distraction. "We were looked after like kids at a boarding school," she said. Still, they did manage to sneak out a few times without Mrs. Taylor finding out: "My wildest dissipation was to go out dancing until four o'clock, and that happened only two or three times," Thelma remembered.

Having new friendships helped Thelma finally settle into the Paramount School routine, and she discovered that there were some classes she appreciated. She became very interested in the more physical lessons: dance, gymnastics, fencing, and how to fall down stairs. The last of these particularly entertained her, and with a flair for comedy that would put her in good stead for the future, the young woman began falling into the funniest positions she could, just to make her fellow students laugh. Still, she wasn't sure how any of it would further her career. "I don't think the school helped us very much," she told *Motion Picture*. "Learning to swim, fence, dance and ride horseback doesn't add to one's histrionics." At least she enjoyed them; in fact, riding and swimming would become lifelong hobbies that Thelma pursued frequently, claiming they were good for her body and mind.

Thelma's turnaround was swift. Within a month of arriving at the Paramount School, the nineteen-year-old actress had written her aunts and uncles to tell them she was "deeply engrossed" in her work. In September the local media reported that she was one of the school's most promising students. By October her name was being mentioned in several fan magazines, all intrigued by the idea that a prim schoolteacher was being turned into an up-and-coming actress. *Photoplay*, too, described her as one of the most promising pupils in the school, adding, "[She] is a real beauty with a crown of gorgeous golden hair." Reporters descended on the Lowell Normal School and asked Thelma's former principal for a comment. She happily told them that during her time there, the young woman had been a capable scholar and was bound to do well in the film business.

Over the subsequent months, the Paramount School lost three students who had not shown much aptitude for acting. "Curiously enough, the three who were dropped were from Hollywood and Los Angeles," said Jesse Lasky. "I believe the reason for that is that all the really promising talent in Los Angeles manages to find its way into pictures unassisted." (Another student, Marian Ivy Harris, had also wanted to leave; for the first two weeks she did nothing but cry for the comforts of home. The studio finally felt there was nothing it could do except send for her mother, a move that eventually calmed the emotional woman, and she decided to stay at the school.)

Student actor Charles "Buddy" Rogers also decided the school wasn't for him. He had auditioned for the representatives in a park in Olathe, Kansas, and believed himself to be so bad that he wondered why Lasky decided to take him on. He shared his concerns with Thelma, who sympathized but persuaded him to stay. He would eventually be glad he did; Rogers became one of the most famous of the school's graduates and enjoyed a very successful film career.

In December 1925, Thelma garnered a mention in a major newspaper. The *Los Angeles Times* published an article about her long hair, calling it her "crowning glory" and telling readers that she didn't have any intention of cutting it. It's unknown how the other students felt about this little piece of publicity, but around this time Thelma did find herself in a minor rivalry with fellow student Marian Ivy Harris to see who would be the most successful in the quickest possible time.

By now, Thelma had gained quite a lot of weight. The studio was footing the bill for the students' meals at the hotel restaurant, and they were allowed to order whatever food or drink they wanted. Dorothy Nourse told the *Boston Globe* that the girls were eating steak three times a day. The result was that Dorothy gained six pounds in four months, while Thelma put on seventeen. The course director was incensed and called the girls into his office to scare them into losing weight. The wardrobe mistress, he said, had told him they were just too fat and she didn't have enough material to make them new costumes. This was most likely an exaggeration, but it infuriated Thelma. She was five foot four inches, 149 pounds, and in her words "terribly broad," but she told anyone who would listen that her weight wasn't due to fat at all but the muscle she'd built up during her physical training at the school.

Photos from the time show that she was not a large young woman by today's standards. Publicly, at least, she expressed the attitude that her weight was not something she was bothered about. But teasing from other students and the disappointed stares of her tutors started to upset her. Then one day in the cafeteria, she encountered actor Richard Dix, who was working at the studio. His face cracked into a smile, and he told her that she would never act with him looking the way she did. "If you want to be my leading lady, you'll have to reduce," he said, adding that she would also have to be herself and stop acting like a "schoolmarm." Although she didn't care if she acted with him or not, his next jab irritated her no end: he told her she would never be able to lose the weight she needed to.

"It made me furiously mad," Thelma said. She decided that not only would she slim down—or "reduce," as she frequently referred to it—but she'd also be Dix's leading lady within a year. "I might say to Richard Dix, 'You made me what I am today,'" she told reporter Myrtle Gebhart. From that moment on, Thelma studied diet plans said to have been written for Gloria Swanson, and she talked Dorothy Nourse into losing weight too. However, while they were both determined to shed their excess pounds, the girls were certainly no angels. One day when the studio cafeteria was particularly quiet, they ordered every cake and dessert they could find and gleefully ate the lot.

But they eventually lost the weight, and during a later publicity tour, Thelma was asked how she did it. She told everyone in the theater that she would share her secret with those who cared to write to her. Those who did as she requested were rewarded with a diet sheet, signed by Thelma herself, that detailed her strict routine.

Looking at this sheet today, one is amazed that this absurd technique did not land the actress in the hospital. First of all she was instructed to cut down the size of her meals, making them smaller to shrink her stomach. Then the young woman undertook two or three days of eating vegetables only, and then another three days of eating nothing but oranges. If she felt faint, she was told to eat a piece of toast or sip a cup of tea or coffee, before going back to the oranges again. After three days of oranges, she was to go back to vegetables, then oranges again. "After the second week," she wrote in the instruction letter, "you should begin to lose a few pounds, and then your weight should decrease rapidly."

Just how long she stayed on this diet is a mystery, but photographs taken later show that she had slimmed down considerably, and Thelma herself said that she ended up losing a staggering thirty pounds in just four weeks. Her weight remained an issue for the rest of her life, however, and rumors have circulated over the years that as well as dieting, the actress used diet pills to keep her weight on track and eventually became addicted to them. Thelma herself never publicly spoke about it, and it is doubtful that she was addicted by the time of her death. No trace of the pills was mentioned in her autopsy report or death record.

As her studies at the Paramount School continued, Thelma began to think about what kind of actress she would like to be. She was a big fan of Florence Vidor and Irene Rich, both of whom were known for dignity and refinement in the roles they played. Thelma decided she wanted to follow in their footsteps: "I should like to play women with character," she said. But it would be a long time before the young actress had even slight control over the roles she played; for now her teachers required her to study the films that were being made at the studio and re-create specific scenes in front of a camera. Each student would then be asked to watch him- or herself in the projector room, with an instructor standing at the front pointing out any mistakes.

It was an embarrassing and belittling experience at times, and Thelma again felt that her schoolwork was not the best preparation for acting in the real world. She firmly believed that a better way to correct her mistakes would be by watching *other* actors and actresses at work and adjusting her own habits as a result. (One of the things Thelma later discovered by watching others work was that she often moved too fast; scenes would be over before she had even really begun. She started to slow down her movements, and her comic timing improved dramatically as a result. "I do honestly feel that I have learned all my real lessons while I have been actually at work in front of the camera," Thelma said.)

Unfortunately, the Paramount School actively discouraged its pupils from seeking out any real-world experience. Throughout their time at the school, the students were visited by directors who were making movies on the lot. They would often ask the youngsters to take parts as extras in their films, but before they were able to say yes, the head of the school would step in. Ushering the young actors away, he'd insist the idea was nonsense and send the directors back to their own sets.

Future employers weren't the only ones who were interested in paying Thelma and her classmates a visit. For the duration of the course, stars such as William Powell and Gloria Swanson would saunter into the room or gawp through windows, eager to see exactly what was going on inside. Thelma later said that she felt awful during these visits; she likened their stares to being "as if we were monkeys at the zoo."

After some time, the studio felt that its pupils were ready to be featured in their very first film. All sixteen students would star in the project, under the watchful eye of director Sam Wood. He nicknamed his cast "the substitute team," as in the players waiting on the sidelines for their big break.

The story would be crafted by screenwriter Byron Morgan, who at first resisted any involvement. "It's going to be pretty tough writing a story for sixteen stars," he told *Photoplay*, before joking, "and when they start to cast the picture, I'm going to leave town." Although he didn't actually go anywhere, he was right to expect trouble over the casting process. Thelma later recalled that there was a huge amount of bickering among the students over who would get the best parts. "I've seen a lot of studio jealousy in my time," she said, "but never in all my life have I seen so much envy, jealousy, hatred and malice."

Thankfully the students had Wood and Morgan to help iron out their differences. Morgan in particular spent a lot of time chaperoning the students around town, studying their personalities, advising them about the movie business, and eventually coming up with a comedy called *Fascinating Youth*. It is the story of a young man (played by Charles "Buddy" Rogers) who wants to save his father's hotel by turning it into a successful winter business, so he organizes a risky ice-boat race. In the process, of course, he wins the girl of his dreams, even though he has previously been promised to an heiress.

Wood began filming on November 23, 1925, at various locations, including Lake Placid. Thelma plays Lorraine, the heiress's sister, someone she later described as a bad girl. Also appearing—much to the students' surprise—were several full-fledged stars, among them Richard Dix, Chester Conklin, and Clara Bow. Despite the excitement of having real stars on set, the young students were often bored during filming, and Thelma took it upon herself to organize outings such as bobsledding and skating. (Later, when her career finally got going for real, Thelma would learn to play bridge so that she and fellow actors had something to do in the long hours between scenes.) Filming ended on Christmas Eve.

Around the time that the class was making *Fascinating Youth*, the *Boston Globe* sent reporter Marjory Adams to visit local girls Thelma,

Dorothy Nourse, and Jeanne Morgan. She found them to be three rather nervous young women, who described their time at the school as happy, but they were still wondering if they would be lucky enough to win a film contract afterward. When they took the reporter back to their hotel for tea, the girls amused themselves by shuffling along a pile carpet and giving each other electric shocks. However, while Thelma was happy to take part in such childish activities for a time, the reporter noted that she was quick to settle the other girls down when they caught a fit of giggles. Thelma was also the one who seemed to be fairly confident in her future abilities, predicting that in a year's time, if she wasn't working in New York, she would certainly be in Hollywood.

On March 9, 1926, the students of the Paramount School gathered in the grand ballroom of the Ritz-Carlton hotel. The room was packed with movie industry insiders, and at a huge table along one wall sat the young actors alongside Adolph Zukor, Will Hays, Sam Katz, Sidney R. Kent, and Jesse Lasky. Lasky stood up and congratulated everyone involved with the course, adding that it was "the answer to the cry for new faces on the screen," and solved the question of how a person could break into the movies. He presented the students with a diploma in the form of a movie contract for one year's appearance in Famous Players–Lasky films.

Then the president of the class, Charles Brokaw, thanked Lasky for the opportunity given to all the students, told him how grateful they were, and presented him with an inscribed cigarette case. Before the evening was over, *Fascinating Youth* was screened and the newly signed actors and actresses received a standing ovation.

While the friends and family of the students seemed to love the film, the same can't be said for some of the critics in attendance—most notably those from *Picture Play* magazine. In the June 1926 issue, *Fascinating Youth* was described as feeble; "These youngsters are utterly without magnetism or distinction of any sort," the review said. The real stars of the film, according to the magazine, were Chester Conklin and the other established actors who cameoed. "The pupils didn't really count. I don't want to be harsh, but they were exactly like so many little shadows running in and out of the picture."

The reviewer continued by saying that if any of the students went on to become stars, he would "return to my home and children." He granted that he did enjoy meeting the graduates after the screening; he wrote that Charles "Buddy" Rogers stood out from the crowd and that Thelma and Josephine Dunn were the best of the actresses. However, this too was a backhanded comment, as he added, "They aren't anything to rave about, goodness knows, but each seems to get across the possession of a sense of humor."

This early battering of the movie made other critics rub their hands together with glee. They queued up to see *Fascinating Youth* for themselves, mainly so they could shoot the film down in flames and call the school a massive, impractical, and costly mistake. But unlike the critics at the graduation ceremony, many of the later reviewers actually found things to like about the film. *Motion Picture News* wrote, "It can stand on its own feet" among the studio's new releases. The *Film Daily* called the story trite but gave credit to the direction and the performances of the students, particularly Charles "Buddy" Rogers and Marian Ivy Harris.

The *Film Daily* review added that with the right publicity the film could be a commercial success—and Famous Players–Lasky had the same thought. The studio's publicity machine would soon go into overdrive, whisking the students off to various different towns and cities, all to make appearances in support of the movie.

4

FASCINATING YOUTH

*A*fter receiving her contract, Thelma decided to stay in New York for the foreseeable future, and John and Alice Todd moved to the city to be close to their daughter. The young actress took time off so she could travel with them to Lawrence to pack up the remainder of their belongings.

Almost as soon as she arrived in her hometown, the actress was met with a rumor that she had become engaged to a young local man. It was a fabrication, contrived by the man in the hopes that it would help make a name for him in the movies. Thelma laughed off the reports and got on with the task of greeting family and helping her parents. Their effects gathered, the Todds returned to New York and set up a permanent home in the Jackson Heights area of Queens.

A few weeks later, another rumor emerged: it was reported that she and former classmate Robert Andrews were an item and had recently become engaged. This story, too, was fanned by Thelma's supposed beau: he told a local newspaper that the only reason he stayed at the Paramount School was so he could see his sweetheart, Thelma Todd.

Reporters flocked to her parents' new home, and the humor with which the first "engagement" had been met was now nowhere to be seen. Mrs. Todd told reporters that neither she nor Mr. Todd was impressed by the stories, and that if there had been any truth in them whatsoever, their daughter would have told them long before she made it public. The reporters were sent scurrying back to their offices with their tails between their legs, though relationship rumors were something Mrs. Todd in particular would quickly have to get used to.

Thelma's success at the Paramount School was the biggest thing that had happened in Lawrence for a long time. With that in mind, several local businessmen, including the managers of a local theater, campaigned for *Fascinating Youth* to be shown in the town. Studio publicists agreed, and not only was the film booked into the Palace Theatre for the week of May 16, 1926, but also Thelma and her classmate Greg Blackton were to appear there in person.

There was only one problem: the newly built Metropolitan Theatre in Boston was due to show the film and host its stars at the same time. Thelma had campaigned vigorously to have the studio list her as being from Lawrence rather than the much bigger Boston, so there was no way she would miss supporting the film in her own town. A solution was found in local car firm Bruno Motor Co., which came forward to volunteer its services, shepherding the young actors and Thelma's parents between the two locations.

Thelma made it to Lawrence in time for her appearance at the Palace, where the anticipation for a film had never been greater. For many hours people lined up outside, and afterward it was announced that the theater had never done a bigger day's worth of business. Inside the building, Thelma was introduced to the cheering crowd by the former leader of the Elks Lodge. Overwhelmed with gratitude, she told everyone about her experiences at the Paramount School and assured them that a part of her heart would always belong to the people of her hometown. "I will never be conceited and think I am bigger than I was when I was a schoolgirl," Thelma told them. Afterward, she answered questions from the audience, collected flowers, and looked amazed at the applause she received.

For the next few days, Thelma and Greg Blackton made appearances at the Boston and Lawrence theaters, walking onto the stage numerous times a day to greet fans, dance the tango, and most of all, publicize the film. The Paramount School graduates were also starring in *Alice in Movieland*, a Boston stage production based on the famous Lewis Carroll novel. With all the work being put into the busy week, nobody could ever accuse the former students of being lazy in their approach to publicity. As it turned out, they made more appearances in support of *Fascinating Youth* than many huge stars did for their own movies—and seemed happier to do so.

The Massachusetts tour was a success, and by the summer Thelma's efforts had moved farther afield. On July 29, 1926, she celebrated her twentieth birthday while promoting the film on tour. Back in New York, John Todd was walking in the city when he collapsed, stricken by a massive heart attack. He passed away shortly thereafter.

A shocked and heartbroken Alice wired her daughter and relatives in Lawrence to tell them that John had died. The telegrams contained no details as to the cause of death, so confusion abounded. From the very start it was rumored that he had been killed in the middle of a busy street or in some kind of subway accident. To this day, details such as the location of his death are unclear. But this much is certain: John Todd suffered a heart attack that took him away from his family on his daughter's twentieth birthday.

John's brothers, Adam and Henry, traveled to New York to make the necessary arrangements to bring the body home. The funeral was held in Lawrence on August 2; mourners set out from 22 Bowdoin Street, where various Todd family members still lived. The amount of flowers the family received was so staggering that the local newspaper dedicated an entire column to naming everyone who sent bouquets and sprays. Among them were two tributes from Thelma and Alice, with the simple but eloquent words DADDY and MY JOHN.

No sooner had Thelma attended her father's funeral than she herself collapsed and was rushed to the local hospital. Doctors determined that her appendix needed to be removed immediately. Confined to a bed following the operation, Thelma had time to reflect on the recent tragedy and think about her future.

Just like her brother's passing, her father's death had a profound effect on Thelma. There had certainly been times when John was not particularly supportive of her forceful nature or her eagerness to entertain, but he had always loved her. The fact that he and Alice had accompanied her to various publicity appearances and that they had moved from their Lawrence home to be near her, were testament to that. Thelma worried what was to become of her mother, and she found herself longing for the comfort of her hometown more than ever.

Still, she knew that a career in acting was something she wanted to pursue. "My father died, and I was too proud to go home with my tail between my legs," she wrote. "So I sat down, thought things out and went ahead with a scheme in my mind." Her plans were big, but her sense of loyalty to her hometown was something she would never lose. "I am still very much a Lawrence girl," she said, explaining that since her father's family all lived there, she could return whenever she wanted to. She would continue to talk about her love for Massachusetts for the rest of her life, and when she joyfully told hometown fans to come visit her in California, she meant it.

By September 1926, the media and fans of *Fascinating Youth* were starting to question when the stars of the film would reunite for another project. Jesse Lasky was very interested in the idea, and he had already told the students during graduation that all sixteen of them would be involved in three productions together before the end of the year. This had not yet happened, but now the producer announced his plans to fly all of them out to Hollywood to make a movie with producer Hector Turnbull. It was an interesting thought, but not one that had any hope of coming true.

By this time, some of the former students were busy working on other projects, while others were beginning to complain that acting was not for them after all. Various producers and directors refused to work with them, claiming that the Paramount School graduates were not official members of the film industry. Parts were drying up for many of them, and by the end of 1926, the original sixteen graduates had been reduced to eight: Thelma, Marian Ivy Harris, Iris Gray, Josephine Dunn, Jack Luden, Walter Goss, Mona Palmer, and Charles "Buddy" Rogers. Rogers quickly became one of the school's most distinguished alumni when he was hired to star opposite Clara Bow in the highly successful movie *Wings*. The other graduates, including Thelma's friends Dorothy Nourse, Jeanne Morgan, Robert Andrews, and Greg Blackton, were all free to sign with other studios or give up their film careers altogether; Famous Players–Lasky didn't seem to mind one way or the other.

Thelma's star continued to rise, albeit more slowly than Rogers's, as she booked small roles in *God Gave Me Twenty Cents* and *The Popular Sin*. The former is based on a story by Dixie Willson that *Cosmopolitan* magazine had recently published to some acclaim. Unfortunately, the clever romance did not transfer well to screen (which *Motion Picture News* attributed to a fear of censorship by director Herbert Brenon); leads Lois Moran and Jack Mulhall end up mired in a predictable girl-meets-boy, girl-loses-boy scenario. Thelma's part in the feature was so minor that while she was mentioned in magazines during production, by the time it was released she had effectively vanished from the cast lists and reviews.

The Popular Sin, meanwhile, was set in Paris and stars Florence Vidor as a divorcée tangled up in several unsuccessful marriages. Thelma's role was not particularly notable—but that was just as well, because the reviews felt the same way about the film itself. "Perhaps it isn't to be taken seriously," said *Picture Play* magazine, "but it isn't good fun. And placing the story in Paris, and calling the characters Yvonne, Jean, George and La Belle Toulaise doesn't count for anything."

Despite having had no substantial parts to date, the actress was becoming more popular in the media; the *Film Daily* announced that she was showing much promise. Thelma used this early publicity to her advantage, and when she was approached to star in a series of beauty ads for Black and White Cold Cream, she immediately said yes. These small items ran in newspapers and featured a photo of the upcoming star and some questionable quotes, including the revelation that the cold cream gave her skin "the fine, soft texture of a baby's."

When 1927 rolled around, Thelma was cast in a bigger role in the movie *Rubber Heels*. The film starred comedian Ed Wynn and also featured Chester Conklin and Thelma's Paramount School friend Robert Andrews. Since being dropped by Famous Players–Lasky, Andrews had toyed with the idea of becoming an assistant director or even giving up his career altogether, but his part in *Rubber Heels* changed his mind, at least for a while. Their reunion once again set the rumor mills in motion; *Picture Play* was quick to report that Andrews and Thelma had fallen in love. This time the magazine preposterously claimed that Wynn had given them a nudge in the right direction.

Ed Wynn had been a successful vaudeville and Broadway performer for years, but *Rubber Heels* saw him going in a totally new direction, acting in his first motion picture. The lack of sound presented a special challenge in Wynn's case, given that his fans were used to both seeing *and* hearing him onstage. Many critics would be watching to see whether Wynn's transition was a success, and that meant many critics were sure to review Thelma's first significant role, that of Princess Anne.

For the first time at the Long Island studio, the actress was presented with her very own canvas chair, cementing her status as leading lady. Thelma was slightly embarrassed to have it but ultimately excited to star opposite Wynn, whom she had once seen on the Boston stage, during his show *The Perfect Fool*. "I never in all my life expected to be so far in such a short time," she told Marjory Adams from the *Boston Globe*, before adding that she had felt sure it would take at least three years to become a leading lady. She said it didn't seem possible that it was all true. But true it was, and when Thelma walked onto the set of *Rubber Heels*, she was met with a distinct shift in attitude among the others on set. Throughout her time at the Paramount School and in the few minor roles she had been in since then, she had always been known by her first name. Now suddenly everyone called her Miss Todd and avoided chitchatting with her. The hurt actress took this to mean they thought she was conceited because of her growing popularity, and it took another actress to tell her that this was just the way people treated you when you found success.

Ed Wynn took to Thelma immediately and declared his feeling that she had "It." "She is a mighty clever girl," he remarked, before adding that he had selected the actress because she did not slouch like a flapper girl. According to him, she was the only girl in the studio who could walk well enough to play the role of a Russian princess.

When the film was released later in the year, publicity posters called it the "greatest thrill of the year." Meanwhile, ready-made studio reviews gave Wynn glowing notices for his role as Amos Wart, a bumbling detective who becomes tangled up with a gang of thieves, headed by Chester Conklin. Although Thelma's name was in the studio publicity, it was really only to tell viewers she was supporting Wynn.

Although the publicist-authored reviews were glowing, the real-life critics gave *Rubber Heels* mixed notices. *Motion Picture News* liked it but criticized Wynn's obvious stage mannerisms and dialogue. The *Film Daily* said that the story was full of weak gags, "good for only occasional laughs," and decided the best part of the whole movie was the ending. *Photoplay* pulled no punches: "Five gorgeous moments, in an hour of boredom," it boomed, concurring with the *Film Daily* that the only good thing about the movie was the final scene.

None of the weak reviews were aimed at Thelma, and although the film did nothing to advance her career, a big move was just around the corner. Shortly after finishing *Rubber Heels*, she was called into the studio office and told she would be leaving Long Island and heading for Hollywood. Thelma was thrilled to leave the East Coast and the restrictive confines of her Paramount School training. "I had always felt so cramped, as if the walls were pressing in upon me," she told Myrtle Gebhart at *Picture Play* magazine. "While I had not been conscious of any urge to be wild, I wanted to be where one didn't have to consider always the proper thing to do."

Shortly after the actress was told her fate, it was announced that various other members of the studio would also be leaving for the West Coast during the first week of March. Thelma and Josephine Dunn were to follow shortly behind. At their Jackson Heights home, while Thelma and her mother packed their suitcases in anticipation of their trip to Hollywood, she had never been so excited. "As the train carried me farther and farther away [from the East], I wondered if out here among new associations I might shake off a little of the primness and preciseness," she later recalled.

5

WELCOME TO HOLLYWOOD

On April 17, 1927, the *Film Daily* announced that twenty-year-old Thelma had arrived in Hollywood, the town where dreams could be made or broken in the blink of an eye. She settled into an apartment with her mother and felt immediately that she would enjoy the journey ahead of her. The climate was wonderful, the surroundings inspirational, and Thelma felt that the whole atmosphere "stimulated me instead of enervating me, as it does many. I felt a freedom I had never known before."

Unfortunately, the initial excitement wore off when it became apparent that she would not be welcomed with open arms by any of the players already in residence there. She was one of many actors and actresses who were migrating from the East Coast at the time, and this caused Hollywood's brightest stars to look at these interlopers with great suspicion. They were especially suspicious of Thelma, as she had not entered the business in a traditional fashion.

She also discovered that Los Angeles was very different from New York. She would later tell fans in Lawrence that at first she found Hollywood to be a strange land and had no friends there at all. As a result of the loneliness she felt, the actress would often cry and tell her mother that maybe they should move home—that trying to make it in Hollywood wasn't worth it at all. Surprisingly, it was Alice who encouraged her daughter to stay and see what movies could offer her. "She is the one who is entitled to a great deal of my success," Thelma said.

The young actress tried to put aside the feelings of isolation and thought about her fans back home. She spoke about these days often in the years to come and always assured the press and public that it was the thought of the people back in Lawrence cheering her on and hoping for success that kept her going during a difficult and strange time. She had also inherited an Irish sense of humor from her father's side of the family, which helped her see the funny side of life in Hollywood. "It has been a life-saver in many an instance," she told a fan in a 1931 letter.

On May 18, one month after she arrived in Hollywood, it was announced in the *Los Angeles Times* that Thelma was most likely to star opposite Gary Cooper in *Nevada*, a western from silent film director John Waters. Also on the credit list was William Powell, one of the actors who had once gawped into the classrooms of the Paramount School. The film, shot over several weeks in Utah, revolved around the story of a young gunfighter (Cooper) who takes a ranch job looking after the owner's daughter (Todd). This new development angers ranch foreman William Powell, who sets out to destroy the interloper's reputation. After several plot twists, Cooper saves the day and wins the girl, and they all live happily ever after.

Thelma's part was fairly small, though she caught the attention of reporters who were covering the shoot. She joked with them that her corsets were so uncomfortable that she could hardly bear to wear them for more than an hour or two. While they enjoyed her interview banter, unfortunately the media didn't think too much of the western, and the film did nothing to further the career of any of the actors involved. As it turned out, Thelma didn't really think much of her early roles either; she later admitted that at the time she was merely imitating an actress, not actually being one. "There was nothing up here. . . . I hadn't the faintest idea of what I was doing or why," she said. Thelma had voiced her early reservations on the set of *Nevada*, when she told Cooper that she considered the movie camera to be the enemy. The actor found this highly amusing, as he had always believed it to be his friend.

Also in May 1927, Thelma again made the pages of the *Los Angeles Times*, this time in the influential column of Grace Kingsley. Thelma's career would be mentioned there often in the years to come, but for now it was her hair. The golden tresses that she had so carefully looked after all these years were said to be the envy of bobbed-haired flapper girls everywhere, especially now that Thelma was developing into a leading lady.

Still, while Kingsley may have looked at the actress's appearance with some affection, Thelma herself was getting bored. As she had planned while departing the East Coast, she wanted to shed her prim and proper image and make herself into someone new. "Gradually I began to come out of my shell," she said. "People looked at youth and beauty, I noticed. While brains and learning are the fundamental values, there seemed to be others worth considering. I had determined by then to succeed in pictures, and therefore I must adopt some of the new rules."

Off came the sensible clothes, and on went new and stunning outfits bought from the best stores in town. This metamorphosis was witnessed by reporter Cal York when he visited the set of *Fireman, Save My Child*, in which Thelma was again playing an uncredited role. While in New York, he said, the actress was very much like vanilla ice cream—an interesting comment, since one of her later nicknames in the media was "the Ice Cream Blonde," apparently a reference to her pale skin and pillow-white hair. York noted that before the move, Thelma had worn "black velvet, a slow smile and dignity." The woman he met on the set of her latest L.A. production, however, was the complete opposite, wearing a shorter skirt, sporting plucked eyebrows, and vigorously chewing gum.

Reporter Myrtle Gebhart remembered that when Thelma first came to Hollywood, "she was a shadowy figure, hovering in the background of the brilliant personalities. The very word schoolmarm scared people away." On meeting the actress again a few years later, Gebhart would be shocked at her transformation. It was at a tea party when she first saw Thelma sitting "tall and graceful, golden head against the black satin of a high-backed chair." The reporter noticed that she had cast off her inhibitions and was making every effort to be witty and charming. Gebhart was impressed, and others had begun to notice too.

Sporting her newfound glamorous look, Thelma heightened her profile by attending several film premieres, among them the July 22 showing of Richard Dix's new movie *Man Power*. Dix was the actor who had laughed at her at the Paramount School, saying she was too overweight to ever be his costar. How wonderful it must have felt to now be on the guest list at his premiere, among the likes of W. C. Fields, Constance Talmadge, Mabel Normand, and Gloria Swanson.

In August, Thelma proved Dix wrong when she won a rare credited role opposite him in *The Gay Defender*. Dix plays a young Spanish aristocrat who becomes a bandit to right the wrongs done to his people by American desperadoes, and Thelma is his lady love, the daughter of the US land commissioner.

Initially the filming experience was not a happy one, however, as Dix was becoming increasingly interested in directing rather than acting. "I am an actor now, but no star in the industry has succeeded in maintaining his or her popularity up to the age I shall be ten years from now," he said. "I want to retire while I am at the top, not wait until it is whispered I am slipping. But I don't want to leave the industry. My desire to direct grows upon me and I feel sure there will be a place for me." Dix also complained bitterly that he did not want to play the part of a Latin man, since he believed he did not look like one, and while he did reluctantly appear on set, after just one day of working with Thelma, he shouted at the director, handed in his wardrobe, and left the building. Nobody knew what was going on, especially when he passed on all phone calls to his lawyer.

It took a full day of negotiations and pleading before he returned to the studio to complete the role. Unfortunately, it would seem that Dix was right in his hesitation; when the film was released, some sections of the media declared him to be unfortunately miscast. "Dix has sideburns and a mustache, but it is still a tough job for him to look Spanish," said *Variety*. "He ought to remain this side of the border." But, the review added, "Miss Todd wears crinoline and bonnets and seems satisfied."

The *Los Angeles Times* claimed the direction to be middling but managed to praise Thelma's part, before adding that it would take more films before they could determine whether she really could act. The *Film Daily* was slightly more positive, praising Dix, "who does the most improbable feats with such snap and assurance that the absurdities are easily forgiven"; while nothing was said about Thelma's performance, she was given a small mention as "a pretty senorita."

Rumors began to circulate that Dix and Thelma were in a relationship, but it was work that was firmly on her mind. She continued to make movies and take part in publicity appearances and social events. She was frequently spotted out and about in Hollywood, and in late summer 1927, she attended a barbeque at the home of actress Julia Faye, where she received a great deal of attention from actors Kenneth Thomson and Barton Hepburn (no relation to Katharine or Audrey). Also in attendance was actor Ivan Lebedeff, who would be romantically linked with Thelma on several occasions in the future.

The actress was finally beginning to enjoy her life and the freedom she found on the West Coast. "California has given me the youth I had missed," she said. "I have shed the years that had been added to me only by atmosphere and association."

Thelma may have become a lot more relaxed in the Hollywood atmosphere, but several issues still bothered her. She was shocked by how common it was for married men and women to have affairs and disturbed by the constant gossip aimed at bringing down the careers of one's rivals. She made a decision very early on that she would not go down that road, and by the time Thelma passed away, a reporter would have been hard pressed to find any negative remarks she ever made about her coworkers.

She did have harsh words, though, regarding the rude and forthright nature of the men she encountered in the business. "Their attitude lacks the courtesy and respect which I've always expected from men," she said. From the time she moved to New York, Thelma had noticed a vast difference between men who spoke to her as a schoolteacher and those who knew her as an actress. She brushed off their comments, but since arriving in Hollywood, she found that the problem had only gotten worse.

When actors came up to talk to her and put their arms around her, she was at first shocked, but she soon accepted that it was just part of being in an acting company. However, while she could live with the attention of her fellow performers, she didn't feel so good about the other "wolves" in Hollywood. She quickly grew to hate "the business men—the outsiders—who smirk suggestively when they learn that your work is acting."

Thelma had fought off the amorous advances and vulgar conversations of various men since she arrived in the city, including a photographer who invited her to talk about human biology after their photo session. But the worst aspect of Hollywood, she found, was the dreaded casting couch and the willingness of various women to jump right on if they thought it would further their career. The whole process infuriated her, and she couldn't understand those who chose to go that route. "Girls out here have cheapened themselves by permitting too much familiarity," she said, "girls who can't get anywhere by their own merits, who'll be nice to anybody if it will advance them the slightest bit."

The young actress's own experience with the casting couch was swift and traumatic. She had only been in Hollywood a short time when she was called to a meeting at the studio. When she arrived she was taken straight to an office where there was a party in full swing that included music, bootleg alcohol, young women, and several executives. Thelma knew exactly what was going on, so she made her excuses and left, though not before one of the men tried to cajole her into having a drink and told her to be "a good fellow."

After arguing with the executives in the room that evening, Thelma was threatened with blacklisting. She was told that she would never work in the town again. "Hollywood hath no fury like a director scorned," *Photoplay* later said of the incident. Thelma herself knew the risks: "You can't be openly offended; you need the good will of everybody in this game." Still, she chose to leave the party with her dignity intact.

If further proof were needed that Thelma was an outspoken young woman, unafraid of saying what she thought, it is presented in several articles printed after the casting couch incident. In 1929 she gave a revealing interview with *Motion Picture*, telling Dorothy Lubou that "movie men are so crude." Then several years later at the height of her fame, she relayed the entire story to *Photoplay*, which went on to publish her vivid memories in its February 1932 issue.

Thelma didn't let the threats keep her down. She continued to be seen out and about in Los Angeles on a regular basis. In October 1927 she was in the audience of a fashion show at the Café Montmartre, alongside actresses Joan Crawford, Billie Dove, and Sally Blane. Then on October 30 she was featured in the *Los Angeles Times* with fellow Paramount School alum Josephine Dunn, modeling jewelry and showing how styles had changed over the years. Thelma was becoming a hit with advertisers; during the course of 1927 she had also posed with Dunn to advertise the Peerless 6-60 roadster and then on her own to show off the new Arborphone radio unit.

Toward the end of the year, Thelma embarked on what was to be a huge movie in the years to come, making stars of just about everyone in the cast, including one particular actress. The movie was *Hell's Angels*, but the actress it made a star of was Jean Harlow, not Thelma Todd.

The World War I epic *Hell's Angels* was the brainchild of eccentric businessman Howard Hughes. His intention was to produce a war picture the likes of which nobody had ever seen before, complete with daring aerial footage and adventurous action shots. Though the movie is now known as one of the earliest smash hits of the sound era, it was originally planned as a silent film. Shooting began around November 1, 1927, and was slated to take just three months, with a cast that included Ben Lyon and Greta Nissen in lead roles and James Hall and Thelma in supporting parts. From the very beginning, it was something of a nightmare shoot.

On November 3, Thelma had just completed a scene on set and was released so she could go home and collect a change of clothes. The actress was driving her own car, but as she pulled out of the studio gates, an ice cream truck lost control and plowed straight into her, throwing Thelma to the floor and almost overturning her vehicle. Studio security heard the commotion and came running; they saw the actress's car totally wrecked but no damage to the truck whatsoever. Amazingly, though Thelma was bruised, she wasn't seriously hurt, and after receiving first aid at the scene, she was taken back into the studio to recover. The other driver was sent on his way, shocked to have hit a movie star but otherwise unscathed.

Just days after the crash Thelma was at work on publicity appearances, this time traveling to the Southern Pacific Train Depot to welcome actors Bernard Gorcey and Ida Kramer. They were in Hollywood to make their play *Abie's Irish Rose* into a movie. Nearly five hundred members of the public turned out to see them, along with celebrities, including young stars Charles "Buddy" Rogers and Ivy Harris, but it was their former classmate Thelma who stole the show. Posing for photographs with Gorcey and Kramer, the actress was seen with her arms around the joyful Gorcey, while his screen wife stared daggers at his new admirer. It was all pretend, of course, but it ensured that the young actress was the only one of the players to get her photograph in the movie magazines afterward.

On November 8, the *Film Daily* reported that Thelma was one of the busiest girls in Hollywood, working on several movies in quick succession. The newspaper added that her scenes in *Hell's Angels* had been completed during the first week of November—though production would continue without her for some time. Shortly thereafter, she and Richard Dix traveled to Victorville, California, for location work on the film *The Traveling Salesman*. In one scene, the actor was required to drive his car through water, get out of the vehicle, and climb onto a rock. Everything worked as it should until the last part of the scene, when Dix suddenly slipped and fell straight onto his back. The actor injured his spine, though he managed to get through location work quite successfully.

The same cannot be said for Thelma. In the desert she was photographed looking happy and relaxed in her canvas chair, reading a book and surrounded by a ring of rope to scare off snakes. In the end, though, it would seem that she had to contend with reptiles of a different kind. Shortly after the photo was taken, the actress was unceremoniously fired from the film and sent back to Los Angeles. She was later quietly replaced by Gertrude Olmstead, who went on to earn good reviews for her role in the movie (later retitled *Sporting Goods*).

There was never an official explanation as to why Thelma was fired from the movie, but the timing of her casting couch experience and the termination of her employment on *The Traveling Salesman* cannot be ignored. It seemed as though Thelma was lurching from one disaster to another, and it was beginning to grate on the young actress's nerves. One day when asked by a reporter about the luck she was having in movies and in life, she surprised him by saying, "I have lots of luck—but it's all bad." The reporter shook off her comment, stating in his column that he was sure Thelma was just joking. However, given the unpleasant experiences she had encountered in the past year, it is easy to believe that the actress was in fact serious.

Thelma was in something of a down mood toward the end of the year, but she kept up appearances at various events around Los Angeles during November and December 1927. During a birthday party for actress Shirley Dorman, Thelma joked with reporters that the presents were so great that she might decide to have a birthday herself the following week. This was her more typical mien when dealing with the press—a happy acquaintance that endeared the actress to them—and as a result, the regular Hollywood columnists always seemed keen to write about Thelma in a positive light.

Thelma's mood must have lifted at the beginning of 1928 when she discovered that First National wanted to buy out her contract from Famous Players–Lasky, which by this point was known as Paramount Famous Lasky, or simply Paramount. Several magazines, including the *Film Daily*, broke the news to film fans: "First National is dickering to take over from Paramount, that company's contract with Thelma Todd." The two studios had long been in conflict; in fact, First National was founded specifically to stop Paramount head Adolph Zukor from browbeating theaters into showing only his movies. Zukor was furious, but he began to see the power of his upstart rival when theater owners actually began boycotting Paramount films.

First National started signing huge stars such as Charlie Chaplin, and then in 1918 its executives managed to persuade Paramount's Mary Pickford to join them too. Zukor tried to win her back with the promise of a five-year vacation and $250,000, but First National instead gave her the opportunity to write, produce, and star in her own films and took out several full-page ads to tell the world about her first film there. "Miss Pickford paid more for the screen rights to *Daddy Long Legs* than is spent on the entire production of many pictures," it announced. "Hereafter she will appear only in stories of her own choosing." Over the following years, major stars came and went from First National, but it continued to expand and eventually opened a full-blown studio in Burbank.

Although Mary Pickford had long since departed by the time the studio extended its offer to Thelma, the idea that such a strong company wanted to steal her away from her current studio must have been thrilling for the twenty-one-year-old. The deal with First National was finalized by early February 1928, but there was just one problem: the contract noted that her current weight was 122 pounds and stipulated that it must never go three pounds above or six pounds below that mark. For someone who had struggled with weight issues before, this would be quite a challenge, but Thelma signed the contract and bade farewell to the studio that had given her her break.

6

WHAT'S YOUR DREAM?

*A*fter her new contract was signed, Thelma dove headfirst into a string of movies for First National. *Vamping Venus*, a comedy about a politician (Charlie Murray) who is propelled back to ancient Greece after receiving a bump to the head, received considerable press attention during production. Thelma received third billing after Murray and actress Louise Fazenda; Todd plays Madame Vanezlos the Dancer and the goddess Venus. Photos of her in full Grecian dress were distributed to magazines such as *Screenland* and the *Film Daily*.

Thelma loved working on the film and went to work each day confident that she would enjoy what lay ahead. She got along very well with actor Charlie Murray, a naturally funny man who kept everyone laughing on set. That, she felt, was the hardest part of all: trying to keep a straight face while he made jokes as they filmed.

When the upcoming release was announced, several comparisons were made between the actress and the "original" goddess—as exemplified by the famous sculpture the Venus de Milo. Thelma was nothing like her, people said, and newspapers explained that the original had a totally different figure and would be considered dowdy by 1920s standards. When the film was released, it did make money, but some audiences and most critics seemed to hate it.

Exhibitors Herald and Moving Picture World asked various theaters around the country to disclose their customers' reactions to the film. While none mentioned Thelma, they were vastly disappointed in the cast performances as a whole. A theater in Elgin, Illinois, reported that most of their patrons had simply gotten up and walked out of the cinema altogether: "If anyone could enlighten me why they made this thing, I would be pleased," wrote the manager.

Another First National release, *The Noose*, starred actor Richard Barthelmess and was based on a play about a boy who becomes tangled up in a plan to murder his long-lost mother. Actress Lina Basquette plays a cabaret girl with great success, while Barthelmess gives what the *Los Angeles Times* described as "one of the finest performances of his career." Thelma, meanwhile, was given the small role of Phyllis, which saw her receiving last billing in the "Others" section of print reviews. Nevertheless, critics enjoyed the film; some claimed it to be one of the most gripping films of the year: "A mighty fine production," said the *Film Daily*. While Thelma's role may have been small, she did gain a few positive reviews, particularly from the *Film Spectator*, which said, "Thelma Todd, who is one of my favorites, is satisfactory in a small part."

The next few months passed in a haze of acting jobs and social events. Thelma was becoming a regular at the Café Montmartre on Hollywood Boulevard, which was seen as one of L.A.'s most prestigious nightclubs, a direct competitor to the Ambassador Hotel's Cocoanut Grove. Café Montmartre was popular with just about every celebrity in Los Angeles. It was not at all out of place to see a young Joan Crawford doing the Charleston there, and before his death in 1926 even Rudolph Valentino had spent many hours on the dance floor. Of course, these were also the days of Prohibition, so imbibing alcohol was illegal. Still, this did not stop most nightclubs from supplying it, and at the Café Montmartre there was always a bootlegger on standby to procure whatever libations a clubgoer desired.

———— ∞⧜∞ ————

Thelma loved not only the Café Montmartre but the Ambassador too, and the parties at both venues gave her a chance to keep her face and name in the magazines. And she did need to spend time away from her ever-present mother. However, outside of her party appearances she actually lived a relatively quiet life in the apartment she and her mother shared. Her typical day involved getting up early, having breakfast, and readying herself for work. Then she would drive to the studio, pop home at lunch if there was time, and finish work around five.

Evenings would be spent answering her own fan mail, arranging her favorite flowers—violets—in a vase, baking cakes, or reading books such as *The Story of San Michele* by Axel Munthe. "I guess a certain amount of success does change one outwardly," she said. "But I've still got the New England conscience. I like to stay home and read and play the piano and have quiet little dinners. I'm always buying china and linens and things." And if she needed to "break up the monotony of the quiet evenings," she might just take her car out on the road. She would explain her need for calm in 1929, telling reporters there was so much mental work required in filmmaking that she always needed to regroup in the evenings. "Sometimes you get so nervous that when you hear a noise you want to jump," she said.

While at the studio, Thelma always seemed to have everything in order. She knew everybody on set; she was conscientious and reliable and always handled herself in a professional manner. Because of this, executives asked her if she would look after Otto Kahn, an investment banker with an interest in the performing arts, during his trip to Hollywood. She was happy to help out and arranged everything herself, seeing to it that a party was held in his honor at the Café Montmartre on March 28, 1928. Thelma reveled in getting everything ready for the big event and personally saw to it that the tables were decorated "just so" with a variety of flowers, including red tulips and sweet peas. The party was a success, due mainly to Thelma's happy disposition, supervising skills, and eye for detail. Humorously, people in attendance that day were quick to comment that she directed proceedings just like a schoolteacher would.

On May 24, Thelma was one of the guests at a party given for Watterson R. Rothacker, vice president of First National. The event was in recognition of his building plans and reorganization of the studio, and it was attended by stars such as Theda Bara, Charles "Buddy" Rogers, and Colleen Moore. Thelma actually had more to celebrate than most. She had just passed the dreaded "microphone test" and was officially approved to become an actress in the "talkies."

Film audiences enjoyed seeing their favorite stars on screen, but as they sat in the dark cinemas enthralled by the likes of Theda Bara and Clara Bow, there was one very big thing missing: sound. "I venture the suggestion that the great public was unconsciously hungering for sound when the talkies arrived," wrote Benjamin B. Hampton in 1931, adding that radio and the record player had evidently created an appetite for noise.

Production companies started to experiment, and great strides were made with short movies. Then in late 1927, Al Jolson's feature-length film *The Jazz Singer* was released, which while still partially silent, also explored singing, music, and dialogue. "This Al Jolson picture is the worst wallop the silent drama has ever had," wrote critic Delight Evans, and she was correct. Audiences flocked to see the movie and came out of the cinema wanting more. Word reached Hollywood that audiences would no longer be happy with silent movies. Films that were already finished were recalled to have sound inserted at key points. The production of new films slowly adjusted, and it changed the industry in drastic ways.

First of all, the introduction of sound meant that special filming stages had to be built, engineers had to be employed to work the audio recording technology, and new cameras had to be installed. Designers had to create new sets that would provide the actors with the best surfaces on which to work without creating extraneous noise, and props had to be carefully placed so that they would not tumble and upset the silence on set. The cacophony of sounds—wind, animal cries, etc.—caused by exterior filming was no longer acceptable, so productions were moved indoors, meaning that it was no longer possible to make westerns on the cheap. This resulted in cowboy actors being fired.

The advent of sound affected everybody and everything. Directors needed to learn not to shout at their actors once the cameras were rolling, and the actors had to adjust not only to talking on camera but to learning lines, too. Previously it hadn't much mattered what was being said during filming, and some eager lip-reading fans would often complain that they could see the stars using foul language. Actors also had to jettison the overacting that had been necessary to convey emotion in silent pictures. Studying lines and delivering them in a subtle way was now the ideal, and many actors found themselves totally out of their comfort zone. "Old reliables wobble, new names on wing as sound alters star values," read *Motion Picture News*. "Many silent performers flounder in rough waters kicked up by talkers."

At First National Pictures, actress Corinne Griffith had a contract for three more films. However, after making the transition to sound, she was able to make only two before executives decided things weren't working out and canceled the remaining movie. Around Hollywood, other actors were dealt the same hand. Karl Dane's thick Danish accent meant that overnight he went from the biggest draw on screen to an actor nobody wanted to employ. He tried to gain jobs outside the industry just to make ends meet and at one point even worked at a hot dog stand by the gates of Metro-Goldwyn-Mayer, the very studio where he had once reigned supreme. After trying unsuccessfully to kick-start his career, he ended up taking his life surrounded by photos and scrapbooks detailing his past achievements. "He stepped off the oblivion end of Hollywood last Saturday night," said the *Motion Picture Herald*. "[He was] a penniless, hopeless relict of the silent drama. The microphone did not like his voice. 'Success' gave him $1200 a week, and took everything."

Even Clara Bow, born in Brooklyn, worried that her accent would be too much for some mainstream audiences. She did successfully make the transition (going on to act with Thelma Todd), and her voice on film was actually quite beautiful. However, the fear of the microphone never left her. She began referring to it as an enemy and on several occasions appeared to break down at the thought of having to perform in front of it. Various personal scandals and breakdowns haunted her, and the fear she experienced on film sets became too much. She eventually gave up her career and for a time left Los Angeles in favor of life on a ranch in Nevada.

While some silent actors were pushed aside, others surprisingly found their careers on the rise. Performers who had been working in small parts during the mid-1920s were called upon to do a test in front of a microphone, and some were found to have the very vocal talent that executives and audiences were looking for. One example of this was a young woman named Bessie Love, who had tried to make a name in movies for ten years before talkies came along. During the transition, she made a calculated leap into several stage productions, training her voice and learning new techniques in the process. On her return to film work, she performed a mic test that went so successfully that she was given a role in a musical film titled *The Broadway Melody*, which went on to win the Academy Award for Best Picture. The same good fortune came to vaudeville acts, dancing girls, choreographers, and songwriters, as musicals became the new big thing.

By the time the transition was complete, *Motion Picture News* had interviewed several moguls to gauge their views on the new industry. Thelma's former boss Jesse Lasky said, "Talking pictures have hit their stride and their popularity has been proven beyond any doubt at the box office. Our studios have come through the transition from silent to sound in a manner most gratifying to those of us primarily interested in production."

Louis B. Mayer, vice president in charge of production at Metro-Goldwyn-Mayer, went further: "About a year ago motion pictures had reached a crisis, with pessimists predicting that sound films would bring chaos and disintegration. Every company has gone through this period of transition and emerged triumphant. Pictures are now being made in ways that were never dreamed of five years ago. Tremendous progress has been accomplished without any of the drawbacks which often go with such a rapid advance. The long-faced prophets have been silenced and the entire profession stands on a new pinnacle of achievement."

When it was discovered that Thelma was to take the talkies test, various newspapers wondered in print if she would make the transition from silent movies to talkies. Reporters asked for a comment from the studio, and finally an unnamed motion picture official told them, "I think Thelma would do well in speaking movies. She is a good talker." He was indeed correct. She had experience with public speaking, modeling, and stage work. She also had a clear New England accent; she later told interviewer Alice L. Tildesley how fortunate she was to come from a part of the country where "we naturally use good diction. . . . I watch my voice more carefully than I watch my facial expressions," she said.

While other actors and actresses were crippled with fear about the test, Thelma refused to let herself be fazed by it. She later told *Picture Play* magazine what was going on in her head during this time: "Something refused to let me fear, amid all the fear that was gripping my fellow players at the time. I seemed to walk alone, unterrified by 'dat ole devil' mike, even as time approached for my voice test. Not that I didn't have plenty of reason to worry, if I had let myself—but I just didn't. Finally the hour drew near; the minutes were flying fast and at last the crisis was at hand. I said my little speech. Then came the play-back. That was a nerve-racking moment."

Nerve-racking or not, on June 7, 1928, First National wrote to tell her officially that she would now be employed in movies with sound. (Though it should be noted that some of her silent pictures were still to be released.) As she signed her name below the signatures of the vice president and secretary, Thelma must surely have felt grateful. During the next few years, the actress would watch as many silent-film stars faded into the background. In an article for *Film Weekly* in 1933, she gave her opinion on why they had been forgotten. "I think the answer lies in the fact that the screen is no longer silent," she wrote. "It is no longer possible for a clever director to mold his material as he could before the talkies came. The captions that once helped the screen actress along are gone. She has to put her own captions across . . . she has to do a great deal more for herself than she had in the old days."

By July 1928, *Hell's Angels* had been in production for eight months and was now almost complete. Thelma's small role had long since wrapped, but Howard Hughes was still not happy with how the film was working out. Like everyone else in Hollywood, he had become enthralled with the concept of sound movies and decided he wanted to add sound and even several color scenes to his film. *Exhibitors Herald and Moving Picture World* and *Motion Picture News* both told readers about the exciting development, noting that Thelma was still going to be in the production (along with other original cast members).

At that point, *Hell's Angels* was slated to be shown in New York in November 1928, though it would not include female lead Greta Nissen, as her Norwegian accent meant her performance did not translate well to sound. She was eventually replaced by Jean Harlow (though Hughes insisted Nissen would still be present in a silent version released to those theaters that did not accommodate sound). Harlow's star-making turn would have to wait, however, as production on the film stretched on through the end of the decade.

In summer 1928, Thelma and her mother dined at the Café Montmartre, where insurance man and playboy Harvey Priester was seated at a nearby table. He would soon become a regular fixture in the actress's life, but for now it was another young man who was joined with Thelma in the headlines—and infuriated her at the same time.

Though the actress was still extremely busy with her career, the newspapers and magazines became more and more obsessed with her private life, in particular who she was—and was not—dating. False engagements were becoming a regular thing, and in August 1928 the *Boston Globe* reported that Thelma had rekindled her love with a "childhood sweetheart" and was about to be married. The man involved was James Ford, an actor who had recently played his first important role in *The Outcast.* An outcast was what he soon became when the news of the "betrothal" reached Thelma's home.

According to the newspapers, Ford had dated the actress when they were young schoolkids, and they had put their romance on hold while she made her name in Hollywood. Meanwhile, he had worked as a baker and driver before dramatically hiking across the country to find his love—and an acting career in the process. He won a five-year contract, and now "he has won the girl," announced newspapers, before sending reporters off to bang on Thelma's door for a statement. She wasn't at home, but her furious mother was. "This is about twenty times they have had Thelma engaged," she said, before adding an exasperated, "and we are sick of it!"

By the time they caught up with the actress, she was equally annoyed. Denying that there was any truth in the story, Thelma went on to say that if she ever were to get engaged, she would be more than willing to tell the whole world about it. Furthermore, she denied ever being friends with Ford at school and said she had met him only a few times in Hollywood. "Jimmy is a boy from my home town," she later said. "That engagement was a press agent's dream."

Friends got in on the rumor too and said that Thelma was most certainly not involved with Ford. Instead, they said, she had been seen out regularly with screenwriter Jules Furthman. This was just what journalists wanted to hear. They rushed to his door, only to discover that it wasn't actually him Thelma's friends were talking about; it was writer *Charles* Furthman she was supposed to be dating. When the reporters finally caught up with the correct screenwriter, they were bitterly disappointed. There was simply no truth in the matter, he assured them, and Thelma was quick to confirm his comments.

Although Thelma had successfully made the transition from silent movies to talkies, still she worried about her future. Rumors circulated that First National had called her to a meeting to discuss her weight. "If you don't get thin, you can get out of pictures," executives reportedly told her. She would later explain that she began to suffer from anxiety, fainting spells, and throat problems. "I began to get ambitious, to worry if I wasn't given a good part, if someone else got that bit I had my eye on," she later said. "[I] had a nervous breakdown. Pictures seem to affect girls like myself who are rather reticent and quiet."

The stress she felt during the latter half of 1928 was magnified when First National merged with Warner Bros. Though the studios would continue to operate separately until the mid-1930s, stars began to fall from the First National roster, and over the next year revised production policies would see the departure of actors Mary Astor, Billie Dove, Corinne Griffith, Colleen Moore, Charles Murray, and many others. Actress Alice White was built up into a full-fledged star, while other starlets found themselves out in the cold. Would Thelma be one of them?

The anxiety caused by this uncertainty was exasperating for Thelma, and eventually she visited a doctor. He examined her persistent throat problems and found that her tonsils needed to be removed. This was done in late October 1928, and during her time in the hospital, the doctor also decided to look for a physical cause of her anxiety and fainting spells. He ran tests and came back with the diagnosis that Thelma had a heart murmur, which he said might be due to the problems she had suffered with her tonsils. The actress was released from the hospital shortly after the operation but continued to be the victim of fainting issues for some time to come.

By the end of the year, several of Thelma's First National pictures were released, including the silent movies *The Crash* and *The Haunted House*. Numerous stills and portraits were released of the star in support of the latter, which saw Thelma in second billing as a nurse working in a creepy old house. Silly stories were released from the set, supposedly describing how Thelma's screams were a result of someone touching her sunburned shoulder. These tales were Hollywood fluff, of course, but it was all in the name of publicity.

Film Spectator called *The Haunted House* "a clever picture," praised the director Benjamin Christensen, and said it was sure the film would receive "a hilarious reception by the public." *Motion Picture* magazine explained that while the film began with some pointless gags, it ended "in a burst of screams from the audience. . . . There's a laugh for every shiver." However, *Exhibitors Herald-World* was not so kind. "It seems quite plain that I have nothing positive to utter about *The Haunted House*. Therefore I'll say no more about it."

While the reviews in general were mixed, for one of the first times in her career thus far, Thelma received significant positive mentions, not only for *The Haunted House* but also for her role in *The Crash*, a film about a man who meets and marries a burlesque dancer. The *Film Spectator* said Thelma was "a First National contract artist who is being built up and who has enough ability to justify it," while the *Exhibitors Herald and Moving Picture World* described her as "the new leading lady, gives a good performance as a traveling show girl." The *Motion Picture Almanac* for 1929 said the young actress had done so well in *The Crash* that she almost stole the picture from star Milton Sills.

First National's *Naughty Baby* was about a coat-check girl in a hotel who tries to win the heart of a millionaire. Alice White and Jack Mulhall played the two leads, and by all accounts they were at loggerheads during the making of the film, due to the fact that Mulhall had wanted to work opposite actress Dorothy Mackaill instead. This caused a lot of tension on set, but Thelma—who had third billing in the movie—took it all in stride, "by saying nothing, smiling at everyone and listening to everyone," she said.

When the film was released, the reviews proved to be as temperamental as the stars. They were at best average and at worst abysmal. *Motion Picture* magazine called it "worthless, save for a couple of creditable close-ups of Alice White." It also said that none of the stars (including Thelma) had anything to do—"an excellent example of how human material may be wasted in the movies." To cap it all, the magazine stated that the editing had been done with an ax, the direction was amateurish, and the story was "three cents worth of cat's meat." The *Film Daily* was less aggressive, saying that *Naughty Baby* would undoubtedly appeal to the "flapper trade" but (rather insultingly) added that the film really belonged to the "shop girl school of screen entertainment. Made expressly for the five and ten cent shop girl vote." While the reviews from the *Film Daily* and *Motion Picture* were not personal toward Thelma, the one *Motion Picture News* printed definitely was. "Thelma Todd displays her blonde loveliness and there seems to be an awful lot of it," the reviewer wrote. "That girl better go into training to keep her weight in hand."

With the weight clause in her contract, and knowing how prone she was to put on extra pounds, this review should have devastated the young actress. However, by the time it was printed, the clause would no longer be an issue: Thelma had become a free agent.

7

THERE'S NO PLACE LIKE HOME

On January 5, 1929, the *Exhibitors Herald-World* announced, "Thelma Todd, who until a few days ago was a First National star, is finding it profitable in the freelance field. She has had three calls during the past three days to appear in leading roles for various producers, but had already signed to play the starring role in *The House of Horror* for First National." Unfortunately, by the time the movie was released, it did so to terrible reviews. So too did *Seven Footprints to Satan*, in which a couple gets mixed up with a strange gentleman who seems to have superhuman powers. *Photoplay* described it as a "hodgepodge mystery story," though the reviewer did give Thelma something of a compliment by writing, "[She] manages to look beautiful and frightened while Creighton Hale makes his knees stutter."

Socially, however, 1929 got off to a good start. As a regular Café Montmartre customer, Thelma was asked to appear at its anniversary party on January 23. She was happy to oblige and not only attended the event but took an active role in the proceedings too. As young men and women took their places, Roy Fox and his orchestra kicked into action and off they went, dancing around the café floor under the watchful eye of Thelma, who was acting as a judge for that evening's dance competition. Afterward a fashion show was held by the May Company, which showcased styles designed to show off the "charm" of sunburn. If the sunburn stories that came from the set of *The Haunted House* were at all true, then Thelma must surely have appreciated that segment.

By this point Thelma had a manager, S. George Ullman and Associates, putting her forward for various projects, including a cinema advertising feature called *Fashion News*. It was also announced that Thelma would begin working on the First National Pictures talking feature *Careers*, alongside Billie Dove, Antonio Moreno, and Noah Beery. Thelma was given fourth billing, though her part was minimal and did not garner any attention from reviewers. This was probably just as well, since the story, a murder mystery about a boss who likes to sleep with his employees' wives whenever they want a promotion, proved to be exceptionally controversial. When it was released, the *Exhibitors Herald-World* would go so far as to declare it "a rotten story of a diplomatic chief whose methods of promoting inferiors was not a fit subject to be thrown on the screen for the entertainment of ladies, gentlemen and children."

The movie was a test run for Dove, who had just taken her talkies test, and according to *Picture Play* she succeeded "quite nicely . . . even to the extent of a great, big case of hysterics." While the reviews were decidedly mixed, Dove did find something of a friend in Thelma, who had liked her from the beginning—and later wrote her a letter. In it, she described Dove as "the sweetest and most charming woman I have had the pleasure of working with," then told her costar that she hoped life gave her a great deal of happiness "and all good things upon you."

By early April 1929, rumors circulated that Thelma was about to sign a permanent deal to make short films with master producer Hal Roach. Born as Harry Eugene Roach in Elmira, New York, in 1892, Hal had worked as an extra and assistant director during the early days of moviemaking. An ambitious young man, he saw a way into producing after inheriting a large sum of money. In the coming years, he and his partner Dan Linthicum produced many short films with actor Harold Lloyd, before Roach took an almighty leap into constructing his own film studio. The Hal Roach Studios began collecting a stable of talented performers such as the aforementioned Lloyd, then Charley Chase and Laurel and Hardy. The studio went on to have its films distributed by

Hollywood giant Metro-Goldwyn-Mayer, making it one of the most successful companies in Los Angeles.

Thelma had been persuaded to meet with Roach after talking to friend and fellow actor Marshall Neilan. He had watched one of Thelma's dramatic roles and advised her to stop trying to be serious and stick to doing comedy. While she appreciated the introduction, the actress wasn't sure about signing with Roach, as she had just received an offer to make four feature films for a studio in England. Friends encouraged her to sign that deal, but Neilan was adamant she would be better off with Roach. Thelma met the movie mogul, and together they discussed the terms of her contract. It was decided that although Roach would have first dibs on her talent, she would still be able to act in movies for other studios. The situation was perfect for the actress, and she agreed to the deal.

Reports released on April 8 described her as working on two unnamed comedies for the studio, and then on April 25 the *Los Angeles Times* announced that, sure enough, the star had just signed a five-year contract. (That report also mentioned that she had been talent-spotted by the Victor Talking Machine Company, which signed her to work on records after a successful test of her singing voice.)

When Thelma first walked into the Hal Roach studio, the organization was still in the early stages of incorporating sound and dialog into its shorts. As a result, several of the stock actors were in the midst of training their voices accordingly, some turning to Clark Gable's then-wife, Josephine Dillon, who was a successful drama and voice coach in Hollywood. In spite of any difficulties their transition may have caused, Thelma seemed to revel in the new experience of making slapstick comedy. "I didn't know what a good time I was missing," she told *Picture Play* magazine.

The first short film Thelma became involved in was *Unaccustomed as We Are*, with Laurel and Hardy. Stan Laurel and Oliver "Ollie" Hardy were then, as they are now, celebrated as comic geniuses. The two actors had been successful in their own right when they were teamed together by Hal Roach in the mid-1920s. The two worked so well together that they soon became a regular slapstick duo in Roach's silent shorts. Audiences loved their particular brand of hilarity, and even today, DVDs of their films are still sold all over the world.

By the time Thelma arrived at the Hal Roach studio, Laurel and Hardy were at the top of their game. They had recently worked with Jean Harlow in the silent comedy *Double Whoopee*, so the sight of a glamorous actress like Thelma on set did not cause much of a stir. "They were fond of Thelma Todd, as was everyone at the studio," said Stan Laurel's daughter, Lois. "She was an exceptionally nice person."

Unaccustomed as We Are just happened to be the first speaking part the famous duo had ever taken part in. It was a learning experience for everyone concerned; nobody but Thelma was really prepared for the need for absolute quiet on the set. Just dropping a pencil or bumping into a tea trolley would ensure the whole scene had to be done again. "The talkies are much more different than the silent pictures," Thelma later said.

The actress's role put her right in the middle of the slapstick shenanigans. She plays Mrs. Kennedy, a neighbor of Ollie's from across the hall. When his wife storms out of their apartment after a huge argument, he and Stan try to cook themselves dinner. Unfortunately they end up blowing up the kitchen, so Mrs. Kennedy comes over to help them out. Of course, nothing goes to plan, and before long her dress is on fire and she is left wearing only her underskirt. When Ollie's wife comes home unexpectedly, Mrs. Kennedy hides in a trunk to avoid detection, but then her own spouse arrives and begins bragging to Laurel and Hardy about his affairs with other women. Once she gets her husband alone, it becomes clear that Mrs. Kennedy has overheard the conversation: she begins throwing things at her husband. Finally, a bruised Mr. Kennedy calls the boys into the hallway for some payback, but as he prepares to clobber Stan, Mrs. Kennedy shatters a vase over his head. The comedy in *Unaccustomed as We Are* stands up to this day, and reviews at the time were very encouraging. *Motion Picture News* said that all who were involved in the film could "throw their chests out a bit."

Thelma's next Roach short was *Hurdy Gurdy*, filmed during the first week of April 1929. It stars Edgar Kennedy, one of the actors who had turned to a voice coach to prepare him for the microphone on set. He plays the part of a retired policeman who is encouraged by some apartment-dwellers to find out why their upstairs neighbor (Thelma) is always ordering buckets of ice. Has there been a murder or something else grisly and obscene? No, the young woman just needs the cold water for her pet seal, that's all. *Motion Picture News* called it a "crackerjack affair," and Thelma's character was mentioned in good favor throughout.

It was clear that Thelma had found her niche as a short-comedy actress. She continued to shine in appearances with talented comedians, including longtime Roach star Charley Chase, with whom she starred in one of his first talking shorts—*Snappy Sneezer*, about an unfortunate soul who suffers greatly from hay fever—and various projects thereafter. She enjoyed working for Roach, whom she described as "a really wonderful man." She quickly became one of the most valuable and approachable actors at the studio. One employee said that during her entire time there, Thelma clowned around constantly and never complained or asked for a stunt double.

Things were definitely looking up professionally, but Thelma had something of an inferiority complex when it came to her acting. On occasions throughout this period, she complained that she wasn't good in any of the films she had previously appeared in. When pressed, however, she was quick to add that if she were satisfied with the work she had done so far, she would have nowhere to rise to. "Instead of progressing," she said, "I would slowly but surely fade out of the picture."

Adding to her feelings of inadequacy were the constant claims in the press that she had gotten into movies by winning a beauty contest. The references bothered her enough that she gave several interviews over the years pushing back against it. "I have never heard of a beauty contest winner getting very far in any other line," she told Alice L. Tildesley. "The fact that I was Miss Massachusetts had nothing to do with [my career]." She also gave advice to future winners, instructing them to forget the fact that they had won a competition and to just get on with their work.

"Work alone will get you some place," she said. When reporter Dan Thomas brought the subject up, she told him, "I worked like a Trojan in that training school in order to get my contract, and I want the credit that is due me."

Despite the ambivalence about her reputation as a contest winner, Thelma was never shy about showing off her beauty and style—or even being judged for them. One of Thelma's next social appearances was at a fancy costume ball held at the Beverly Hills Hotel, with awards for the best and most original costumes. No records can be found as to what Thelma wore that night, but by the end of the evening it was actresses Ruth Chatterton and Marion Davies who won the prizes and the headlines.

On May 11, Thelma dressed up and walked the red carpet at the Pantages Theatre in Hollywood for the premiere of *Trial Marriage*, a silent movie she made for Columbia. In it she plays a woman whose half-sister (Sally Eilers) is always stealing her boyfriends; the film garnered some nice reviews for its "interesting story" and "good cast," and even skeptical critics seemed to enjoy the "sexy scenes." Together with Eilers and actor Jason Robards (father of the Academy Award–winning actor of the same name), Thelma not only wowed the crowds outside the Pantages but also took part in a personality competition several days after the premiere. The hopefuls paraded up and down in front of the actors, and then ten winners were chosen to be given parts as extras in a Columbia picture. For Thelma, the opportunity to be on the other side of the judges' table must have given her a great deal of satisfaction.

Next came an appearance on radio station KHJ on June 29, 1929, at which Thelma put her voice to good use in various comedy numbers. She was in great company, as celebrated actress Marie Dressler sang songs and concert pianist Jack King played during the same show. Then on July 10, just as the Hal Roach team was winding down for a summer break, Thelma was seen with Billie Dove, Lina Basquette, and June Collyer at a fashion show at the Cocoanut Grove in honor of the wives of visiting Elks. Since her father had been an Elk, this must have been a particularly meaningful event for the young actress—but not as meaningful as when she boarded a train with her mother to head back home to Lawrence for a much-needed holiday.

Around the time she was leaving Los Angeles, an article appeared in *Hollywood Filmograph* that called Thelma "an outstanding example of the new school of motion picture women evolved in Hollywood during the past year." The advent of sound movies had provided a wonderful boost to the actress's career, and as a result, by the time she reached Massachusetts not only her friends and family but also the public at large were all eager to meet and greet her.

There were many parties and get-togethers to celebrate Thelma's return as a successful movie star, but it would be the quiet times she came to appreciate most, such as when childhood friends came over to spend time with her. "[That is] the greatest feeling in the world," Thelma said. Together the young women talked about their lives since school, and the actress tried very hard to show she had not changed. She also made sure her friends and other visitors knew that it wasn't all smooth sailing in the industry—that the failures and disappointments far outweighed the successes. "It is only to the very few—the lucky ones—that Hollywood brings success and happiness," she said.

Thelma also enjoyed seeing the schoolteachers she'd trained with at Lowell Normal School, though she became discouraged by her old pals' favorite topic of conversation. "I found that the gossip about the school teachers was just as rampant as about the people in Hollywood," she said; it was strange to hear the same sorts of rumors whispered about actors and actresses directed at schoolteachers instead. "Not that it is really deserved in either case," she added.

After visiting her friends from the Normal School, Thelma started to reassess why she had ever considered teaching as a career. When asked about it on a visit to Scotland a few years later, she said that teaching was "fine but you can't keep it up and be sincere." She then expressed her view that all teachers should stop by the age of thirty-five or else they will eventually start to resent the students for their youth.

On days when there were no visits from family and friends, the young woman would slip out of her uncle's house on Bowdoin Street and make her way downtown to the various places she used to visit as a child. Walking past Lawrence High School, she would stop for a while and think about the times she spent as a student there, back in the days when her father was alive and her most pressing concern was spending time with friends or taking part in amateur theater.

The actress would also revisit the stores she had both frequented and worked in during her youth. She loved nothing more than ambling down Essex Street, a road she had walked many times during her childhood years. One day when she was out, a young boy came running up in great excitement. He had just seen *Hurdy Gurdy*, he told her—could she please send him her pet seal when she returned to Los Angeles? Thelma was so tickled that she shared the story during multiple publicity appearances she made before her Lawrence trip came to an end.

In late August 1929, shortly before her return to Los Angeles, Thelma appeared several times at the Broadway Theatre, where she was mobbed by so many fans that traffic was stopped and police had to be called to help her to and from the building. Introduced by manager Jim Carney as "Lawrence's own Thelma Todd," the actress walked onto the stage to an ovation that lasted several minutes. Afterward she thanked local residents for making her trip so worthwhile and for the support that had kept her going during the times when she just wanted to give up trying to be an actress. "I thought of your faith in me and it stirred me on," she said. "In my discouraging moments I think of the people back home and it gives me renewed strength."

The crowd loved her heartfelt speech and cheered when she turned the spotlight onto her mother. However, things turned a little sadder when Thelma told them that she would not be returning to Lawrence again for several years at least. The disappointment in her voice was genuine; the actress would always love returning to her hometown, and while she had lots to do in Hollywood, it must have been bittersweet knowing she once again had to leave her friends and family behind.

Immediately after her final appearance at the theater, Thelma (and her police escorts) headed to the Roseland Ballroom, the same venue where she had been crowned Miss Lawrence just four years before. There she repeated her words of gratitude, only this time she invited her mother onto the stage and thanked her publicly for everything she had done throughout her life and during their time in Hollywood. She then took a bow and left the stage, only to be crowded by many of those who knew her during her childhood. After such an exhausting round of publicity appearances, Thelma could have been forgiven for making a hasty exit, but instead she stopped and talked to each and every person, asking after their parents and for news of their lives.

8

QUEEN OF SLAPSTICK

Several of Thelma's films had been released while she was in Lawrence for the summer, including *Her Private Life* for First National and *The Bachelor Girl* for Columbia. Back in Hollywood, the editing of *Hell's Angels* rumbled on. On August 25, 1929, Howard Hughes announced that he was recalling Thelma and other cast members to the studio. His idea was that they would reshoot all of the scenes that had previously been shot in silence. The actors would be expected to come in at the beginning of September, Hughes said, and he would then be able to finish up production. While it cannot be confirmed whether Thelma was able to comply with Hughes's wishes, in the coming months her name certainly remained on the cast lists.

At the same time, Thelma returned to work at Hal Roach Studios and made sure her name and face stayed in the public eye, making trips to the Café Montmartre and to a housewarming party at the beach home of director Wesley Ruggles. The twenty-three-year-old was spotted at the opening of the RKO Theatre on September 11, 1929, and in newspaper and magazine ads for everything from the latest fashions to Brandes radios. However, it wasn't all work, and before long Thelma had found romance with one of Hollywood's most affluent men, believed to be a millionaire several times over.

In 1929 Harvey Priester was a thirty-year-old insurance salesman and confirmed bachelor who frequented Thelma's favorite restaurant, Café Montmartre. There he sat at the "bachelor table," courting the attention of eligible women diners. His wealth was legendary, especially when he purchased Rudolph Valentino's yacht for $2,300 after the actor's death. His love interests were rumored to include actress and socialite Dorothy Dunbar, and he was frequently mentioned as a party guest in the society pages of the *Los Angeles Times*.

Harvey came from an interesting family. His grandfather was one of Hollywood's first settlers; his father was a rancher, and his mother was heavily involved in social work and the women's movement. Perhaps it was his sister, Alma Dorothy Priester, who ended up being the most interesting, however. During the 1920s she was known as yet another Hollywood socialite, frequenting parties and nightclubs just as her brother did, but over the next forty years she become known as an accomplished pianist and patron of the arts, a civic activist, and the president of a mining company.

Thelma and Harvey moved in the same circles for a number of years before they finally started to be seen as a couple toward the end of 1929. They were spotted dancing up a storm at the Cocoanut Grove, dining quietly at the Brown Derby, partying at the home of friends, and watching a performance of the play *New Moon* at the Majestic Theatre. The relationship gained many mentions in the society pages, and people began to wonder aloud if, after all the rumored engagements of her past, Harvey was the man to finally win Thelma's heart.

In February 1930, a party was given at the Biltmore Hotel in honor of actor Neil Hamilton. Thelma arrived not with Harvey Priester but with her mother and actor/director Emory Johnson. Wearing a dramatic, tight-fitting blue gown and long black gloves, Thelma joked that the guests felt rather "wild and wicked," that evening, as everyone had been seated well away from their partners.

Her next appearance was equally fun: she and several other actresses were called upon to entertain Alister Gladstone MacDonald, the married son of Britain's prime minister, at the Breakfast Club. He openly kissed the young women, which shocked at least one journalist into claiming he was "apparently dangerously devoid of inhibitions." However, anyone who believed the meeting would end up embroiling Thelma in a political scandal was mistaken.

In April 1930 she went to a party at the home of actor Harry Langdon, back on the arm of Harvey Priester—though again she refused to give anything away about the nature of their relationship. One enterprising journalist, hoping for an exclusive, sidled up to her and exclaimed, "Things look serious between you two." Thelma smiled politely and said, "Yes they do," and that was the end of that.

While it could have looked as though Thelma was spending 1930 at play, she was actually working hard for Hal Roach and as a freelance artist. She was one of the busiest actresses in Hollywood, though her appearances were mostly in supporting roles. This didn't take away from the joy Thelma felt when acting, however, and her confidence was growing at last. She said she couldn't imagine being happier in any other career, but added that while others might dream of having their own film company, she had no ambitions in that direction. She enjoyed making comedies and hoped that all the training she was receiving at Hal Roach would put her in good stead for the future, but she had no ambitions to be a star. Instead her favorite parts to play were character roles that required a degree of research and thinking. "Character work is hard work but I seem to thrive on it," she said.

In a later interview, Thelma described how, at the beginning of her career, she was getting ready to do an emotional scene that required her to cry. The director sent her off to the corner to prepare when the leading man came up and asked if she had ever lost anyone or anything close to her. The actress had recently lost her father, and so she was told to think of that loss to bring on the tears. Or maybe the loss of a pet. Thelma was mortified. "I don't belong in this business if that's the way you cry," she said. "What's the matter with believing in what you are doing? If I believe in this girl, I ought to be able to cry over her grief, not drag in a puppy dog." Thelma then worked on her character and was so convincing with her tears that she had to be helped out of the studio when they finished for the day.

At the Roach studios, 1930 saw her teaming up with Charley Chase over and over again. One successful collaboration came in the comedy *Whispering Whoopee*, which also features actress Anita Garvin, a frequent Roach player who worked with Thelma on various occasions. The story revolves around Charley's efforts to sell his property to three representatives of the Chamber of Commerce. The men are renowned for their party antics, so to help them on their way, Charley hires three girls to "whoop things up." However, tipped off that their envoys like to mix a bit too much business with pleasure, the board sends three sour-faced gentlemen instead. As a result, the appearance of Thelma and her two wild friends threatens to derail the whole operation. Even as part of a trio of wild girls or acting opposite veteran comedian Chase, she holds her own, switching from the role of giggling youngster to society lady to tough talker in the blink of an eye. The reviews were suitably positive: "The laughs are plenty," said *Motion Picture News.* "Not especially new but the guffaws are there."

In early May Thelma and Harvey Priester went to the reopening of the Café Montmartre together, and then later in the month the actress was invited to the wedding of Louis B. Mayer's daughter Edith to producer William Goetz. A vast array of stars were in attendance, including Mary Pickford, Douglas Fairbanks, Ramon Novarro, and Norma Shearer. Friends, family, and most of all the press began to wonder if Thelma and Harvey would soon be married too, but they were left disappointed. While the couple became engaged for a short time, it would seem the actress never had any real interest in marrying her fiancé. "He's too much a playboy," she told reporter Catherine Hunter in 1932. "No sense of responsibility, and much too agreeable to make life interesting."

Shortly before that particular interview, Thelma told *Picture Play* magazine she had come to the conclusion that juggling a home life and a professional one was a losing proposition. "It can be done of course, but one or the other is bound to suffer. I don't believe myself capable of dividing my love. For the present, my work is my master." And so it was that while Harvey and Thelma made great dinner companions, their interests were just too different to make things work on a permanent basis. As a result, the engagement was quickly called off, but they remained friends and continued to date off and on for the rest of her life.

Although Thelma remained on the cast list for *Hell's Angels* throughout production, by the time 1930 rolled around, Howard Hughes had decided the footage he had was simply too extensive to be made into an acceptable movie. He trimmed the film so considerably that Thelma's part disappeared altogether. Jean Harlow, on the other hand, was much luckier. While she was actually billed third, it was her face that graced the movie posters, and the public loved her. Harlow would go on to become one of the most legendary of all Hollywood stars, appearing in films such as *Platinum Blonde* (1931), *Red-Headed Woman* (1932), *Red Dust* (1932), and *Bombshell* (1933). Her tragic death in 1937 at the age of just twenty-six caused an outpouring of grief usually reserved for presidents and members of the royal family.

Although the *Hell's Angels* experience was obviously a disappointment for Thelma, she did still take time to celebrate the release of the movie by joining Clara Bow, Inez Courtney, Lina Basquette, and others as hosts of a special supper party held after the glittering premiere at Grauman's Chinese Theatre. Then days later she was a guest at the Beverly Hills home of actress Carmel Myers and her husband Ralph Blum, where she arrived in a daring black lace gown and took part in their masquerade ball.

By summer 1930, *Hollywood Filmograph* was predicting a long future ahead for the actress. "Miss Todd is looking her very best these days and is showing a marked improvement in every talkie that she appears in. Some company will be signing her up one of these days to a long-term contract and they will have a winner." And her love life was again causing a stir when she was photographed with actor Ivan Lebedeff at the premiere of *Dixiana*, held at the Orpheum Theatre. Maybe *this* time she had found "the one."

For now, though, it was her friends' romantic lives that were making the real headlines. On August 6, actress Dolores Del Rio tied the knot with her relatively new boyfriend, art director Cedric Gibbons. Just days before, Thelma had joined the couple and a party of friends at the High Hat restaurant. They dined quietly and no one said anything about an imminent wedding, but as Thelma made her way home afterward, she happened to see an EXTRA sign with the news that Del Rio and Gibbons were to marry. The media went wild about the hasty decision and phoned Thelma for a statement. "I was astonished," she told reporter Mayme Ober Peak.

On September 10 the actress was to be guest of honor at George Olsen's club in Culver City, with friends Nora Lane and Lina Basquette. However, before she could relax that evening, Thelma had to go to court to give evidence in the divorce of Basquette and her husband, cameraman J. Peverell Marley.

On May 10 of that year, Thelma had been spending a pleasant evening at the Embassy Club, seated at a table with Basquette and Marley. The couple got up to dance, and suddenly Basquette began screaming at her husband over a woman who was dancing fairly close to them. "If she speaks to you or touches you, I will slap your face," she shouted, while Marley—in an attempt to calm her down—told his wife that he had no idea who the woman was and led her back to the table. Thelma immediately tried to soothe the jealous woman and calm the heated situation, but it did no good.

Basquette was well known around Hollywood for her scandal-laden life and at one point was all over the news for her marriage to studio head Sam Warner, with whom she had a daughter. After Sam's death, she handed the child over to the Warner family, then fought a long and convoluted legal battle to regain custody. After marrying Peverell Marley, the actress became extremely possessive and jealous. Her behavior was so extreme that Marley ended up quitting his job as a cameraman to become a dancer on her vaudeville tour. When the tour came to an end, he decided to resume work in Hollywood, trying desperately to find a job that would bring him into contact with no women whatsoever to avoid upsetting his wife.

Thelma had known Marley for two and a half years and was privy to the mental torture that he had been put through by Basquette. Shortly after the nightclub incident, a separation was announced (though the two were subsequently seen out together at numerous Hollywood functions). A few months later the actress tried to commit suicide, claiming she was depressed over her ongoing child custody case, and several days later her estranged husband filed for divorce. Marley told the press that she was a lovely woman and he wished it could be different, but he'd come to the decision that the marriage was over.

So it was that on September 10, Thelma was called upon to give her version of events during divorce proceedings. While Basquette later claimed that the two women were the very best of friends, it would seem that on the day of the hearing, Thelma was there to support Marley: she stood up in court and told the judge about his wife's jealousy and threats of violence.

Years later, Basquette would tell negative stories about her "best friend." (The two were certainly friends and often spotted at the same social events, though Thelma was seen far more with Billie Dove, Sally Eilers, and Sally Blane.) She claimed, for instance, that Thelma was obsessed with boasting that her ancestors came to America on the *Mayflower*, a habit that supposedly aggravated Basquette no end. It is interesting that Lina should mention this as one of her friend's annoying habits, as a few years after the divorce hearing, Thelma wrote a short article in which she addressed this very same topic. In the article, the actress explained that her "favorite occupation has always been expressing annoyance at people who boasted of coming from families who booked or stow-awayed passage on the Mayflower." It seems strange that Thelma would annoy her own friend with the exact same genealogical stories she herself hated to hear.

Lina also said that Thelma had a terrible drinking problem and made a drunken embarrassment of herself at parties. This claim, too, seems suspect. Thelma herself was typically frank about her shortcomings, but she never made any mention of such a problem in interviews. She also had a strong work ethic, and there doesn't seem to be any documentation in the Hal Roach archive to suggest that Thelma's drinking had an impact on her employment. And while the supposed substance abuse problems of other Hollywood actors became fodder for newspaper and magazine gossip, the media never directed those allegations at Thelma. Finally, none of her other friends seem to have noted such behavior—which cannot be said about Basquette's public rages.

Perhaps Lina's own reputation for drama persuaded her to take Thelma down a peg. She may also have wanted to get back at her friend for siding with Marley during the divorce. After Thelma's appearance in court she and Lina were publicly spotted together on only a handful of occasions—such as the party given in Thelma's honor on the very evening of the divorce. What the two said to each other during the event is unknown, but Thelma's support of Marley must have been something of a sticky topic.

Thelma spoke about her difficulties with female friendships to reporter Gladys Hall: "Women never trust women who are beautiful," she said. "Friendship with other women is all but impossible." She added that other ladies seemed to fear her, concerned that she was about to steal their boyfriends or husbands. One wonders whether this relates to Lina Basquette's jealous eye.

Autumn 1930 arrived, and Thelma was busy making comedy shorts for Hal Roach and features for other companies. The intense drama *Aloha* saw her playing the sister of a young man (Ben Lyon) whose love affair is not approved of by his family. Acclaim in dramatic productions continued to elude her; on its release the following year, the *Los Angeles Times* would describe Thelma's character as "a thoroughly disagreeable person."

Another feature, *Her Man*, was set in a dance hall in Havana, Cuba, and revolves around the fortunes of a young woman (Helen Twelvetrees) who wants to find an improved life for herself. It fared well and gained a large selection of positive reviews: *Film Daily* called it "the best drama of its kind to come along in quite a while," while *Exhibitors Herald-World* said it was action packed from beginning to end and offered the most realistic fight scene that had ever been imagined on screen. Unfortunately, Thelma was again cast in a minor role, this time as Nellie, a brunette vamp who is seen in the club. She was occasionally mentioned in the reviews, though those who did give her column inches focused on her appearance rather than her dramatic abilities.

Hot on the heels of *Her Man* came *Follow Thru*, one of the first films shot entirely in Technicolor. The feature-length comedy centers on a golf tournament, with Charles "Buddy" Rogers and Nancy Carroll in the lead roles. Thelma plays Ruth Van Horn, Carroll's rival both on the golf course and for the affections of Rogers. The film received mixed reviews, with several reviewers describing it as only fair or "pretty dull." The *Los Angeles Times* thought the two main characters were particularly irritating but liked Thelma, describing her as "quite a woman." *Exhibitors Herald-World* enjoyed the film and described Thelma's portrayal of the vamp as "excellent work."

At Hal Roach Studios, she reteamed with Charley Chase for two more shorts, *Dollar Dizzy* and *Looser Than Loose*, then reunited with Laurel and Hardy for *Another Fine Mess*. This last film was a funny piece in which Stan and Ollie play vagabonds who take cover in a mansion when the owner goes on holiday. All is well until Lord and Lady Plumtree (Charles K. Gerrard and Thelma) turn up to see if they can rent the mansion themselves. Ollie is then forced to pretend he is the lord of the manor, while Stan goes from playing the butler to playing Agnes the maid in quick succession.

In perhaps the funniest scene in the short, Agnes and Lady Plumtree sit down for some girl talk. The scene consists of Thelma interrogating Agnes on the running of the house, while the maid succeeds in poking herself in the eye with a feather duster and ripping her bloomers while trying to perfect a curtsy. Thelma plays the role of Lady Plumtree with a posh accent and regal bearing. Her talent was noticed by the reviewer of *Exhibitors Herald-World*, who described her as "a reliably good actress for comedy roles [who] adds to the humor of many of the sequences."

Thelma's comic abilities were also coming in useful in her role as an early and active member of Hollywood's newest dramatics organization, the Dominoes. The club was the female equivalent of the Masquers, an organization that allowed actors to come together to perform and socialize. Together with friends Sally Eilers, Billie Dove, and Inez Courtney, Thelma would often visit the Dominoes headquarters at 1791 North Sycamore Avenue to take part in small comedic skits. The club grew steadily and by September 1930 had reached 175 members—not bad for an organization that had only been in existence for seven months.

The members decided that it was time for an invitation-only revue, and Thelma was first in line to offer her services as an actress. In a sketch titled "His, Hers and Theirs," she was teamed with several other players, including Mae Busch; the women played both male and female parts. The *Los Angeles Times* called the sketch "saucy," while *Picture Play* relayed the (probably much exaggerated) tale of Busch being stopped by police officers on her way to the clubhouse and having to explain why she was currently dressed as a man in full tuxedo. The revue was a big success and became an annual event.

Thelma enjoyed being part of the club and also made a point of supporting other, similar organizations, such as the Film Welfare League. The FWL was composed of prominent women in the film industry, and on October 29, 1930, Thelma appeared at a charity benefit for the group at the Roosevelt Hotel. The evening included a bridge game and a fashion show, and Thelma opted to act as a model, showing off elaborate costumes while Ted Weems and his orchestra played the accompanying music. Thelma appreciated the opportunities these clubs afforded her to keep one foot in the worlds of modeling and theater. Of course, the groups also allowed her to mingle and get to know many other women in the business—including actress and comedienne ZaSu Pitts, who would soon become a very important part of her life and career.

January 1931 saw the release of two features, the comedy *No Limit* and the drama *Command Performance*, in which Thelma played minor roles. The following month she was invited to take part in an event to celebrate the Summer Olympic Games, which would take place in Los Angeles the following year. The "Kingdom of Olympia" presentation at the Biltmore

Hotel was billed as one of the most fantastic events on the social calendar and was attended by actresses such as Dorothy Mackaill and Loretta Young. The elaborate—if not slightly pretentious—affair involved socialite Peggy Hamilton being crowned Queen Olympia, while John Steven McGroarty was made King Zeus. (The overall aim was for the new king and queen to promote celebrations for the 150-year anniversary of the founding of Los Angeles.) Ivan Lebedeff was the master of ceremonies, while Thelma was the Greek goddess Hebe.

The Laurel and Hardy classic *Chickens Come Home* was released just days later, and Thelma enjoyed a fairly small but funny part as Mrs. Hardy. Husband Ollie is being blackmailed by an ex-girlfriend (Mae Busch), and the inevitable antics give Thelma many opportunities to show off her comic facial expressions. But her film work outside the Roach shorts continued to flounder; she received some positive reviews for her performance as the female lead in *Swanee River*, but the film itself was not a popular one. *Photoplay* declared that while Thelma and costar Grant Withers did try, they just could not save the film from being anything but ordinary.

Hal Roach's *The Pip from Pittsburgh* gave Thelma the role of a woman set up on a blind date with a very reluctant Charley Chase. While her role is not large compared to Charley's, the actress holds her own and gives audiences something to smile about, particularly toward the end of the film when the slapstick reaches mammoth proportions. *Photoplay* was fairly impressed: "Two tried and true troupers on the Roach lot manage to get a good deal of fun out of a slim script," it reported.

The reviews for the Roach short *Love Fever* were particularly kind, describing Thelma as "especially effective" in the story of three young couples who think that "love is buncombe." The man from each couple finds his way to Thelma's apartment, falls in love, and decides to marry her. *Exhibitors Herald-World* enjoyed her performance, saying that she was "the cleverest of the new line of comediennes. She is again in a role of half vampire and half clown. Her reading of lines is head and shoulders above most of the silent players who have transferred their talents to the recording devices."

In April, Thelma attended a high-profile tribute to pioneering film-maker Carl Laemmle at the Fox Carthay Circle. Abe Lyman was there with his band, but the biggest draws had to be Thelma, Bette Davis, Jean Harlow, and Gloria Swanson. Being on the bill with this new generation of glamorous stars was a big deal, and it is clear that Thelma was enjoying the limelight. She attended numerous other parties during spring 1931, including several get-togethers in support of the Dominoes and one event at the Embassy at which she joined the Hollywood Women's Press Club. There she enjoyed a game of bridge while dressed in a bright yellow sporting costume and white turban.

In most of her party appearances, Thelma was a hoot, a dream guest with a quick wit and a fabulous sense of style. However, sometimes she got fed up with being on display and made her displeasure known. One such incident happened around this time, when she was spotted looking particularly glamorous in a pink and white sports outfit. The party was not much fun, and when she got up to leave, the hostess apparently jumped to her feet. "Don't go," she pleaded. "Do stay around and let people look at you. You're so picturesque. You look like a motion picture star." The actress looked at her hostess with disdain and left the party anyway.

Thelma explained her frustration with this attitude in an interview with Gladys Hall some months later. "When I am invited to parties and large functions I think, why are they asking me? Because they really want me or because I make a good showing? I even dislike going to opening nights and the Mayfair and other public places because again I think, 'Why is he inviting me? Is it because I look spectacular and it's good publicity?'"

While some of the demands of her career were beginning to grate, Thelma was pleased to start a new chapter when Hal Roach teamed her up with comedienne ZaSu Pitts, a brilliant actress who could have the audience laughing or crying with just a look. The partnership began tentatively with *Let's Do Things*, part of a Hal Roach series called Boy Friends. The short film was released in June 1931 and established the basic conceit of the women's partnership: Thelma would be the sophisticated, quick-witted blonde, while ZaSu would be the insecure and somewhat dim brunette.

The pairing worked so well that Roach decided to make the two full-time partners, a female version of Laurel and Hardy. To that end, he took out huge ads in film magazines, promising that "Hal Roach doesn't rest on his Laurel and Hardy's! He's created another team that's equally sensational." He flaunted the duo's early reviews, telling the world how wonderful critics already thought the new act was going to be.

Thelma and ZaSu had known each other briefly from earlier work and their mutual membership in the Dominoes, but when they were teamed as a full-time pair, they became extremely fond of each other. They shared a fearless commitment to the rough-and-tumble nature of slapstick. When the scripts called for them to end up neck-deep in river water or be thrown around the dance floor by partners with two left feet, they took it all in stride. When their clothes ended up messy and often torn, they didn't complain. But they didn't take themselves too seriously, either; they'd often spoil scenes due to their inability to keep a straight face, then have to avoid eye contact with each other lest the uncontrollable laughter start right back up again.

Of course, while the media were keen to report on Thelma's professional partnerships, they were even more eager to talk about her private ones. During 1931 numerous reports were published about her connection to Ivan Lebedeff. The Russian actor was known to be eccentric. Dubbed "Hollywood's champion hand-kisser," Lebedeff used a monocle and carried a walking stick, had his clothes and cigarettes made to order, and required hotel staff to fill his room with fresh flowers. He could only ever live in a hotel or a mansion with full staff, he said—the idea of living in an apartment with just one or two servants was simply too much to bear.

Thelma enjoyed Lebedeff's company, but around the same time she was also in a relationship with—and rumored to be engaged to—bandleader Abe Lyman. Born Abraham Simon in 1897, he was a popular entertainer on records and at venues such as the Cocoanut Grove. Of Jewish descent, his religion threatened to clash with Thelma's Christian beliefs, but the actress refused to let it interfere with their courtship. As she told friend and reporter Catherine Hunter, "I had a few qualms about religion at first, but these days people are broad-minded and I dismissed that scruple." Still, while spirituality would not keep the couple apart, his life of travel did, and the courtship was swiftly called off. "I want a home. How could I have a permanent one anywhere in the country with his band? A traveling salesman would be equally as effective as a husband—if not so harmonious."

In early summer Thelma herself found time to travel to San Francisco and San Diego. Once back she spent time in the Knickerbocker Hotel's recently opened Terrace Café and continued to see friends. However, by July 1931 she had begun work on a movie that would change her life forever.

9

ALISON LOYD MEETS
A MARRIED MAN

For quite some time Thelma had been complaining that she was being typecast in her roles and was finding it hard to break out. Her madcap romps were looked on with great amusement, but she was not being taken seriously as a dramatic actress. In 1931, however, the twenty-four-year-old performer was given the opportunity to change not only genres but her whole persona—and her future too.

Roland West was a forty-six-year-old film director best known for his silent movie *The Bat* (1926). He was married to actress Jewel Carmen, and though to the outside observer they seemed to be a happy showbiz couple, behind closed doors there were most certainly problems. Wife Jewel was a dramatic, intense woman. Nine years older than Thelma, she had been involved with motion pictures since the very beginning of the industry, first working as an extra under the name Evelyn Quick. Very quickly she gained the attention of executive Mack Sennett, who was so impressed by the blonde actress that he placed her under contract. From there she changed her name to Jewel Carmen and worked for a variety of different companies, making her—for a time—one of the busiest actresses in Hollywood.

Given her talent, the woman could have become one of the most famous players in the world, had it not been for her unprofessional behavior. In 1918, she played two film companies—Fox Film Corp. and the Keeney Corporation—against each other, which resulted in her breaking an existing contract with the former in order to sign with the latter. Fox was understandably furious and refused to pay her salary. In retaliation, Jewel went to a New York court, claiming that she had been underage when the Fox contract was signed, and therefore it was invalid and she was free to sign with Keeney. The court agreed in her favor and insisted that Fox pay her a full year's salary, despite the fact that she had not worked for them in quite some time. This was the beginning of the end for Carmen's film career; she went on to play only small roles until her husband cast her in *The Bat* in 1926. After that she seemed to disappear permanently from the screen—though not the headlines.

Husband Roland West, meanwhile, had been an office boy for a Cleveland wholesale company as a teenager before being cast by his aunt in a stage production. After a shaky start he soon got a taste for the spotlight, and it wasn't long before he decided to go into show business full time. He acted often in sketches he wrote himself and became friends and colleagues with up-and-coming producer Joseph M. Schenck. The two worked together for years, and West directed various movies before trying his hand again at theater. Although he consistently worked, West's career never reached any huge heights, and he was known more because of his refusal to wear a tie. Although *The Bat* received positive reviews, it would not be until his association with Thelma some years later that he really started to make headlines—though probably not in the way he had hoped.

It seems that West met Thelma in 1931 while casting his latest project. (Film magazines would mistakenly claim that he had acted with Thelma in the 1929 movie *Her Private Life*, but that was actually actor Roland Young.) The drama *Corsair* was the director's passion project, the story of an unhappy Wall Street broker who decides to throw away his career and take to the high seas to go after notorious Prohibition rumrunners. In the part of stockbroker John Hawks, West cast Chester

Morris, with whom he had previously worked on the movie *Alibi*. To play Alison Corning, the daughter of Hawks's Wall Street boss, he chose Thelma Todd.

West was bothered, however, by the fact Thelma was renowned for her comic talent rather than her skills as a dramatic actress. One might wonder why he'd cast a comedienne in the first place if this was such a major concern, but the director had a solution: shortly after Thelma was cast, West asked her to abandon her comic aspirations—and to change her name as well.

It is hard to understand why West believed that dumping her famous name would be good for business. But Thelma, eager to prove her commitment to dramatic acting, agreed. West immediately set about finding a name he deemed suitable for a serious performer. He settled on Alison Loyd, created with the help of a numerologist who combined the name of Thelma's character with the name of a member of the *Corsair* crew. West told numerous reporters that it was "to take the taint of comedy away from her and give her a chance as a dramatic actress." He also explained that it was all something of an experiment—that he wanted to make Thelma forget she was ever a comedienne. He then added, "It is an attempt to change her personality and psychological outlook as well." As far as he was concerned, West said, Thelma Todd was dead; he would not allow any mention of her original name for the duration of the production.

Shortly after joining the cast of *Corsair*, Thelma gave an interview to *Picture Play*, during which she fretted again that she wasn't giving her best: "I've yet to be entirely pleased with my performances," she told the magazine. "You see, I have to build up my little niche in straight work all over again, having been submerged in comedies for more than a year." To columnist Dan Thomas she said, "Everyone has always thought of Thelma Todd as a rowdy comedienne. She never could get an opportunity to do anything else. But as Alison Loyd I at least have a chance of being dissociated from my past roles."

When Hal Roach heard news of Thelma's name change, he laughed. There would be various Pitts/Todd shorts coming out later in 1931, so he had no intention of declaring Thelma Todd "dead." The actress could be anything she liked outside his studio, he said, but while working at Hal Roach, she would always be known as Thelma Todd. When he heard that West wanted to "take the taint of comedy away from her," he retaliated with a quip of his own: "I'll have to change her name to Susie Zilch to guard against the taint of drama!"

Roach wasn't the only one who took the name change with a pinch of salt. Theaters alternated between the two names in the publicity materials for the forthcoming *Corsair* (once the film was released, reviewers would take to listing both names in the literature, just in case readers got confused). Even Thelma was confused, it seems, as she began signing letters as both "Thelma Todd" and "Alison Loyd" simultaneously.

Aside from her desire to break away from her comedic roots, there may be another reason why Thelma agreed to Roland West's name change. While making *Corsair*, the actress fell in love with her director and was surprised to find that the feelings were reciprocated.

What she saw in West is not obvious; he was a small man with a thinning hairline, gnarly features, and small, hooded eyes. His face often unshaven, his shirts tieless, he looked casual at best and scruffy at worse. Actor William Bakewell later described Thelma as very sweet and warm, but he called West a "kind of odd guy." His brother-in-law's son, Rudy Schafer Jr., described him as "a sinister, sneaky kind of guy and not well liked by most people."

Still, he possessed a charm that had won him the heart of beautiful Jewel Carmen some years ago, and now Thelma felt the same pull. But the director was married, and for someone who had once turned her nose up at the seedy goings-on behind the closed doors of Hollywood, the feelings Thelma was experiencing must surely have had her conflicted.

For the moment, however, the couple apparently put aside any feelings of guilt or remorse and embarked on a full-fledged love affair. The relationship took place right under the nose of Jewel Carmen, too; during the coroner's inquest into Thelma's death, Jewel spoke about being on location for a scene in which Todd is swimming off the coast of Catalina Island, and having various conversations with her.

Privately, Thelma was clearly pondering the future of this new relationship. Reporter Alice L. Tildesley came onto the set to write a feature about Thelma for her column. Halfway through the conversation and without any prompting, Thelma started to give her views on marriage. According to her, a second marriage would be more successful than a first, as the couple would have more experience and make more allowances for each other. "I believe in divorce if it is a case of severing marital relations or living together in eternal warfare," she said. This was revealing enough, but what came next was extraordinary. The actress added that if she had a husband who had fallen for another woman, she would be wise enough to tell him to go to her. She then explained that if he found he really did prefer the other woman to her, then she would step out of the picture and allow the new couple to carry on their relationship.

There was only one problem: Mrs. West was not the sort of woman to step aside for anyone, especially not a young woman her husband had just met on the set of his latest movie. Still, regardless of her determination to hold on to her man, shortly after the making of the movie the Wests' marriage began to degenerate into an estranged, on-again-off-again relationship.

The interview with Tildesley also betrayed some signs that Thelma's feelings for Roland were ambivalent, as she ended the conversation with a declaration of independence. She claimed that while she was blonde, she had a very brunette personality, uninterested in clinging to a man for protection. "So far as I can see, the only person you know you can depend on is yourself."

Thanks to Thelma's veiled comments and the gossip of cast and crew, rumors began to circulate that she and West had fallen for each other. West had once said that a goldfish had more privacy than an actress, and this was proved true when several gossip magazines repeated the stories they'd heard, though they declined to share the name of Thelma's forbidden love. *Photoplay* told readers that the actress "was rumored to have been quite fond of a man who directed her in a recent picture. Hollywood never knew for sure, but the community gossiped," before adding that "today Thelma is hardened against gossip."

Modern Screen was more brazen: it printed a short article about Thelma's name change and then directly underneath reported on "a real Hollywood Mystery Romance." In it the magazine revealed that a well-known director had been leaving his car in the garage and renting a limousine to visit a famous blonde actress. "Don't look at us—we can't tell," they exclaimed, knowing full well that the placement of the story was a dead giveaway.

With no happy ending in sight, by the time the film came to an end the affair had fizzled out. West went back to his wife, who accompanied him on various trips on his yacht, while the heartbroken actress tried to get on with her life. She never mentioned Roland by name to any media outlets but did allude to the relationship during an interview with Gladys Hall in early 1932. When asked if she had ever been in love, the actress assured the reporter she had been—but only once. She wouldn't say who the object of her affection was but said it wasn't occasional boyfriends Abe Lyman or Ivan Lebedeff. "It just didn't work out—but I know now what real love means," she said.

In another interview around the same time, she was asked who her ideal man was. Thelma replied, "One who's about ten years older than I. Who is understanding and tolerant. One who works, but also knows how to play. . . . But most essential of all, one whose intellect I can thoroughly respect, a man who will know when to cater to my whims and when not to." Apart from the age (West was more than *twenty* years older), Thelma had just described her lost love, whether the reporter was aware of it or not.

10

I LOVE YOU, I LOVE YOU NOT

*A*s she awaited the release of what she hoped would be her breakthrough dramatic film, Thelma returned to the world of comedy, playing a small role in *Broadminded*, a feature starring Joe E. Brown about two party boys traveling from New York to California. Thelma's turn as Gertrude, an actress who helps the boys out of a pickle, was barely mentioned in reviews—which is probably just as well, since even the preview audiences were lukewarm and critics seemed to hate the songs and music interspersed throughout the story.

Back at Roach Studios, the actress argued with Hal about whether she would be known going forward as Thelma Todd or Alison Loyd. For a time the actress argued for the latter, though Roach made it clear that the name on her contract was Todd, her movies had been sold to distributors with that name, and that was how she would be billed in Roach movies. In an interview with journalist Dan Thomas, the producer was even more adamant, telling him that while he wanted to cause no unnecessary trouble, if Thelma's new name proved to be detrimental, "I will take the necessary legal steps to prevent her from using it." Eventually she agreed to abandon the name Alison Loyd altogether, though she would still be billed as such for the forthcoming release of *Corsair*.

It was around this time that Thelma was introduced to Mae Whitehead, an elegant African American woman in her early thirties, who would act as Thelma's maid and companion for the rest of her life. Mae had been through a lot; on more than one occasion in her childhood, she watched as her home in Hemet, California, was burned to the ground by racist neighbors who wanted the family to move away. The racial abuse was so bad that her mother, Sara, would walk her to school every day and sit at the back of the class with her, sewing, anxious that Mae's classmates and teachers would treat her fairly.

Understandably, Mae chose to leave her hometown as a young woman, moving to Los Angeles to be close to the movie industry. She had no interest in becoming an actress herself, instead setting her sights on doing domestic work for those in the business. Mae was a caring woman, and it didn't take long for her to earn the trust of various actresses and thereby employment as a maid. Thelma and Mae bonded immediately, and from that moment on, the woman was employed to look after the actress's clothes, take care of her personal affairs, and generally make sure that everything ran smoothly for her busy boss.

With Mae now in charge of Thelma's everyday life and the relationship with Roland West at an end, Thelma could devote more time to her professional partnership and friendship with ZaSu Pitts. The two comediennes were spotted at a variety of parties in the latter half of 1931, including a lavish anniversary event for the president of the Dominoes. They were frequently seen together shopping and lunching around Hollywood, which led columnist Grace Kingsley to nickname them "the Sarsaparilla Sisters." *Photoplay* told readers that the two had gone on a beach outing that ended with ZaSu playing a trick on her unsuspecting friend: the girls stopped off at a store and ZaSu jokingly drove off, leaving Thelma stranded wearing nothing but her bathing suit. Whether the story had any truth in it is another matter, but it shows the extent to which the two comediennes were gaining the attention of the media.

By fall 1931 Hal Roach had released a number of Pitts/Todd comedy shorts, among them *Catch as Catch Can*, *The Pajama Party*, and *War Mammas*. They all followed the tested Roach formula for madcap romp and slapstick comedy, and audiences seemed to enjoy them. The *Film Daily* announced that *The Pajama Party* "has many laughs mainly due to

ZaSu's unique style of droll delivery" but hoped that future outings for the pair would include stronger writing to show the duo at their best.

The autumn also brought the release of *Monkey Business*, a movie Thelma had made with the zany Marx Brothers earlier that year. The film is something of a mishmash, set on board a ship to America. The brothers are stowaways who eventually get mixed up with gangsters. Thelma's part is fairly minor, and she seems to have been there mainly to provide glamour, plus the occasional dance and gag with Groucho. Despite the lack of story, however, the reviews were fairly positive. *Silver Screen* took the corny route by deciding that *Monkey Business* was "funnier than a barrel of monkeys," while the *Los Angeles Times* called it the funniest film to reach the screen in quite some time. Thelma gained a small mention in the *Times*, described as a very pretty comedienne who was playing it straight.

Toward the end of September, the Dominoes club moved its headquarters to a new house on North Crescent Heights Boulevard. As always, Thelma was there to show her support, watching as the club flag was hoisted in a lavish ceremony. Her association with the club pleased her, and it was a definite confidence boost to be able to spend time with such a diverse and interesting group of women.

Still, her professional life was bothering her again, and on October 30, 1931, she poured out her thoughts to a fan who had written to her earlier that year. "Some of the roles are not too pleasing, nor offer much opportunity," she wrote. But she added that she always needed to give her best, as "no matter what capacity you are in, you are quite necessary to make the wheel go round." *Corsair* must have been on her mind, because although her name change had been abandoned, the actress signed the letter as both "Thelma Todd" and "Alison Loyd."

Someone else who had *Corsair* on his mind was Roland West. His film was set for a November release, so he'd soon find out how the critics and public would take to him "killing off" Thelma's comedic nature and replacing it with a more serious persona. When the reviews finally began to come in, they were mixed. The *Film Daily* told readers that the story was far too fantastic to be taken seriously but praised Thelma's part of a society girl as "stunningly portrayed." On the other hand, *Screenland* enjoyed the movie ("It never lets you down for a minute") but said of Thelma's role, "The love interest is always secondary." Many of the critiques were splattered with references to the failed name change.

Thelma had invested so much into the movie, not just changing her name but also risking her reputation on an affair with its director, that the reviews must have been disappointing. She didn't give herself much time to fret, however. Professionally she was keeping herself busy, and in her off-hours she was occasionally still being seen with Ivan Lebedeff. She also occupied her time with more volunteer work: the next Dominoes revue took place in December 1931, and then the Assistance League Tea Room announced that Thelma and ZaSu would be hosting a "Star Day" at their De Longpre Avenue building the following spring.

Just after Christmas, another Pitts/Todd short was released, titled *On the Loose*. They play a couple of girls-about-town who are sick and tired of being taken to Coney Island by would-be suitors. The film is an entertaining ride, with a lot of location shots of the amusement park and a cameo by Laurel and Hardy. As always, Thelma plays the straight girl perfectly, while ZaSu continues to perfect her forlorn, perplexed persona.

Rumors surfaced that the duo had gotten themselves real-life jobs as waitresses just so that they could have fun and be fired as a result. This may or may not have been true, but at the end of February 1932 the two women definitely worked together in a café. Every day for a week, the two actresses would finish work at the studio and drive down to Leighton's Arcade Cafeteria on South Broadway, where they hosted a live radio play. The story saw Thelma play a young girl looking for fame and fortune, while ZaSu played a maid in a boarding house.

The women also found time to rehearse for the next Dominoes performance, a burlesque version of *Lysistrata*. The show took place in March 1932, around the time Thelma's next feature, *The Big Timer*, was released. The Columbia movie starred Ben Lyon as a prizefighter and Constance Cummings as his manager. However, their working and personal relationship is almost knocked out when the fighter catches the eye of city girl Kay Mitchell (Thelma). Thelma had third billing after Lyon and Cummings—though her part in the movie was barely mentioned in reviews. All who did mention her agreed she provided good support, but most of the praise was heaped on Lyon, Cummings, and the rest of the supporting cast.

In April it was announced that Thelma was to appear in another Marx Brothers film, *Horse Feathers*. The Paramount musical centers on a collegiate football rivalry, with Thelma playing Connie Bailey, a grass widow who is involved with Frank (Zeppo Marx), the son of the college president (Groucho). Thelma does a good job of playing a sophisticated schemer whose apartment is so popular with men that Groucho suggests they should install a hot dog stand. She also has the somewhat dubious pleasure of having the song "Everyone Says I Love You" performed for her by each member of the Marx Brothers: in bed, at a piano, beneath her window, and in a canoe.

Thelma enjoyed the experience of working with the zany team again, though she did admit that it was difficult to keep a straight face when the brothers started to ad-lib. The film would be an immediate hit, with the *Los Angeles Times* giving Thelma special mention for her beauty, endurance, and comic values, and it would go on to become an enduring classic.

At the end of April, her father's brother David passed away at Lawrence General Hospital at the age of just fifty-two. Knowing that she could never get time off work to attend the funeral must have been a blow for the actress, but she did what she always did in times of stress and threw herself into her work.

Thelma's next feature was the comedy *This Is the Night*, in which she and newcomer Cary Grant play Stephen and Claire Mathewson, a husband and wife whose marriage has lost its spark. When Stephen suspects (correctly) that his wife is planning an adulterous getaway with Gerald (Roland Young), the illicit lovers hire another woman (Lili Damita) to pretend to be Gerald's wife so that they can all go as a foursome. *Picture Play* declared it "a tepid farce" but asserted that Cary Grant showed promise. Of Thelma, who makes full use of her sharp comic timing and expressive eyes throughout the film, the reviewer commented, "Though beautiful, [she] is a lost lady when she speaks." *Photoplay* praised the movie as "sophisticated and highly spiced" but made no mention of Thelma's performance—only that she had "gorgeous legs."

On May 2 Thelma appeared at the May Company in a rather bizarre public outing. Alongside Marian Manners, director of the *Los Angeles Times* Home Service Bureau, she cohosted the Electric Refrigeration Exhibition. Thelma met and greeted eager fans as Manners gave a lecture on the various uses of fridges. Next, back on stage with the Dominoes, Thelma acted with Eloise O'Brien in a sketch titled "Black Outs a la New Yorker." The two actresses played a man and woman in a blackout, with Thelma as the female and O'Brien as the male.

Thelma was still living with Alice, but the continued proximity to her mother didn't seem to hamper her love life. Thelma was still leaping from one relationship to another; one week she would be seen out with Ivan Lebedeff at the Brown Derby, then the next she'd be at a party in Beverly Hills being taught the rumba by writer Jack Quartaro. Then she'd be discussing poetry with celebrated author Austin Parker, closely followed by dinner and a party at the Biltmore with New Yorker Schuyler Van Rensselaer. For the Biltmore appearance she wore a racy outfit of black lace over a flesh-colored slip and a bright red wrap, which she admitted had taken some guts to wear, even for her.

The girl who had once threatened to knock out any boys who dared try to kiss her may have relented somewhat in adult life, but she still found male attention to be something of a mysterious nuisance. She explained during an interview with Gladys Hall, "I have annoying habits. I sometimes don't like to talk for hours at a time. I hate to be touched. I'm cold and not very exciting." When dating she would ask boyfriends why they liked her—what was it about her that they found to love? They would sometimes come up with a plausible answer, but if they dared tell her their love was based on her beauty, the suitors would be out the door in a flash.

One wealthy admirer went so far as to offer all manner of material reward in exchange for her hand in marriage. He didn't love her, Thelma insisted; the only reason he had proposed was so that he could put her on display. "Something he had bought and paid for because he believed me to be a good specimen and worthy of a swell show case. He did not love me. I would not have had a home," she said.

Thelma also found the media's attention to her love life annoying. In early 1932 she was furious when they started to incorrectly speculate about her involvement with recently separated actor Ronald Colman. When asked by *Picture Play* if the two were having an affair, she snapped "No" before going on to explain that she had only met him several times. She had seen him once at a party in the late 1920s and then again when she was making *Corsair* and he was involved with *Arrowsmith* on the same lot. "Naturally we were thrown together a bit," she said, "but I have never dined in public or alone with him. In fact, I don't think any woman has. There is no romance between us and never has been."

Still, she was in her mid-twenties, and after the disaster that had been her relationship with West, she had begun thinking about settling down. She told good friend Catherine Hunter that she was anxious to get married. "[I'm] just like any other normal girl. You know the afternoons we've spent traipsing around the suburbs looking at all the model homes for newlyweds? Yes I want to get married—and have a dozen babies." To the *Boston Daily Record* she expressed her interest in marriage but assured the reporter that it wouldn't be until she had retired from pictures. "Hollywood marriages are not that successful usually, and I don't want to suffer a broken heart," she said.

Unbeknownst to anyone at the time, Thelma actually had a potential husband in mind. Pat De Cicco was something of a mysterious character before, during, and after his relationship with Thelma Todd. He has been described as a polo player, a businessman, an actor, a theater manager, and everything in between. Many have characterized him as a wannabe mobster who hung out with gangsters to make himself look good. He certainly had his hands in many different pies, though by the time he met Thelma he was describing himself as an agent and business manager for actors.

On the outside at least, De Cicco had much going for him. He was a handsome, smartly dressed man who knew how to turn on the charm. When the couple first met, it was in a friend's residence at the Ambassador Hotel; they began their relationship with a full-blown argument. This did not bode well for what was to come, and certainly by the time their association came to an end she had seen more than her fair share of De Cicco's bad moods and violent tendencies. For now, however, he was simply an attractive if somewhat capricious character, someone who could alleviate the boredom of incessant dating and the heartbreak of losing Roland West. The actress quickly fell for him, and it wasn't long before he proposed.

After Pat and Thelma were photographed together at a polo match, the press started to speculate that they were going out together. But when the couple suddenly eloped to Prescott, Arizona, Hollywood was agog. Jean Harlow had recently tied the knot with producer Paul Bern, and everyone was surprised because celebrated bachelor Bern had never seemed like the marrying kind. But when De Cicco and Thelma married, it was the *bride* who gave cause for astonishment. Yet there she was in July 1932, smiling broadly with her new husband, sitting in the passenger seat of the large car they had used to drive to Arizona. The *Los Angeles Times* lamented the taming of Hollywood's most eligible woman by joking that all her old broken-hearted lovers had attended a party at the home of Billie Dove, where the actress was very happy to console them.

Right from the beginning, the marriage between Thelma and Pat was a difficult one. She had previously stated that once married she would concentrate on her husband rather than her career, but now that she'd actually tied the knot, she was busier than ever before, working on a great number of projects all at once. De Cicco wasn't as busy, so he became frustrated with the long hours she spent at the studio instead of settling down with him and upset that she claimed to be far too busy to make a trip to the East Coast to meet his family.

De Cicco liked to be in charge, which was always going to be an issue for someone as headstrong as Thelma. She had once broken off a relationship with a broker by the name of T. Sulley because of his possessiveness—"He was insanely jealous, and you know you can't live like that," she said—and she certainly wasn't going to accept jealousy from her husband. In fairness, however, she didn't make things easy for him. Shortly after the wedding, they went on their first public outing as a married couple, attending a party at the Hillcrest Country Club. While the two were seen in each other's arms, she was also seen whirling around the dance floor with various other admirers. That kind of behavior was never going to sit well with De Cicco, but for now—in the public eye at least—he remained quiet.

On August 5, 1932, Thelma was thrilled to appear as a host at the Olympic International Ball, held at the Shrine Auditorium. Together with Bebe Daniels, Anita Page, and dozens of others, the actress greeted friends and guests in a pavilion dedicated to her home state of Massachusetts. Then, on August 27, Thelma was dining in the Brown Derby when a fire broke out in the kitchen. It quickly filled the entire establishment with billowing smoke, and two hundred people, including Thelma, Tom Mix, Lew Cody, and Thelma's old love Ivan Lebedeff, all spilled out onto the pavement, where tourists and fans caused such a scene that police had to be called.

Meanwhile, her films continued to hit theaters. In the feature *Speak Easily*, she was teamed with Buster Keaton and Jimmy Durante in a hilarious behind-the-scenes look at putting on a musical. Keaton plays Timoleon, a college professor who is in charge of the production, while Thelma is Eleanor, a young vamp eager to progress in her career and gain the attention of the wealthy professor. It was one of her larger feature roles, filled with copious demonstrations of her comic timing—and her physical fitness too.

During one scene, Timoleon and Eleanor become drunk and she tries desperately to seduce him. Despite being inebriated, he seems to want nothing more than for her to just go away. This results in the actress being dragged across the floor, picked up and bent in two, and otherwise roughly handled. The film received good reviews; *Photoplay* called it a "goofy picture that stands up in a month of screen comedies." But all too typically, the magazine praised Thelma only for her body, declining to mention her fabulous performance.

Show Business, the latest Pitts/Todd short, features the girls as out-of-work actresses looking for their big break. When they are booked onto a show with their pet monkey, all three need to catch their train in just an hour to make the engagement. This of course leads to all kind of scrapes and monkey business. With much of the action taking place in the bedroom compartment of a train, it evokes the early scenes in the 1959 classic *Some Like It Hot*. Since it was a short movie, reviews were limited to a sentence or two, but audiences still enjoyed the girls' adventures, and for now the two were happy to continue making them.

Klondike, a melodramatic love story, was less well received. Lyle Talbot plays Dr. Robert Cromwell, a disgraced surgeon who finds a chance for love and redemption when he crash-lands in the Alaska wilderness. Thelma was cast as Klondike, the object of his affection, who also happens to be engaged to a man whose life could be saved by Dr. Cromwell's surgical skills. While some critics—such as those from the *Film Daily* and *Hollywood Filmograph*—seemed to like it, others absolutely hated it. *Photoplay* called the film "an old melodrama from the silent days, made into a talkie, and it limps from sheer old age. . . . Thelma Todd is unfortunately cast as the sweet young thing." *Educational Screen* was just as brutal, calling it an "unskillful attempt at a melodramatic problem play. Elementary in acting and direction, improbable and unconvincing, and largely uninteresting." In retrospect, the reviews seem a little harsh. While the film is no masterpiece, it doesn't pretend to be, and the actors make the most of the far-fetched premise. Thelma is relaxed and confident in one of her more substantial dramatic parts.

Another drama, *Call Her Savage*, fared better. In it, Thelma was teamed up with fiery redhead Clara Bow, with whom she also happened to share the same birthday (though a year apart). The film explores the outrageous and troubled life of Nasa (played by Bow); Thelma plays Sunny De Lane, Nasa's rival in love. Critics enjoyed the movie, but it was a scene between Thelma and Clara that garnered the most headlines.

Sunny is introduced to Nasa in a nightclub. Nasa greets her very sweetly, but Sunny replies, "They tell me you're dynamite. . . . Dynamite doesn't frighten me. I've been in a lot of explosions." The two eye each other, then Nasa retorts that she was wondering why Sunny looked so scarred. More insults follow, until the two actresses are just an inch away from each other's faces. The camera pans away for a moment, and when it returns, they are fighting, pulling hair and throwing each other around wildly. Before the fight is over, both actresses' hairdos are totally destroyed, Thelma's corsage is gone, and the front of her dress is so badly ripped that for a moment it looks as though her breasts may be revealed.

It is a scene of such intensity that reviewers and columnists began spreading rumors that the two actresses were not acting at all—that they did not get along on set and were captured fighting for real. The rumors grew louder when a columnist got hold of the script and noticed that another actor was supposed to break up the fight immediately after it started. In the final film, he doesn't do so; the fight ends only after Bow and Todd succeed in kneeing each other in the stomach.

Thelma tried to pour water over the story, calling the rumors nonsense. According to her, she had discussed the scene with Clara ahead of time, and both agreed that the fight should be as realistic as possible. If anyone thought it was real, she said, that just showed what good actresses they were. Clara, meanwhile, joked to the *Los Angeles Times* that the only thing that bothered her about the incident was the fact that Thelma kept pulling her face out of view of the camera.

By autumn 1932 Thelma was in the midst of a fight that was all too real: a battle to save her life. On October 14 it was announced that

Thelma was gravely ill in the hospital. The official story was that she had been admitted with an abscess, which was operated on promptly only to become infected and turn into peritonitis, a serious condition that can spread quickly and cause multiple life-threatening complications.

The actress lay in the hospital throughout mid-October, and every day doctors would share the latest developments: "She is getting along very nicely," said one, while another added, "She is now past the crisis." Her husband and mother visited Thelma regularly, and when the actress was finally released, she praised friends Sally Eilers and Minna Gombell for coming every day to see her regardless of how busy they were.

Nothing more was ever said about the incident, which has led to various rumors over the years about what exactly had caused her illness. Some authors claimed that it was appendicitis, though this cannot be true, since she had her appendix removed in 1926. Hal Roach theorized that it was the result of a termination of pregnancy or a miscarriage. He told author and screenwriter Jim Brubaker that he believed Thelma's marriage to Pat De Cicco had been something of a "shotgun" affair.

Whatever the case, the actress was considered well enough to attend the funeral of friend Belle Bennett on November 6, 1932, and by mid-November she was well and truly back on her feet, signing on to make *Air Hostess* at Columbia and dancing at the Beverly Hills Hotel with her husband. She also attended a musical event at the Roosevelt Hotel on November 17, dedicated to musician Leo Carrillo. There the actress listened to a tango and rumba band and was treated as one of the guests of honor, along with Mae Murray, Bert Wheeler, Gilbert Roland, and old Paramount School friend Charles "Buddy" Rogers.

At the beginning of 1933, Thelma and Pat went to numerous social events, including a party given by Jean Malin and a Hollywood film premiere. After the latter, the *Lowell Sun* described De Cicco as not "as wise to the ways of these openings as Thelma," which must have come as an insult to the man who believed he was just as much of a celebrity as his wife. He considered himself such a Hollywood insider, in fact, that during this time, he decided he should start overseeing Thelma's career interests—something that for a time she seemed happy enough to go along with.

⤛⤜

Perhaps one of the reasons she was determined to make the marriage work is that it had afforded her a certain amount of freedom, in that she had finally moved out of the home she shared with her mother. Alice was a woman who had experienced great loss in her life; with her husband and her only son gone, she could be somewhat overprotective of her only daughter, even if she didn't always mean to be. Thelma herself never publicly said a bad word about her mother but hinted at a little discord during an interview in 1931: "[My mother] is a companion, pal and one of the bestest mommas that ever lived. The only thing I can't forgive her for is that she still insists I'm a baby." Alice would remain a major player in her daughter's life, and the two were said to speak every day, but Thelma surely appreciated the bit of distance her marriage provided.

She was now living with her husband in a beautiful apartment, and publicly at least the couple seemed to be getting along nicely. In reality, however, they were headed for a fall.

But first they were headed for a crash. In the early hours of January 22, 1933, De Cicco was driving the couple home from an evening out, and as they headed toward Hollywood Boulevard, another vehicle suddenly appeared in front of them. To avoid crashing, De Cicco jumped the curb, and the car headed straight into a palm tree.

An ambulance rushed the couple to the nearest hospital, where Thelma was initially treated for a lacerated ear and chest injury and her husband for just minor scratches and bruises. It was announced that they had been lucky and would be allowed home later that evening. But further examination found that Thelma had been more seriously injured than originally thought, and she was kept in for more tests. "Examination has revealed that three of her ribs on the left side were broken, that her shoulder was broken and that she received internal injuries," her doctor said.

Thelma was in a serious but stable condition, but she was tough and determined to make a full recovery, which in due course she would. In the meantime, however, her friends in the Dominoes were concerned.

They gave her special mention during their next meeting, sending her a book titled *Troupers of the Gold Coast* to cheer up her recovery.

As the actress regained her strength, she went back to working for Hal Roach. The Pitts/Todd partnership continued during the first half of 1933, with the two appearing in shorts such as *Asleep in the Feet, The Bargain of the Century*, and *One Track Minds*. In *Asleep in the Feet* the two women take on jobs as taxi dancers at a local club to raise money for a neighbor who cannot afford her rent. Thelma, being the more glamorous of the two, has many young men who wish to dance, while poor ZaSu has to make do with a bearded old man and a huge hulk with two left feet. In *The Bargain of the Century* they accidentally get a policeman fired and feel obliged to take him on as their butler until he finds another job. All manner of things go wrong, particularly after ZaSu brings home a convict, thinking he is the policeman's ex-boss.

By now Thelma and ZaSu had become a reliable and well-polished team, capable of the same amount of madcap comedy as Laurel and Hardy—though perhaps on a subtler scale. Thelma was the straight woman, while ZaSu with her extraordinary comedic timing provided the hysterical quips and gullible tendencies. However, in spring 1933 ZaSu went to Hal Roach and told him she was having second thoughts about her participation.

ZaSu adored her costar and would remain friends with her until the end of Thelma's life. However, she wasn't happy with her employment conditions, and by the end of March—when the studio announced it was closing for a two-month break—she was seriously negotiating her position. As she and Thelma wrapped up their latest short film and said their farewells, it must have been bittersweet, as both actresses knew that they might not work together again.

While ZaSu had some time to think about her options, Thelma was unable to fret for long, because she had just received word that she was to head to England to publicize a feature movie she had made with Laurel and Hardy and Dennis King, titled *Fra Diavolo* (a.k.a. *Devil's Brother*).

Not only did this give Thelma an opportunity to visit London, but she also heard that British International Pictures wanted her to star in one of their movies at the Elstree Studios. Excited about this prospect, in April 1933 the twenty-six-year-old actress applied for a passport, using her married name of Thelma De Cicco. Many people assumed she'd be traveling with her husband, but they were mistaken. It is unknown what Pat thought of his wife's idea of going to England without him, but given his possessive personality, it likely wasn't favorable.

The two were certainly not on speaking terms when Thelma departed Los Angeles on the Santa Fe Railway headed for Chicago, and by the time she reached the Windy City, by her own admission she was feeling "a little jittery." Instead of passing quickly to the waiting New York train, she found herself crowded by newspapermen, all waving their notebooks and demanding quotes. Thelma—surrounded by two fur coats and seventeen pieces of luggage—was open to answering their questions. She told of her intention to play "real lady" parts in movies, but when the subject of her marriage came up, she was less than ladylike. When asked about the state of the union, Thelma answered, "I'm going to marry, just as soon as I get rid of the husband I have." She refused to say any more on the subject, but as she left for New York, newspapers were buzzing with stories, claiming that De Cicco would be filing for divorce while his wife was abroad.

When Thelma departed America on the *Berengaria* at the end of April, she was all smiles and gleefully waved her handkerchief to waiting fans. If the actress was worried about any comments she had made in Chicago, she didn't show it, and as the ship sailed slowly out of the dock, Thelma knew she was about to embark on the adventure of a lifetime.

11

LONDON CALLING

The luxurious *Berengaria* docked in Southampton, England, on May 3, 1933. Thelma stepped from the liner and set out for London, where she was booked into the Carlton Hotel. While Thelma was known in the UK, she was not as famous as stars such as Clark Gable or Jean Harlow. As such, little fanfare accompanied her arrival; the first real mention in the press came on May 9, when the *Daily Mirror* reported that she'd been sipping cocktails in the lounge of the Dorchester Hotel with her good friend Sally Eilers, who was in London to make the British International Pictures vehicle *I Spy*.

This lack of publicity came as a relief to Thelma, who spent the first couple of days in London making herself at home and anonymously taking in the sights. She quietly visited Westminster Abbey and took pleasure in gazing at all the artifacts on display at the British Museum. Thelma later said that while she had never really thought about reincarnation before, she began to believe in it as she wandered through the streets of the British capital—wherever she went, she had a feeling that she had been there before. She would also tell reporter Nora Laing that the only place she ever got homesick for was London. "It's a queer thing," she remarked later.

Never one to shy away from a good laugh, Thelma took it upon herself to instruct the waiters and staff at her hotel to call her Countess

De Cicco. This joke came from a discovery, some five months into her marriage, that Pat was rumored to come from Italian nobility. A friend of his told the actress that this meant she was officially a countess, and whether or not this was actually true, Thelma later admitted that she got "a bit of a thrill" from the discovery. And what better time than on her trip to take advantage of it, she reasoned: "When in England, do what the English do."

Despite Thelma's enthusiasm for the country, she wasn't there as a tourist, and before long the actress was headed to Elstree Studios, where she was to act in *You Made Me Love You*, a film starring British actor Stanley Lupino and loosely based on *The Taming of the Shrew*. Lupino plays an entertainer who must win over his new bride, played by Thelma, who happens to be as temperamental as she is beautiful. Thelma herself was anything but; from the beginning of filming, she built up a good rapport with everyone on set, from the director, Monty Banks, to the cast, to the whole crew.

This did not go unnoticed by members of the Elstree team. Later, Ronnie, one of the studio electricians, wrote to *Picture Play* and gave his views on all of the American actresses he had met during his time at the studio. Sally Eilers, he felt, was rather high-hat to reporters and autograph hunters, Bebe Daniels became completely absorbed in her work, and Jeanette MacDonald had a "slightly superior attitude." But the one star who had made the best impression on the crew member was Thelma, who he said was "one of the most charming girls I have ever met in any studio in and around London. If she sees this, the best is wished her from her many friends in Elstree." Thelma returned the love when in 1935, she announced that the only movie she really enjoyed making was *You Made Me Love You*. Considering the actress had made more than one hundred films and shorts by this time, that was quite a statement to make.

On May 19, Thelma made an appearance at the Empire, Leicester Square, where she was to publicize *Fra Diavolo*. Together with actors Dennis King and Jimmy Finlayson, she wowed the crowds, which included King George V and his wife, Queen Mary. "I've never had such a thrill in my life," Thelma said. Another delight came when the actress accompanied director Monty Banks to the Café de Paris, where recording star Morton Downey was giving a series of midnight appearances. British Pathé was there to film the event, which shows Thelma dancing happily in the arms of Banks to the music of Jack Harris.

The dance was purely platonic and the newspapers made nothing of it, but the same couldn't be said when they discovered the actress had been spending an awful lot of time with actor Dennis Banks (no relation to her director) and writer Jerry Horwin. On June 1, the *Hollywood Reporter* announced that Thelma had been robbed of $500 while at the Dorchester Hotel but that she was now having a "grand time" and giving her "divided attention," to Dennis and Jerry. Then on June 15 they told readers that Thelma and Dennis were "billing and cooing" their way around town together. Far away from her husband and his moods, Thelma was kicking up her heels and having the time of her life.

It wasn't all fun and games, however. Actress (and Stanley Lupino's daughter) Ida Lupino told author William Donati that Thelma collapsed on the set of *You Made Me Love You*. The story goes that Dr. Eric Wornum visited the actress, examined her, and informed the Lupino family that there was a problem with her heart. It was unlikely, he said, that she would live a long life. Whether a doctor could make such a definitive and tragic diagnosis during a simple checkup is questionable. However, not only had Thelma already been diagnosed with a heart murmur and suffered from fainting spells, the role she played in the film was particularly demanding. On various occasions she was required to smash numerous amounts of crockery, push around her staff, and hurl a breakfast tray down the stairs. She and Lupino were also seen racing down a station platform while hanging on to a moving train, so if ever there was a production likely to provoke a performer to collapse, it was *You Made Me Love You*.

By June 19, Thelma was well enough to travel to Scotland by train. Headed for Glasgow on the Royal Scot, the actress must surely have been thrilled to discover that Professor Albert Einstein was also on board. A fan of his work, she devoured biographies of him and other scientists and once told the Hal Roach publicity department that she was deeply interested in relativity and the study of planets.

The famous professor was traveling to Scotland to receive an honorary degree, but he arrived a day earlier than expected, meaning that there were no fans waiting to greet him. When the train stopped at Glasgow's Central Station, Einstein slipped out with barely a rumble. The same cannot be said for Thelma, who was crowded not only by the press but also by countless fans and curious members of the public.

Wearing a grey flannel suit and a fur coat trimmed with a sable collar, Thelma tried to keep her balance and her cool, but it was a hard job, especially when the throngs of people crowded in so much that her bouquet of flowers was totally crushed. She later laughed that she was relieved her "toes weren't trampled on," but admitted that she was quite scared for the safety of the fans who had come out to greet her.

Reporters were quick to bombard the actress with questions about the quiet arrival of one of the world's leading scientists, demanding to know why she received more attention than he did. She was apologetic: "I'm really sorry to think I should get such a reception while the professor slipped away," she said, before cheekily adding, "I don't know anything about relativity, but I can give people a laugh and that's what Einstein can't do." The quote was meant in fun, but the press was outraged.

So furious was the *Glasgow Herald* that it mentioned the incident on two consecutive days, pointing out that there was once another Thelma Todd in the movie business who was now long forgotten. The reporter rudely advised Thelma to "gather her carefully arranged bouquets while she may." Embarrassingly for the paper, however, the story was mistaken; the other actress it was referring to was actually forgotten silent star Lola Todd. (Lola was no fan of Thelma's either; at one point she was so angry to be confused with her that she considered changing her name to Carol Mason.) Still, the venomous intent of the *Glasgow Herald* was quite clear: a lowly actress was not entitled to more publicity than Albert Einstein and that was that. In a similarly dismissive move, the *Aberdeen Press and Journal* managed to write a whole complaint about her arrival without ever actually mentioning her by name.

The press coverage wasn't all bad, however. One reporter who didn't jump on the "I hate Thelma" bandwagon was "Kinoman" of the *Glasgow Evening Times*, who devoted a long article to an interview she gave him on the night of her arrival. Sitting in the suite of her hotel, several reporters, including Kinoman, shook Thelma's manicured hand, took photos of her rubbing her weary feet, and asked a variety of standard questions about such subjects as Hollywood he-men, the Marx Brothers, and her days as a schoolteacher. It was all rather average stuff, but one brief passage in Kinoman's article stood out.

"Thelma speaks at first-hand knowledge of the gangsters of the USA," he said. The article went into no further detail on this strange admittance, except to note that Thelma felt if not for the gangsters, everyone would be able to be respectable and go to church. More light was shed by the *Daily Record*, however, in which an unnamed reporter wrote that Thelma had told of some "thrilling instances" involving gangsters in Los Angeles, and said that some leading people in film had to pay protection money to the various hoods in town. She then added that in the 1920s, she herself had met a gangster, which had been an "interesting experience," but he was now doing time in Sing Sing Prison. According to Thelma, as she was leaving New York for England, four of the gangster's representatives had arrived at the dock with a large bouquet of roses and were told to ensure she was seen safely onto the boat.

This was an intriguing story, and it ties in with something Paramount School graduate Greg Blackton later told author William Donati. According to the book *The Life and Death of Thelma Todd*, during a publicity trip to Chicago in 1926, a man approached Thelma and tried to persuade her to dance at one of his establishments. She turned him down flat, though word soon spread that the man involved could have been notorious gangster Al Capone. Records show that Capone was indeed working in Chicago during 1926, and by 1933 he was in prison after being found guilty of tax evasion. He was not in Sing Sing, however, but this could very well have just been a mistake on Thelma's part. Capone or not, the comments during the Glasgow interviews show that as early as the mid-1920s—when she was at the start of her career—Thelma was at the very least aware of the presence of gangsters in her midst. By 1933, she was well versed in their operations in Hollywood, perhaps thanks in part to her marriage to would-be hood Pat De Cicco.

While gangsters seemed to be playing on her mind during the press interview, Thelma was happy and relaxed while attending a banquet for the Cinematograph Exhibitors Association and making an appearance at Glasgow's Regal Picture House. For the rest of her time abroad she was free to explore, and she traveled to Edinburgh on a sightseeing trip and then Ayrshire, telling reporters she had friends there and joking that one of them was the late poet Rabbie Burns.

Thelma's trip to the UK came to an end on June 27 when she met up with Sally Eilers and actor Charles Laughton at London's Waterloo station. Together they posed for photographs before heading to Southampton to catch the *Europa* for the long trip back to the States.

For the next five days, the actress had a lot of time to digest not only the events of her trip but also what was waiting for her when she got home. Her marriage was a disaster; there was no denying that. Even *Photoplay* was starting to spread rumors that the couple were not happy, showing a picture of them at the Cocoanut Grove captioned with the words "When Thelma Todd and her husband Pasquale De Cicco were still good friends." Thelma's travel records are also enlightening: on the way over to England, she had been booked as Thelma De Cicco, but on the return journey she gave her name as Thelma De Cicco Todd.

While Pat waited for his wife to return, he spent time playing polo at the Riviera Country Club, no doubt wondering what was about to happen to his marriage. On board the *Europa*, Thelma made the decision that on her arrival in New York, she would not go straight back to Los Angeles but would instead travel to Massachusetts to visit friends and family. As soon as the boat docked on July 2, Thelma made her escape, and before long she was ensconced in her uncle's home on Bowdoin Street in Lawrence, where a room was always kept for her just in case she needed it. There Thelma spent time with her cousins and visited a

Mrs. Thomas Wilson, who had been her classmate during the brief time she'd spent at Lowell Normal School.

After four days she bid her friends and family good-bye and headed to Boston, where she checked into the Hotel Statler. There she told newspapermen that Pat had called her at 3 AM and she was confident there would be no divorce. "You would be too," she said, "had you heard my Pat talking to me over the phone." The press weren't convinced and bombarded the frustrated actress with more personal questions, which she answered quite calmly, given the nature of their queries. Yes, she said, she was still in love with her husband; she described him as a "great fellow" for letting her fulfill her ambition to make a movie in England.

Finally, however, her patience came to an end, and she took a huge swipe at the reporters present—and the media in general. "In Hollywood one has as much privacy as a goldfish," she complained (the same saying Roland West had used several years before), and then added that she had always known her trip would cause rumors to start. She then exclaimed that any reporters making up stories of divorce deserved to be punched in the nose, warning that her hot-headed husband would not appreciate any rumors about the state of their marriage.

Despite her bravado, Thelma must surely have been just a little apprehensive when she finally arrived at Boston Airport for her flight back to L.A. Nevertheless, she cheekily winked at reporters and joked that it wouldn't be worth her while to announce a divorce at that moment. "With so many being discussed in Hollywood, I wouldn't have a chance to get any sort of publicity," she laughed, then climbed aboard the plane.

At Los Angeles airport on July 9, Pat De Cicco waited for his wife impatiently. The plane eventually landed, and as she disembarked, her husband and the world's press were waiting. There is little doubt that the pair would have liked to slip out anonymously, but that was not possible with photographers clambering for a shot, so instead they greeted each other, amicably and somewhat awkwardly. Thelma gave her husband what can only be described as a quick peck, to which De Cicco asked, "Is that the best kiss you have for me, dear?" Thelma smiled and replied, "Certainly, darling, you don't expect me to make a scene here."

Shortly after came the couple's first wedding anniversary, which they celebrated quietly at home. Later in July, Pat arranged a birthday party for his wife at the Miramar Hotel, prompting mention in the gossip columns that perhaps everything was OK between the couple after all. In the days following, they were spotted dancing at the Cocoanut Grove, but while the gossip columnists were happy to report such sightings, they seemed equally delighted to mention Thelma's frequent outings without her husband. For instance, she attended Minna Gombell's tea party with friend Sally Eilers, and then a Jascha Heifetz violin concert at the Hollywood Bowl, and if De Cicco was with her, the gossip columns were uncharacteristically silent on that point.

Feature film *Cheating Blondes* had been released while Thelma was in England and had the actress playing the unusual role of twin sisters: one falsely accused of murder, the other a pregnant cabaret singer. While the dual roles gave her maximum exposure on screen, the story left some viewers unimpressed. The *Film Daily* reported that *Cheating Blondes* "fails to click with forced dramatic situation. . . . [There is] no excuse for the offering." *Variety* was somewhat kinder, though it did suggest that the film seemed far longer than its sixty-one minutes. The reviewer's only comment about Thelma's actual performance was lukewarm: "Miss Todd is as pictorial as ever, walking through a tense role without great credit but enough to get by."

Mary Stevens, M.D., released shortly after Thelma's return to the States, is another melodramatic tale; it's about two doctors, Mary (Kay Francis) and Don (Lyle Talbot), who after graduating together set up adjoining offices. Mary struggles as a female doctor, but Don sees an opportunity for money from his friend Lois (Thelma), who just happens to be a politician's daughter. Thelma's role as the woman who temporarily comes between the leads was a small one, and reviewers again mentioned her only in passing, choosing to spend most of their column inches on the two main characters. The continued lack of good reviews must have been frustrating for Thelma. She had been working steadily since 1926 and yet she was still struggling with small roles and mediocre scripts.

Thelma was also still struggling through her marriage to Pat De Cicco. On August 13 the actress made an effort to show an interest in her husband's activities by traveling to the Riviera Country Club to give trophies to the winning polo teams. The club became the couple's spot; they would be seen there frequently cheering on and partying with the teams. With all these public appearances together, the press reluctantly decided that perhaps they were happy after all and got off their case—at least for a while.

Thelma vamps for the camera on a day out with family and friends. Her unsmiling father (far left) looks on. *Courtesy of James and Joyce Brubaker*

Thelma, age ten, with her mother (right) and family friends. *Courtesy of James and Joyce Brubaker*

Thelma was a student teacher before becoming an actress. This early publicity photo shows her with a prim and proper look. *From the collections of the Margaret Herrick Library, Academy of Motion Picture Arts and Sciences, courtesy of James and Joyce Brubaker*

Thelma sat on a tractor for this unusual publicity photo, taken at First National Pictures in 1928. *Author's collection*

Thelma was immensely proud of her long hair, though shortly after moving to Hollywood and changing her image, she decided to cut it short. *Courtesy of James and Joyce Brubaker*

"Honey - you don't know what you're doing---"

This publicity photo for *Follow Thru* (1930) shows Thelma leaning on a barrier, looking disdainfully at the character played by fellow Paramount School graduate Charles "Buddy" Rogers. *Courtesy of James and Joyce Brubaker*

Thelma was a very popular actress on the Hal Roach set. She is seen here on the far right, helping to publicize the studio in the 1930s. *Author's collection*

This publicity photo for *The Big Timer* (1932) shows Thelma in the arms of Ben Lyon. They acted together several times. *Author's collection*

LEFT: In this publicity photo for *Speak Easily* (1932), Thelma sports something of a "gangster's moll" look. In reality she was anything but. *Courtesy of James and Joyce Brubaker*

BELOW: Thelma had a short but dramatic marriage to Pat De Cicco (left). They are seen here at a Hollywood party in 1933 looking happy enough, but in private it was a very different story. *Author's collection*

Thelma sits with actress Marion Shilling and several other guests at a party celebrating Shilling's birthday. *Courtesy of Michael G. Ankerich*

The garage where Thelma Todd died. Her body was found in a car behind the right door. *Courtesy of James and Joyce Brubaker*

Pat De Cicco (left), Harvey Priester (middle), and Mae Whitehead (right) visit the garage where Thelma died on the day her body was discovered. *Author's collection*

Roland West's estranged wife, Jewel Carmen. She gained a lot of publicity by claiming to have seen Thelma in a car hours after her death. *Author's collection*

Roland West gives evidence at the inquest into Thelma's death, December 1935. *Author's collection*

Thelma Todd was one of the most talented comediennes of her generation. Sadly the gossip, rumors, and notoriety of her untimely death have gone on to eclipse her life and career. *Author's collection*

12

MARRIAGE DOES INTERFERE WITH A CAREER

W hile Thelma had been whooping it up in England, all hell had broken lose at the Hal Roach studio. Negotiations between Roach and ZaSu Pitts collapsed, and it was clear that she would not be returning to the lot. Henry Ginsberg, general manager of the studio, told the *Hollywood Reporter* that the talks were called off when they refused to pay ZaSu $8,000 per script. The actress bade farewell to the shorts, and the studio found a new costar for Thelma: New York stage star Patsy Kelly.

Patsy was a good sixteen years younger than ZaSu, but the executives felt she would be an excellent wise-cracking partner for Thelma. Patsy's agent approached her with the idea, explaining that a movie scout had spotted her and wanted her to move to Hollywood. Patsy was a proud New York theater actress and turned him down flat. However, after some negotiation, during which the studio made it clear that she'd be paid far more in Hollywood than she ever would in New York, Patsy agreed to give it a go. Before long the actress had loaded herself onto a train bound for Los Angeles, where she met her new costar and began work almost immediately on their first short, *Beauty and the Bus*.

As filming began, Patsy worried that the cast and crew were so close to ZaSu that they would not take well to her replacement. Thelma was indeed sad to see her friend leave, but she was careful never to take it out on the newcomer. Later Patsy would tell journalist Dena Reed that the people on set were "swell to me." Even so, the young actress was very much aware that ZaSu had left a considerable hole in the studio's everyday life, and she wasn't sure she could ever fill it.

Patsy was also shocked to discover just how physical the part would be. *Beauty and the Bus* is a madcap romp that revolves around the two ladies winning a car in a raffle and then getting into all kinds of trouble, including being stopped by a policeman for speeding and then crashing into a car owned by a gentleman played by Don Barclay. The altercation quickly devolves into a physical disagreement that requires Patsy to pull the fabric roof from his car, smash a headlight, and then throw various pieces of large furniture from the back of a nearby truck. The actress was unaccustomed to such demands and later said, only half joking, that the studio should have hired a clown instead of an actress.

On the first day of filming, Patsy needed to trip over a roller skate and fall flat onto her back in the middle of a theater. Once she had pored over the script, the shocked actress asked the director why he couldn't use a body double for the scene. His response—to break out laughing—sent her into a panic. "I never fell in my life, except accidentally," she told him, but her plea for a stand-in fell on deaf ears. The entire experience was scary and depressing, she later told reporter Sara Hamilton. "Those first days on the set were awful for me. I didn't know a thing about movies and I was miserable."

Even as she resigned herself to the inevitable injuries and humiliations, Patsy encountered another problem. The theater actress was used to having an audience applaud and cheer after every scene; at the end of her performance, if she was lucky, she would receive an ovation. On the film set, however, no matter how good she thought she'd been, she was met with only silence. The whole thing was very disconcerting, made no better when she'd make a joke or comment off camera and be told to keep it down—or even to shut the hell up. Added to that, Patsy was used to working at night and sleeping for most of the day, but Hollywood kept the opposite hours. As a result, there were many times when the actress had to make her way out of her house so early that she needed a lantern to light her way. It did not take long for Patsy to wonder if she had done the right thing by relocating to California.

After a few weeks—during which, the actress said, she was "blue, busted and disgusted"—she decided enough was enough. She vowed to admit defeat and return to New York on the first available train. But being the considerate person that she was, Patsy did not want to leave without first explaining her actions to her new costar. Returning to the studio, she pulled Thelma aside, and the film veteran listened intently as Patsy explained how miserable she was, what a failure her experience with Hollywood had been, and how she was determined that she couldn't stay another moment. After begging Thelma to stay quiet until she was safely away, Patsy left the lot.

Thelma stewed over what had just happened. She knew how hard it was to make the transition from New York to California—she had done it herself years before—but she also knew that things did get better. So instead of telling the studio executives that Patsy was gone, she decided to take action herself: she jumped into her car and shot off in the hope of catching her costar before she left town. By the time she reached her apartment, Patsy had already gone to the train station, but not even that deterred Thelma. She drove on to Pasadena, hoping to catch the train as it pulled into the next station.

She was in luck, and as she jumped on board, there was Patsy surrounded by her luggage. Thelma looked at her intently, told her that under no circumstances would she be leaving California, and proceeded to grab her bags. "Get off, Kelly," she said. "Come on." And with that, she bundled the shocked woman off the train and into her car.

The two women drove back to Hollywood and sat up all night talking about Patsy's problems—the largest of which, it turned out, mainly revolved around her finances. She had somehow managed to get herself into serious debt before moving to California. Thelma advised the young actress not to declare bankruptcy, that it would only make things worse for her credit rating. She then added that no matter what happened, she must never run out on anything again. Thelma made a promise to help sort out her finances with the help of her agent, and for the next six months she would be in charge of Patsy's money, giving her only enough cash for small treats and nothing else.

It was not the only time Thelma went out of her way to help a coworker. Many who worked with the actress over the years commented on her giving nature, and Thelma herself spoke about the reasons for aiding others in a 1933 article titled "How I Was Groomed for Stardom." She said that too many established stars were happy to ignore the calls for help from the actors and actresses coming up behind them. She put this down to a fear of the younger generation, that new faces "may creep gradually on, ousting today's favorites from their position." Thelma never thought that way about any future star, instead musing that it would be nice to look back during her retirement with "pleasant memories, rather than on petty jealousies and the creation of bitterness."

At the end of *Beauty and the Bus,* the two women watch in horror as their recently won car goes rolling down a hill, careers through a fence, and hurtles over a cliff. In the movie it is funny, but just two weeks after shooting, on August 10, 1933, the scene became reality for Patsy, and suddenly it wasn't so funny anymore.

The actress had gone to see her friend entertainer Jean Malin (a.k.a. Gene Malin) in his farewell performance at the Ship Café at Venice Pier. After watching him perform, Patsy, Jean, and his friend Jimmy Forlenza all climbed into Malin's sedan, which was parked outside the café. The vehicle had trouble starting, and the entertainer called upon two parking attendants who were standing nearby, hoping that they would be able to give them a push. They were happy to help out, but as they did so, the car started unexpectedly, and Malin was unable to gain control of the gears. The vehicle shot backward along the pier, through the railings, and down into the ocean some eighteen feet below.

As the three friends struggled under the water, the bruised but relatively unharmed passenger Jimmy Forlenza was able to free himself, and together with a quick-thinking lifeguard he pulled Patsy Kelly out and rushed her to hospital. Her condition was said to be serious but stable, and apart from a slight concussion, she made a full recovery and was able to leave hospital after ten days. Tragically, Jean Malin could not be saved; he succumbed to his injuries shortly after being hauled out of the vehicle.

While Patsy's physical injuries were overcome within days, the emotional damage stayed with her forever. "It did things to me," she said in one interview. "Oh sure, I laugh, I joke, I wisecrack. What else can I do but go on? But I feel that it took something out of me that's gone forever."

Thelma continued to support her costar throughout the ordeal. She had suffered tragedy in her own life and knew only too well just how much it could change a person. Shortly after the accident, a government representative came to the Hal Roach set to complain about Patsy Kelly's unpaid taxes. Thelma not only persuaded him to leave without making a scene but also helped the actress work out how to pay back the money.

The two became firm friends. They would watch the daily rushes together every evening before going home. Sitting in the dark, the two women laughed hysterically at their performances. Thelma would turn to Patsy and say she was the funniest comedienne in the world. Patsy would repay the favor by telling Thelma that she was the funniest, and they'd both laugh again. "She was a smart girl," Patsy later told Gladys Hall. "She had a fine brain inside that beautiful head of hers. She was clever in every way."

This esteem was reiterated by others who worked with Thelma during the Hal Roach years. She was always the life and soul of the studio and a huge practical joker. She would pull crazy faces at the cameraman as he tried to shoot her or promise to be sensible and pose beautifully for the still photographers only to twist her face into outrageous contortions the moment they clicked the button. On one particular day, a new publicity director walked onto set just as she was about to shoot a scene with a stack of dishes beside her. As the director yelled "Camera," the actress started throwing plates at the publicity man, who was obliged to catch them before they crashed to the floor.

The entire company would crack up at Thelma's spontaneous and carefree attitude, and when she took time away from the studio, there were always colleagues waiting to greet her when she came back. In return Thelma would eagerly ask about their welfare, how their parents were, whether a wife had had the baby yet, or if a grandmother had come out of the hospital. No one was exempt from the actress's genuine interest in home and family matters, and she was very much loved for it.

Thelma thoroughly enjoyed her work at Hal Roach and her new partnership with Patsy, but certain corners of the media weren't so thrilled about the finished product. The following year, *Variety* declared that Thelma and Patsy would be a great team only if they could "overcome the handicaps of such trite material," an opinion the trade publication reiterated in its review of their short *I'll Be Suing You*. *Variety* later deemed their *Sing Sister Sing* as "lowdown nonsense and some undressing" and complained that the camera in that particular movie was not flattering toward Thelma.

By autumn 1933, Thelma was called to work on the RKO production *Hips, Hips, Hooray*, starring comedians Bert Wheeler and Robert Woolsey. They play two drifters who become tangled up with beauty emporium managers played by Thelma and Dorothy Lee. The combination of the four actors was so successful that they were soon offered the opportunity to go on a nationwide tour with a live show called *Dumb Bells* by Tim Whelan, though the plans ultimately fell through. (This wasn't the first time Thelma was offered such a deal; in 1931, she and ZaSu Pitts had considered a part in a vaudeville act but ultimately couldn't find a sketch they thought was good enough, so that idea was scrapped as well.)

On September 19 the actress went to visit her lawyer, A. Ronald Button, to draw up a new will. Although she was still officially with Pat De Cicco, it was clear Thelma was thinking about a future without him; during the writing of the will, she added the following: "I give and bequeath to my husband Pasquale De Cicco the sum of One Dollar in cash." She then left all her other worldly belongings to her mother, Alice Todd. Once finished, she signed the document as Thelma Todd De Cicco, though she clearly didn't plan on being so for very much longer.

In an article titled "Marriage Does Interfere with a Career," put out by RKO publicity, the actress explained that in the early days of their marriage, her husband would "sulk for a while" if she was required to go to work. However, according to Thelma, he had become more tolerant by the time she was working on *Hips, Hips, Hooray* and did not protest when she was required to spend her Saturdays at RKO.

The article is fascinating, because while it was released to quell rumors that Thelma's marriage was in trouble, the actress seemed to spend a lot of it trying desperately to convince herself that everything was all right. In the text, she explained that marriage not only interfered with a career but with every other activity too, though she was quick to stress that it was all worth the risk. She then wrote that if she had to choose between either marriage or a career, she would let the career go—but only if she knew that it would create happiness in the home.

Regardless of anything Thelma said in publicity materials, by now her marriage was falling apart. She had to endure many arguments, as well as what her lawyer later described as extreme cruelty. Pat hated the press intrusion into the marriage, and photos emerged showing the couple on the street, De Cicco wearing his hat low down and Thelma staring firmly at the floor.

The actress's nerves began to suffer, and she spent more and more time away from her husband. Through it all, Pat threw himself into polo playing and was seen frequently at the Riviera Club, while Thelma was spotted putting on a brave face at the races and at several different parties, including one hosted by friend Minna Gombell. Though she was obviously concerned by the state of her marriage, photos of the event show her smiling broadly, wearing her hair in ringlets underneath a large, floppy hat.

In the midst of all this, the reviews were in for Thelma's British comedy *You Made Me Love You*, and they were fabulous. The *Daily Mirror* called it "a rattling good slapstick comedy with music" and said it was the best film to come out of Elstree Studios since the huge 1930 hit *Almost a Honeymoon*. The *Los Angeles Times* announced that it was as good as any US film of its type and Thelma had given her best performance yet. *Hollywood Filmograph* described it as "A really very humorous semi-musical. . . . One of those rollicking, fast moving yarns; something different from anything you have ever seen before." The *Yorkshire Post* told readers that Thelma played the role of the disdainful newlywed "with a combination of charm and venom." As a result of the positive reaction around the world, *You Made Me Love You* became one of the most successful films of Thelma's career and one she always thought a great deal of.

Watching the movie today, one understands the affection for it. Thelma's role required her to be extremely funny in some places and obtuse to her new husband in others; she shows a wonderful ability to go from drama to comedy and back again without the slightest hesitation. (And Stanley Lupino, it should be said, gives just as good in return, playing her husband.) The film also called for location shoots—around London, on English country lanes, at the nearby Elstree & Borehamwood train station—all of which the young woman took in stride. Thelma shows a talent that is so natural it is hard to imagine she was only in her twenties at the time. Should she have lived to middle age, she surely would have made a terrific character actress.

On December 7, Hal Roach Studios hosted a banquet for five hundred celebrities and other movie notables to celebrate Hal's twentieth anniversary in the business. In an event that was broadcast over the NBC radio network, master of ceremonies Charley Chase introduced speakers that included the likes of Jean Harlow, Laurel and Hardy, Patsy Kelly, and of course Thelma. A good time was had by all, and it is interesting to note that Thelma (along with Harlow and Laurel and Hardy) was cited as being one of the better-behaved people at the party.

Roach released several new Kelly/Todd shorts before the end of the year, and then at Christmas the features *Son of a Sailor* and *Counsellor at Law* hit theaters, though Thelma had only minor roles in both of them. December did see one exciting development in Thelma's career: RKO announced that it would offer her a contract to make feature films. Acting production chief Pandro S. Berman said that RKO had ambitious plans for Thelma and her future as a star. Pat De Cicco took full credit for negotiating the deal, though the amount of input he actually had is debatable.

As 1933 rolled into 1934, several more of Thelma's comedy features were released, including the aforementioned *Hips, Hips, Hooray*; *Palooka*, the story of a young boxer in which Thelma plays an enjoyably wicked vamp; and *The Poor Rich*, a well-reviewed farce about down-on-their-luck aristocrats scheming to regain their wealth. Off screen, meanwhile, Thelma was photographed inviting the local mayor to a beauty show being held at the Biltmore Hotel and spotted dancing with Pat De Cicco at the Clover Club and at a party given by actress Louise Fazenda and her husband, Hal Wallis.

But away from the cameras, the actress's life was crumbling. Thelma and Pat may have seemed happy to the outside world, but it was all an illusion. Their arguments continued, and on February 16, the two became involved in a huge fight at home. This was the last straw for Thelma and she walked out, immediately filing for divorce and citing extreme cruelty as the reason.

Her lawyer broke the news to the waiting press. "It was a case of incompatibility," he told them, though court documents showed it was a lot more than that. "I have been a dutiful and good wife," Thelma wrote, adding that her husband had called her "harsh and opprobrious names" without any provocation and had been particularly rude when they were in the company of friends.

When she appeared in court on March 2, 1934, the actress barely spoke a word, answering a simple "yes" to just three questions asked of her by her lawyer. The judge granted the divorce immediately, and the look of relief on Thelma's face was there for all to see. Smiling broadly, she left the court without speaking to reporters. De Cicco, meanwhile, told the *Hollywood Reporter* that he still hoped to guide Thelma's film career.

What Thelma thought about that remark can only be guessed at, but after the divorce was settled, the subject of her ex would come up in conversation only occasionally. For all intents and purposes, she considered herself free. While a certain amount of bitterness remained, Thelma surprisingly never showed De Cicco any animosity in public and always considered herself to be on relatively friendly terms with him. As for De Cicco, despite initially declaring an interest in continuing their business relationship, he ended up giving his ex-wife scant attention, speaking about her only when pressed to do so by the media.

Days after his ex-wife's death the following year, he would insist that they had remained the best of friends after separating, despite seeing each other only a handful of times. However, he didn't seem to understand exactly why they had divorced in the first place. To one reporter he said it was because Thelma put her career before marriage and had brought the cruelty action against him only so that she would be granted an easy divorce. He explained that she was "pleasure loving and temperamental . . . not the domestic type at all," before adding he agreed to the divorce because of his gallantry. However, the very next day, his story had changed: "All this talk that I consented to it out of gallantry is nonsense," he said. "We reached an amicable agreement."

For the next few months, Thelma forgot her troubles and continued her social and professional lives. A few features and various Kelly/Todd shorts were released, and in April she attended a poetry recital given by Argentine actress Berta Singerman, held at the Philharmonic Auditorium. Then on May 18, 19, and 20 she teamed up with various stars, including Loretta Young, Claudette Colbert, Eddie Cantor, and James Cagney, at a "Film Stars Frolic" at the new Gilmore Stadium. Tickets were fifty cents, and the event consisted of a circus, a rodeo, and a Mardi Gras celebration.

But Thelma didn't have time to play for long. Her life was about to change track once again, this time with the help of a very familiar source offering an extremely unusual proposition.

13

CASTELLAMMARE

On November 23, 1924, a new property development was announced, to be built just north of Santa Monica. Named Castellammare, the estate was to be a tribute to the Mediterranean and include winding streets, bridges leading to the nearby beach, Spanish-style homes, and lots of privacy.

One of the selling points was that the community was to be built onto the hillside, thereby affording stunning views of the ocean and hills. There was little if any concern for the development's precarious position and the likelihood of mudslides; the emphasis was instead on creating an environment where the well-off and famous could while away their spare time, gazing out to sea and splashing in the surf. The future homes were in great demand—and made even more so when it was announced that producer Thomas H. Ince had started his career on the very spot where Castellammare was to be located. It was further revealed that he had even filmed many hours of his early movies on the adjacent beach.

Among the notables interested in buying property on the lot were Roland West and his wife, Jewel Carmen. After securing the land, they built an $85,000 Spanish-style home into the hillside, which was so large that the residence itself was located on Revello Drive, while the garage was located down the hill on Posetano Road. Other neighbors included actress and producer Lois Weber, actress Louise Fazenda, and actor Victor McLaglen, who all set about building luxury homes around the hillside.

To cater to the vast number of people moving into the development, a large building was constructed at the very bottom of the hill, with Malibu Road (later Roosevelt Highway and now Pacific Coast Highway) separating it from the beach and ocean. When it opened to the public, the building housed a restaurant called the Castellammare Inn, along with a grocery store, a pharmacy, and changing rooms for the various beachgoers that came past every day. It was popular with locals and holiday-makers, and early film footage shows the restaurant bustling with lunchtime visitors enjoying ice cream and chicken dinners. The Castellammare Inn continued quite successfully for several years and was considered the place to enjoy reasonably priced food and great views. However, this all changed when disaster struck three years to the very day before Thelma Todd would be seen at the same building for the very last time.

Carl Curtis was the successful principal of a local school. He was popular with staff, parents, and pupils and proud of his institution's commitment to a well-rounded education for every pupil. But he had recently discovered he was suffering from an unidentified illness and became worried that he would not be able to recover. Curtis was friends with Thomas W. Pigg, the superintendent at the Castellammare Inn, and on December 14, 1932, he made the journey from his home on Porto Marino Way to visit Pigg at work. Walking around to the back of the building where the watchman's office was located, Curtis was greeted by his friend, and together they enjoyed what seemed to be a friendly meeting. However, when the superintendent left the room for a moment, Curtis saw the man's gun on the desk, recognized an opportunity, and before Pigg had returned, shot himself in the head. He died instantly.

The death of Carl Curtis sent shockwaves throughout the area, and while it is not known whether this event spurred on the sale of the Castellammare Inn, by 1934 the restaurant, grocery store, and pharmacy were no longer on the property. On May 27 of that year, notice was placed in the *Los Angeles Times* that lawyer A. Ronald Button had applied for planning permission to change the building from several original units into one large restaurant. Permission was granted and work on the development began.

Although Button was Thelma's lawyer, it was not that actress who had bought the building but Jewel Carmen, Roland West's wife. It was a curious arrangement; by now the husband and wife had separated, but they were still considered to be the best of friends and were known to occasionally reunite when the mood took them. Carmen obviously thought the building was a good investment, and it was decided very early on that West would take over the running of the property and create a café on the site. She in turn would collect rent for its use.

West threw himself into the café project, but he was sensible enough to realize that with the United States in the grip of the Great Depression, he needed a good hook to make it a success. This is where Thelma came in. It would seem that Roland and the actress had remained on speaking terms since the end of their relationship, and he hoped she could front the business, publicize it during interviews, and put her name on the front of the building. Meanwhile, he would be behind the scenes, pumping money into the restaurant and buying everything needed to ensure its good running. The café "had the finest and best equipment of any place in this city," he later told the coroner during the inquest into Thelma's death.

Given the passionate affair between Roland and the actress during the making of *Corsair*, it is intriguing to imagine what Jewel thought of the idea of having Thelma as the star of her husband's establishment. When Thelma passed away, Jewel gave a detailed statement on her feelings for Thelma, even going so far as to describe her as a "bosom friend." Though this seems hard to believe, she added that she knew all about her estranged husband's feelings for the actress and had discussed the matter with him on many occasions. "Mr. West was a gentleman at all times. . . . I understand Mr. West and Mr. West understands me," she said. Whether Jewel was fully on board with the idea of having Thelma back in their lives is unknown, but in any case, Thelma was asked if she would be interested in fronting the café, and she responded favorably.

———— ✖ ————

The idea of doing something outside the entertainment business had been growing in Thelma's mind for quite some time. She wanted more control over not only the arc of her career but also her day-to-day life. One reporter visiting the set of a Pitts/Todd short in 1933 had discovered her arguing with the director over the best way to shoot a scene. Thelma wanted ZaSu to perform a particular stunt, while the director disagreed. "We write our own stories," Thelma told the reporter, before ZaSu added that they at least suggested situations. "Yes," replied Thelma sarcastically, "and you see how far it gets us?"

Now, more than a year later, Thelma's frustrations had only intensified. Other actresses were making great strides in Hollywood at the time, including Jean Harlow and Carole Lombard, but Thelma's career never managed to reach such heights. Small roles seemed to follow one another in quick succession, and the positive reviews she received with such films as *You Made Me Love You* had shown her that there was so much more on offer than short movies, if only she had the chance.

Rumors began in earnest that the actress would leave the Hal Roach Studios and move into dramatic roles exclusively. They gathered momentum when an actress by the name of Lilian Ellis arrived in the city, reportedly to take Thelma's place as Patsy Kelly's on-screen partner. However, those stories came to nothing when, on June 8, 1934, it was announced that Thelma had signed a new contract for eight more Hal Roach comedies.

Her decision may have come as a surprise, but it probably shouldn't have. It is clear by looking at her career choices that Thelma did actually enjoy her comedic work. "Comedy teaches one to act and think quickly, to be alert every moment," she'd said only recently. "I think it is the best training in the world and I wouldn't take anything for my experience in comedies." Her partnership with Patsy Kelly was perhaps the most reliably enjoyable aspect of her ongoing comic training.

It was away from the Hal Roach lot that her comic career continued to disappoint. While RKO had made big statements during their signing of Thelma, not much seemed to actually be happening to make her into a full-fledged star. Late July saw the release of the studio's *Cockeyed Cava-liers*, a feature set in medieval England and complete with dancing, sing-ing, and huge petticoats. Thelma was billed third after starring funnymen Bert Wheeler and Robert Woolsey, though her role of Lady Genevieve was yet another supporting part in a middling film. While some cinema managers reported the movie to be fairly funny, others were dismayed as audiences stayed away or actually walked out on the film.

As Thelma struggled to break out, she was also troubled by the ways Hollywood had changed over the past five years. Stars seemed to dis-appear from the screen as quickly as they arrived. "Whoever hears of them now?" she would ask writer Nora Laing in 1935. "Most of them are unhappy and rather bewildered. . . . They're left with nothing but a past—no future." She had expressed similar reservations in her "How I Was Groomed for Stardom" article, describing how many beautiful women failed to do well in their acting careers and eventually drifted into other jobs, with "their hopes shattered."

It was an astute observation. Since arriving in Hollywood, Thelma had seen many stars fall by the wayside, including one of her favorite actresses, Florence Vidor. When pictures transitioned to sound, Vidor failed her microphone test, and as a result her career was all but over. Others had fared even worse, brought down by drug addiction, scandal, or a tragic death. One of those who had not lived to see old age was pio-neering comedienne Mabel Normand, whose death had been announced while Thelma was at a party at the home of comedian Harry Langdon in 1930. Normand was just thirty-seven years old, and the news sent shockwaves around the room. The band stopped playing, the laughter paused, and Mabel's former costar Roscoe "Fatty" Arbuckle exclaimed, "My pal's dead." Just three years later, Arbuckle too was dead at the age of just forty-six, his career never having recovered from his own infamous sex scandal.

The death of these two stars, and the lapse into obscurity of many others, had shaken Thelma and made her evaluate the longevity of her own position in Hollywood. As a result, she seriously weighed West's offer. Thelma loved the sea and thoroughly enjoyed dining out, but she had never found a suitable place by the beach that combined the two. She later told interviewer Molly Marsh that it was because of this that she wanted to get involved. Before long she had made a definite decision: she sat down with West and agreed to front what would soon become Thelma Todd's Sidewalk Café (a.k.a. the Sidewalk Café and Thelma Todd's Inn).

From the moment Thelma came on board, the partners went full steam ahead to prepare the restaurant for its grand opening. The world-famous actress was more than the face of its publicity campaign; she put every ounce of spare energy into ensuring that the Sidewalk Café would be a success. "I like to keep my finger on the pulse of the business," she told Nora Laing. Thelma would work all day at the studio and then head to the building just in time to give the preparations her undivided attention.

When she worked so hard in the evening that she couldn't bring herself to make the trek home, she stayed at the apartment above the café. These rooms also provided her with enough privacy to renew the romance between herself and West, and while his room was separated from Thelma's with a wooden sliding door, it is easy to assume that it was rarely closed. In July 1934 the two raised eyebrows by dining together at the Russian Eagle Café, though they now had the excuse of discussing café business to keep the rumors at bay.

By the time the restaurant opened that summer, Thelma was involved with daily consultations with the head chef, discussing ideas for new food and drink choices. She was also frequently working as a combination kitchen assistant, waitress, cashier, and greeter. "I always did like to cook," she told the *Lawrence Evening Tribune*, "and I have a grand time working out there."

Running the café suited Thelma's personality and her need to keep moving forward. She told friends and reporters that in years to come it wouldn't matter if she got fat or gained wrinkles, because nobody would care what she looked like in her restaurant: "When the studios no longer want me, well, my hungry public will," she said, only half joking. By this point Depression-ravaged Americans were literally standing in long lines for a loaf of stale bread. Thelma foresaw that things could get worse before they got better and prophesized that if the world's finances came to a standstill, "I might have to accept a pair of shoes for six meals, [but] still practically everybody would have to eat."

Customers at the café were greeted by an eclectic menu, starting at seventy-five cents and rising slightly for something with a few extra thrills. However, if they ever dared complain about the food they were served, there was trouble in the kitchen. The Viennese chef enjoyed inventing new, creative ways of serving food but was not so good at accepting criticism. If anyone dared complain that his steaks were undercooked, he'd stamp on the meat with his foot, sling it back into the fire, and then—unknown to Thelma, of course—serve it up again to the unsuspecting customer.

But customers weren't there for the eccentric chef. Visitors arrived from all over the country to catch a glimpse of Thelma Todd. Sometimes they would be in luck and see the star in person, and many times she would joyfully sign their menus and send them on their way with something to tell the folks back home. Tourists weren't the only ones to come visiting. Whenever the actress made her way back to Lawrence, she would invite the locals to come visit her next time they were in California. The café now gave her a base for such visits, and she would always extend a very warm welcome to the Massachusetts fans who chose to visit her there.

Meanwhile, Thelma welcomed some very special visitors from Lawrence: a few members of her own family. One of them was her young cousin Shirley, a film fan whom Thelma made a point of introducing to all the people she knew at the studio. Shirley was delighted when her cousin collected autographs from Laurel and Hardy, and though Thelma hadn't worked with Charlie Chaplin, the actress got his photo too, thanks in part to her friend Catherine Hunter, who worked as his secretary.

When she wasn't working, Thelma drove the family out into the countryside in her Lincoln phaeton and then took everyone to the Mexican resort of Agua Caliente for a short break. Her family was impressed that although she was a world-famous star, Thelma was still very much the down-to-earth girl they had always known. "What a gentle, kindly, loving girl she was," her relatives later said. Sad to say, that happy trip was to be the last time Thelma would ever see her Lawrence family.

In September, the actress returned to dramatic filmmaking with the release of *Take the Stand*, in which Thelma plays Sally, a secretary in the office of a news columnist played by Jack La Rue. When the columnist is murdered after threatening to reveal a scandal, the story turns into a whodunit, and everyone is under suspicion. Thelma's role was minimal, but critics loved the film, praising the suspense of it all.

Just when everything seemed to be going swimmingly, Thelma's ex-husband Pat De Cicco reappeared in her life. He and Thelma were both hit with a lawsuit in October, brought by the owner of 8320 Fountain Avenue, an apartment building the couple had moved to shortly before the end of their marriage. According to the landlord, they owed rent from April of that year, plus money for damages made to furniture and carpets. It was the third time this year that the actress found herself mentioned in legal proceedings. The first had come in February, when two talent agents attempted to sue each other for commissions they felt were owed to them from Thelma's stint in London. Then in March the actress was forced to defend herself against a former lawyer's claims that she owed him $600. As with the earlier problems, she faced the rent suit with a smile, and everything was settled in time for a trip to San Francisco in the hope of finding a location for a possible second café venture. Several days later she announced that it wouldn't stop there; she intended to open another business in Palm Springs and then one more in her hometown of Lawrence.

The ferocity of the pace at which she was working was exciting, but it came at a price. Thelma desperately wanted to make another movie in England, but her workload just wouldn't allow it. "It was nice of you to have air-mailed me to wish me a bon voyage," she wrote to a fan in November 1934. "But as affairs have shaped themselves, the London trip is again indefinitely postponed."

Thelma was disappointed about the trip, but she was happy to star in a film closer to home that played to her comedic strengths while also allowing her to flex her dramatic muscles. RKO's *Lightning Strikes Twice* is the story of an engaged couple whose lives are disrupted by a series of strange incidents, including three apparent murders and the arrival of some imposters. She played one of the two main characters, billed second after costar Ben Lyon, with whom she had acted on other several occasions. "This picture is a sort of farce they say," she told interviewer Molly Marsh, "but to me it is a serious drama." Soon she would be involved in a real-life drama, and this time nobody could confuse it with a farce.

14

ALL GOOD THINGS

*N*ineteen thirty-five began quite pleasantly for Thelma. She was enjoying her rekindled relationship with Roland West, joining him on trips to the Santa Anita racetrack, for dinner at the Russian Eagle Café, and on a short getaway on his yacht, the *Joyita*: "[I] snuck away on the yacht for a week . . . but will be back in the straightjacket any day now," she wrote on a sheet of *Joyita*-headed notepaper. West was not the only former partner she was spending time with; she also accompanied Harvey Priester to various social events and parties. And when she was spotted with a "tall dark gentleman" in the Miramar Hotel, *Picture Play* magazine was intrigued enough to speculate that it could even be Pat De Cicco, though this is unlikely. Thelma was busy and happy, continuing her film work and running the café, which was becoming more successful by the day. However, in the weeks and months ahead, her carefree world would slowly implode.

In February 1935, a resident of New York picked up a pencil and wrote a note that was most certainly not a fan letter. "Pay $10,000 to Abe Lyman in New York by March 5 and live," it said. "If not our San Francisco boys will lay you out." The naming of Abe Lyman as an intermediary made no sense at all, except that the author had obviously discovered he once dated Thelma. To make it look even more menacing, the words "this is no joke" were scrawled underneath, accompanied with a very rough picture of the ace of hearts. This crude doodle thereby ensured that the writer of the note would be known the world over as the Ace. The individual then walked to his local post office and sent the letter to Thelma, care of Hal Roach Studios.

The letter arrived at 6 PM on February 25. One employee showed it to another and another, until finally it arrived at the office of Hal Roach himself. He read it and then took the note straight to Thelma. The actress was confused and said she was "suitably worried," and then the police were called. A week later, on March 6, Thelma and the studio went public with the threat, announcing that a team of security was now on hand to guard the actress and her home.

Joseph E. P. Dunn, head of the Los Angeles office of the US Department of Justice, was suspicious of the letter's authenticity. After the news hit the press, Dunn released a statement to reporters. "This Thelma Todd matter, of which the actress may be an innocent victim, reached my office in a roundabout manner Tuesday night," he said. He then went on to say that if the claim was "bona fide" then his office would work day and night to solve it, but he wanted it understood by everyone "that our office will not tolerate nor be used in any cheap Hollywood publicity stunt."

Thelma was furious that such accusations were being thrown at her, and frightened that the threat was more than someone's cruel prank. On the same day that Dunn was telling the world about his concerns, the actress released the news that a stranger had recently come into her café demanding to know her address. Apparently the man claimed to have a delivery for her, but when Mae Whitehead refused to point him in the direction of her employer's home, he became frustrated and stormed out of the building. Restaurant manager Rudy Schafer then watched him drive away, and Mae told reporters that Thelma was "very upset by the whole matter and does not intend to relax her guard."

More threatening letters arrived, with some corners of the press seeming to relish giving blow-by-blow accounts of the daily goings-on. One columnist, Harry Carr, was incensed that Thelma was going through such pain. Writing in his column in the *Los Angeles Times*, Carr called for tougher laws for would-be kidnappers. Other sections of the media, however, wrote how silly it was for famous folk to worry about kidnap-ping—after all, their familiar faces made them too conspicuous a target for even the dumbest of criminals.

This didn't stop the celebrities of the day from taking every precau-tion to protect themselves. Those with children were particularly careful, creating sunken gardens and high walls where their sons and daughters could play without being observed. They also made sure their kids' bed-rooms were on the top floor of the house, out of reach of even the highest of ladders, and sent them on outings with armed guards and protective dogs (mastiffs being the canines of choice).

Thelma, of course, did not have children to worry about, but she was vulnerable for another reason, in that she was now living alone. Once her marriage to Pat De Cicco ended, the actress had been keen to continue her life outside the confines of parental control. Instead of moving back in with her mother, she shared a home with friend Catherine Hunter for a while, then rented her own house on Tramonto Drive, just a short journey from the Sidewalk Café. Between it and her part-time apartment in the building, she was afforded an independence she'd rarely known, and she was determined not to let the troubling letters stop her from enjoying it.

On March 23 an article written by the actress was printed in the *Adelaide News*, in which the new restaurateur shared her tips on the fine art of making two types of sandwich: cream cheese and pineapple, and stuffed olives with parsley, lettuce, watercress, and chives. The next day she received the good news that her divorce was now final. She continued to work and even invited photographers to the studio to see her happily playing cards with Patsy Kelly. And while her social outings certainly decreased somewhat, they didn't stop altogether.

In late April, Thelma was among a group of stars—which also included Clara Bow, Clark Gable, and Bing Crosby, to name but a few—who made reservations for the Hoot Gibson rodeo show. Gibson was a rodeo champion who had also done very well for himself in movies, as demonstrated by the fact that after the event, Thelma and her colleagues were invited to his ranch, grand enough to entertain thousands of people.

Then, on Mother's Day, she visited the home of friends Clarence Hutson and Eileen Sedgwick for a party in honor of film censor Joseph Breen and his family. There she forgot her cares by playing Ping-Pong and table football on the patio in the company of the other guests.

Things had not returned to normal for the star, however—far from it, in fact. On May 9, having studied the news reports and headlines his letters had garnered around the country, the Ace mailed another letter to Thelma, this time telling her it would be "too bad" if she decided not to pay the $10,000. He had read comments in the paper from Sidewalk Café manager Rudy Schafer, so to add a touch of intrigue the Ace spoke as though the two were old friends. Schafer denied knowing anyone low enough to torment a young woman. But still the letters arrived. One was sent to Thelma's ex-boyfriend Abe Lyman, urging him to persuade her to pay up and warning that she would be killed if he did not do what he was told. "Will be waiting for signal all is well tonight on radio," the letter said. "If we do not hear it we know you fail us." The next letter warned Lyman that he had failed the task and that Thelma would be kidnapped, and yet another made fun of the police's handling of the case.

Determined not to let the strange letters destroy her year, on May 29 Thelma traveled to San Diego with her mother to take part in the latest world's fair, the California Pacific International Exposition, alongside fellow actors Clark Gable, James Cagney, Joan Bennett, Joan Crawford, Ann Harding, and many more. She checked into the La Jolla Hotel, where fellow actors Robert Young, James Gleason, and Bela Lugosi were also staying, before finally heading to the expo to make her appearance. The fair opened with a radio address by President Franklin Delano Roosevelt, and Thelma's part was to greet foreign visitors at the Motion Picture Hall of Fame. There she was photographed alongside her mother, shaking hands with actress Tala Birell and actor George Murphy. She also took part in a fashion parade, modeling a tailored white flannel suit with matching linen blouse and sailor hat. Not to be outdone, fellow actress Ginger Rogers opted for a beige outfit complete with fur collar and brown accessories.

Back in Los Angeles, she made arrangements with Harvey Priester to attend a concert at the Hollywood Roosevelt Hotel. She was also seen with Harvey at the Brown Derby and then sitting quietly alone at Al Levy's Tavern. Friends weren't left out either; she met up with Joan Blondell, Claudette Colbert, and Anna Q. Nilsson before taking in a fashion show in the cocktail lounge of the Knickerbocker Hotel. She was then seen at Sardi's, studying menus for ideas to incorporate into the Sidewalk Café.

Another outing wasn't quite so positive. Thelma received a letter from someone claiming to be the Ace, who asked to meet her on Hollywood Boulevard. Determined to put on a brave face, the actress traveled into town with a one-dollar bill and a gun in her purse. She immediately came face to face with the alleged extortionist, though when he asked if they could go to a secluded spot together, she declined and quickly left.

It would later become evident that the person she met was an imposter, but it had taken a lot of gumption to confront him in person. It was clear that she was trying very hard not to let the Ace intimidate her. Equally clear was the fact that the guards she had told the press were protecting her either had been dismissed or had never existed in the first place. Certainly they were nowhere to be seen toward the end of June, when Thelma's world was turned upside down again.

In late 1934, still negotiating the learning curve of living alone for the first time, she made the mistake of posing alongside her prized collection of perfume for a small feature in December's issue of *Photoplay*. The scents were something she had been collecting for many years, and comprised hundreds of bottles of many different designs, colors, and fragrances. *Photoplay* described the collection, which she kept in her bedroom, as Thelma's "nasal test laboratory" and guessed that it would be worth "hundreds of dollars."

What the magazine didn't know, or perhaps deliberately didn't mention, was that it was actually worth *thousands* of dollars, not hundreds. Unfortunately, some unscrupulous individuals took note of the discrepancy. On June 27, 1935, burglars broke into Thelma's Tramonto Drive home. After cutting through the glass in the front door, they then headed for the perfume collection and spirited away every bottle, also gathering up various coats, a tuxedo, and a suitcase.

Thelma returned from the studio to find her house ransacked and immediately worried that the break-in could somehow be related to the anonymous threats. She phoned the police to report her loss and told responding officers Rosselli and Hoskins that her perfume collection alone was worth around $2,000. Though Thelma feared a connection to the Ace, she was actually just the latest Hollywood name to fall victim to burglars. For several years producers, actors, and actresses had been targeted by one or more gangs who made it their business to know where the rich and famous lived, along with their daily comings and goings. Indeed, just a few days after the burglary on Tramonto Drive, three members of a thieving gang were in court, charged with stealing furs and jewelry from the sister-in-law of Louis B. Mayer.

The burglary problem was further exacerbated by the media's continued insistence on printing the addresses of film stars. After Thelma's incident, the papers quite happily reported the location of the burglary, complete with house number. So now not only had the actress's house been broken into, but she also had to contend with the fact that her full address was in the newspaper for all to see. Shaken to find herself targeted by both criminals and the press, she grabbed some belongings and headed to the apartment above the Sidewalk Café, which she intended to move into on a full-time basis.

It still wasn't an ideal arrangement, as her apartment could easily be accessed by anyone who walked up an exterior flight of stairs connected to a public walkway. And like her home address, her café accommodations could not be kept from the press's inquiring eyes. In a piece in an Australian paper, the *Perth Western Mail*, an individual identified only as "an explorer" revealed that the actress "has a lovely flat built above [the Sidewalk Café], overlooking the ocean, and she lives there." But the article was published on the other side of the world, so it is unlikely that Thelma was aware of it. And at the apartment she had Roland West by her side and various café employees coming and going at all times of the day and into the night, so for a time she felt safer.

The feeling did not last long, however. Another letter from the Ace arrived, giving her until July 29—her twenty-ninth birthday—to pay the ransom or "it will [be] tough on you. . . . We know every move you make." As if that weren't bad enough, one evening an intruder was spotted hanging around on the terrace outside her bedroom window. He ran away when spotted, and West called in builders to install bars on all the windows that faced onto the terrace. Thelma presented manager Rudy Schafer with a Colt pistol, which he carried with him while on the premises.

The actress's life went into lockdown. She went to work at the Hal Roach studio, but the moment her day was over, she was whisked back to the café, where she stayed until the next day. No social engagements were mentioned in the press, and her whole life began to revolve around protecting herself from the Ace.

Her work in feature films was also affected; her only features released during 1935 were *After the Dance* and *Two for Tonight*. Once again the roles were minimal vamp parts, with critics lukewarm about *Two for Tonight* and absolutely hating *After the Dance*. "Thelma Todd has a bit and no more," said the *Independent Exhibitors Film Bulletin*. "Its melodramatics may readily get the ha-ha in better class houses, so it should be avoided. It will even have difficulty in getting by in cheap spots and should occupy the second feature spot in a double bill." *Variety*'s review was no better, though it did give a little nod to Thelma: "Nancy Carroll has little to do. She is never called on for steam until a moment at the finale. . . . Thelma Todd, as the blonde peril, is given more opportunity and she comes across with it. But her costumes are frowsy."

By this time someone had begun telephoning Thelma's café long distance and reversing the charges. It did not take long for the actress to grow convinced that the caller was the same man writing the letters. She refused to take his calls, delegating Mae Whitehead to answer the telephone. Mae was also in charge of checking the actress's food for signs of contamination, which some may say was the height of paranoia on Thelma's part. Not so, it would seem, as one day the maid discovered tiny pieces of glass hidden inside the food. This information was kept out of the press, and no one ever discovered how or why the glass was there, but it surely was enough to make Thelma believe her troubles were never going to end.

Newspapers reported that the Ace had been mailing more and more letters to Thelma and Abe Lyman, asking for $10,000, then $15,000, then $20,000. Terrifyingly, one letter announced the intention of kidnapping "the Thelma Todd dame" on August 25, and demanded that money be paid for her release. The letters were bizarre, many written in an almost illegible hand, but at some point in his psychosis the author made the fatal mistake of making up the fictitious name of Mike Dorgan and giving himself an address of 3118 Newton Avenue, Astoria, New York. This, he said, was where those involved could get in touch or deliver the money. Of course, the moment the letters arrived at their destinations they were handed over to officers, who immediately asked if the actress had received anything from that address in the recent past. She had.

In June she'd gotten a letter from someone calling himself Richard Harding, who addressed Thelma as a "Charming Lady." In the note he expressed his admiration for the actress and told her that he was an actor himself. He had made it a habit, he claimed, of carrying her picture in his pocket. "Recently I had the misfortune to lose it," he wrote, "and since that time have been very much distressed." He then asked the actress to send him a new photo, as he was about to star in a play about Sherlock Holmes and wished to replace the one he had lost. "I will jolly well be grateful if you send one," he said.

The name Richard Harding, it turned out, had also appeared in one of the extortion notes. As soon as the police were informed of the connection, they went straight to the Newton Avenue apartment block to look for anything suspicious. During the stakeout, one man caught their eye: building superintendent Harry Schimanski, a married father of two with no previous convictions. On August 17, the officers swooped in, and though he denied having anything to do with the letters, he was taken immediately into custody.

Two days later, Schimanski was charged with attempted extortion through the mail. Back at the Sidewalk Café, Thelma was notified of his detention and let out a long sigh. "Oh, I'm so relieved," she told reporters. "I hope this stops all this constant worry." Privately, she was so delighted that she immediately began planning her social life again, telling friends that she no longer needed a security detail to go out in public.

The actress gave a short interview to reporters on August 29, revealing that no letters had been received since Schimanski's arrest (even though he was, by this time, out on bail). Thelma added that she would not insist on prosecution but would certainly not stand in the way of the FBI should it want to press forward with a trial. The arrest had given her the satisfaction of repudiating the rumors that the whole business was a publicity stunt, she said—a comment aimed very much in the direction of skeptical DOJ representative Joseph E. P. Dunn.

Two days later the actress stepped out for the first time since the arrest, this time back supporting the Dominoes during a party for local children. There she mingled with the other guests and happily watched youngsters riding on the merry-go-round, taking in a puppet show, and eating ice cream. A week later Thelma and Patsy Kelly attended a barbecue party at the home of actor Pat O'Brien in Brentwood, which was given in honor of singer James Melton. Then she celebrated the wedding of Inez Courtney at one of her favorite restaurants, the Brown Derby. Thelma was beginning to feel good about herself again. So good in fact that she even talked about expanding the café: she and West made plans to put an addition on the back of the building, as well as make $10,000 worth of improvements to the interior.

Thelma began work on the new Laurel and Hardy movie *The Bohemian Girl*, in which she was to play the Gypsy Queen, a substantial role. The shooting of the movie was hard, mainly because several of the actors (including Stan Laurel) became ill and delayed production. Added to that, Laurel and Hardy both refused to do a commercial tie-in for the

Standard Oil Company, which according to studio records would have brought in $40,000 worth of advertising. Executives were frustrated by their decision but finally decided to use Thelma Todd and costar Antonio Moreno for the spot instead.

It was during this time that Thelma met Lee Heidorn, a young lady who ran the official Billie Dove Fan Club. Lee had traveled to Hollywood to meet her idol, but the trip turned into much more than that. Lee was able to spend time with a great many celebrities along the way, including Jean Harlow and Thelma. Despite being busy with the film, the actress made time to not only meet Lee but introduce her to Laurel and Hardy too. Several days later the ladies met for lunch at Al Levy's, and afterward Thelma happily posed for pictures with the young woman.

While her life was slowly getting back on track, Thelma was disturbed that even though Schimanski had been arrested, she and Abe Lyman had started to receive threatening letters again. After Thelma's death, the FBI investigated claims that she had chosen not to hand these over to officers out of fear, instead hiding them in her bedroom. What actually happened, however, was that the actress showed the letters to Roland West, and together they decided that since Schimanski had already been arrested, these must be the work of a crank. "She did not consider it worthwhile forwarding the letters to this office," an FBI investigator wrote. The bureau then asked someone at the Sidewalk Café (probably Roland West) to locate the letters, but without success. "Undoubtedly Miss Todd had destroyed them prior to her death," the report said.

Back in New York, Schimanski appeared in court on October 30 to plead not guilty. He remained out on bail. Meanwhile, at the apartment block where the man had worked, Edward Schiffert, a twenty-six-year-old loner who lived with his parents, was becoming increasingly upset. Ever since the arrest of Schimanski, he had been passionately telling his parents that the man was innocent, that he never wrote the letters and it was all a mistake. During one conversation, he blurted out that he was going to "protect Schimanski," but because Schiffert was mentally unstable, always telling his parents about big plans and ideas, they decided to ignore him. "We thought it was just another one of his ideas and didn't pay any attention," his mother later told reporters.

But it was more than that, and before long Schiffert telephoned a reporter at the *Long Island Daily Star*. Introducing himself as Richard Harding, the man admitted writing the letters himself. "Meet me for the full story," he told the reporter, who thought he was a timewaster and bid him good day. Schiffert called again on November 5 and repeated the same story. By this time the reporter had become intrigued and arranged to meet him later that afternoon at a newsstand in Times Square. At that point he called the FBI, who immediately headed to the location and waited for Schiffert to turn up.

It took only moments to arrest the man, and he willingly accompanied agents to their office, where he told them his real name. In contrast to Schimanski, he not only admitted to writing the notes but also gave handwriting specimens, providing copies of some of the extortion letters from memory. He then told officers that he had never conversed with or collaborated with Harry Schimanski. When told of the arrest, his parents were mortified and protested his innocence, but their son was adamant: it was he who had sent the notes and nobody else. He was correct; shortly thereafter his handwriting was analyzed by experts, who noted that they were certain that Schiffert "wrote all the contents without collaborating with others."

In the weeks after the arrest, psychiatrists at Bellevue Hospital studied the young man and interviewed him intensely. Schiffert told them he had been madly in love with Thelma for four years—that he had never met her but worshipped her photos night and day. He added that the letters were written to gain more publicity for her career, and doctors noted that he had "no insight into the quality of his act." Psychiatrists were concerned. "He is a suitable case for care and treatment in a state hospital," they wrote, and added that even if charges against him were dropped, they would push to have him committed themselves. They need not have worried, as shortly after Thelma's death Schiffert was committed to the Manhattan State Hospital, while the charges against Schimanski were quietly dropped.

With the letters behind her, Thelma's march back to normalcy continued. And for her, "normal" meant a new round of engagement rumors. Reports had begun to circulate in late October that she and Roland West were about to be married—a tricky proposition given that he was still officially married to Jewel, but that small detail didn't faze the press. In the weeks leading up to Thanksgiving, Thelma spent more time with Harvey Priester, and the two enjoyed several restaurant outings.

Thelma also became very involved with events at the First Baptist Church in Hollywood, where she helped them supply food to needy families in the area, taking it upon herself to donate thirty filled baskets. Having done that, she then distributed the hampers herself, and she made sure that the families she gave to were now on her Christmas list for cards and presents.

Her pastor, Harold L. Proppe, took note of all the things she did for the church and later told reporters just how much joy she brought to the children she met. "She always welcomed children wherever she was, with as much hospitality as she would welcome the most powerful of motion-picture magnates," he said. Proppe's church wasn't the only one the actress helped in her lifetime, as she also provided money to a church back in Lawrence so it could build a much-needed stage.

Thelma never forgot her family in Lawrence either. She once sent her cousin a fur jacket made from a coat she no longer wore. After her death, the same girl also acquired some of the actress's jewelry, including several rings. Thelma's giving spirit extended to housekeeper Mae Whitehead; when she learned that Mae had a baby son, she'd insisted on giving her fifty dollars to spend on the boy. Then one day while out shopping, Thelma spotted an expensive overcoat that would fit the child perfectly. Knowing that the maid would never be able to afford such an item on her own, the actress snapped it up and presented it to her employee as a gift—a gesture for which Mae's son still expressed gratitude some eighty years later.

At the Hal Roach studio, fellow employees would be afraid to tell Thelma how much they liked something she was wearing, as they knew she would immediately give it to them. Furs, jewels, expensive gowns— it didn't matter what it was, if someone admired it, Thelma would gladly hand it over. Fans were also included in her generosity; she was well known for being one of the best autograph signers in Hollywood, even signing for fans when she was out dining or spending time with friends.

Once, at the Hal Roach studio, she was told of a young boy who badly needed his tonsils out but the family could not afford the bill. Thelma paid for it immediately, and though she told no one about it, the fact that she was the benefactor soon became common knowledge, purely because she was the most likely person to do such a thing.

On another occasion in the early 1930s, Thelma was out with her mother when a young man approached her. He recognized her immediately and told the star that he had searched unsuccessfully for a job for many months and wondered if perhaps she could hire him as a chauffeur. She had no need for a full-time driver, but she reached into her purse and gave him some money. When he tried to refuse, she assured him that it was a loan; he could pay her back when he was on his feet again. He accepted her kindness and took the cash.

Thelma finished her work on *The Bohemian Girl*, and shortly afterward production began on her next Hal Roach short with Patsy Kelly. In *An All American Toothache*, the two women play waitresses in a café, and Mickey Daniels is a fairly incompetent dental student who enlists their help to prove to his professor that he can successfully pull a tooth. Meanwhile, Thelma's real-life café business was still going from strength to strength; it became such a mecca for celebrities that Thelma began acquiring special plates for them, personalized with their initials. Costars Laurel and Hardy would drop in when they were at the beach, and friend Pat O'Brien was a regular visitor. Thelma loved the café so much that she ordered a variety of exclusive stationery items that sported her face and name, and plans were underway to add several more features to the establishment in the year ahead.

By this time Thelma and Roland West had opened an upstairs room called Joya's. While the Sidewalk Café was for fans and beachgoers, Joya's was a luxurious restaurant designed to cater to a more sophisticated clientele—entrance was by invitation only. Thelma explained the reasoning behind it to reporter Nora Laing: "You see, there is no place in Hollywood or outside where celebrities can go and eat in comfort without being besieged by autograph hunters. And although we screen people wouldn't do without our 'fans' for the world, we do like a little peace sometimes. That's why I thought it would be nice to have a really exclusive place where I can guarantee my guests real relaxation as well as good food."

The partners' expansion efforts included a number of additions to Joya's, including a lounge where celebrities could enjoy cocktails. Thelma planned a huge gala for New Year's Eve so that she could show off everything she had done with the place during the months leading up to Christmas: "I'm going to have some new ideas in effect for our party," she told reporters.

While it was undoubtedly an exciting time for Thelma, she was also sad that the arrangements would keep her away from Lawrence for the holiday season. Her mother had helped ease her homesickness with a traditional meal at Thanksgiving, complete with turkey and all the trimmings, but Thelma missed her family and had planned to go back to Massachusetts for Christmas Day. She had even booked to appear at a local theater in January, but all these plans fell through. The organization and supervision of the café was just too much, and she reluctantly agreed to postpone her trip until May 1936. "She was greatly upset," relatives said. "She never forgot her old home."

The day-to-day running of the café presented other worries as well, and some were far more complicated than ordering new glasses or cutlery. It was a well-known fact that nightclubs and restaurants in many cities across the United States had attracted the unwanted attention of gangsters and gamblers. By many accounts, the Sidewalk Café was one such establishment.

During the grand jury investigation into Thelma's death, which followed the inconclusive coroner's inquest, it was widely reported that the Sidewalk Café building had been the site of a number of private gambling parties. These illicit events were said to be informal, frequented by celebrities and others with whom West had become acquainted during his time in the movies. Years later these parties were confirmed by Rudy Schafer's son, Rudy Jr. Speaking with Thelma Todd historian Benny Drinnon, he remembered being shown an upstairs room by his father, who explained that it was used by Thelma and her friends to play games of chance. He even recalled seeing a number of card tables and a roulette wheel. (There were also a few nickel slot machines in the bar downstairs, he said, and he had even pulled the handle occasionally for people who knew his father. This equipment was illegal, of course, but nobody seemed particularly bothered by its presence.)

After Thelma's death, the grand jury visited a room on the third floor of the building—dubbed the Tower Room—and found it to be apparently under construction, with carpenter's supplies scattered around the floor. It is entirely possible that this was the room Rudy Jr. saw and that the gambling equipment had been removed and the renovation excuse concocted to avoid questions by police. The police—and the press—had similar suspicions about the Tower Room. They further speculated that gangsters had become aware of the private parties and put pressure on Thelma and Roland to bring them on board, hoping to turn the informal gaming sessions into their own professional gambling racket.

It's possible that Thelma was fine with the original gambling parties. After all, she was a fun-loving woman, and she may have seen it as something of a hoot—a harmless activity among friends. But it would have been completely out of character for her to give up any control over her establishment to underworld figures. She had shown from an early age that she never hesitated to stick up for herself and stand her ground, and she passionately believed in the restaurant and wanted to make it even more successful during the years to come. After all, it was her ticket out of Hollywood.

So the speculation about the Tower Room led to one conclusion: if Thelma had been approached by gangsters who wanted a foothold in her restaurant, she would have insisted on having nothing to do with them. According to some, that is exactly what happened. As grand jury foreman George Rochester told reporters, Thelma had been firm, and that attitude had "aroused hostility of gambling interests."

15

THE GANGSTERS

*I*f the café was being approached by local hoods, which gang could it have been? This debate has raged on since 1935. One man often associated with the case is gangster Charles "Lucky" Luciano. Some writers have claimed that he must have been the mobster behind the gambling ring, and rumors abound that the actress had a longstanding relationship with him. Once it cooled, it has been claimed, he ordered a hit on her.

While stories will always be told about Lucky and Thelma's supposed involvement, the fact remains that there is simply no evidence tying the two together, either romantically or professionally. On the evening of her death, the actress apparently told Ida Lupino that she was involved in a relationship with an unnamed businessman from San Francisco, but unless she had got her lover's town wrong (which seems very unlikely) she surely couldn't have meant Lucky. He was known to live almost full-time in New York City and at times in Hot Springs, Arkansas, but not in San Francisco.

There is also no evidence that Luciano ever visited Los Angeles, let alone spent a great deal of time there. By the time 1935 rolled in, he was heavily involved in his East Coast operations, including the Commission, a governing body for organized crime. He was planning a takeover of mobster Dutch Schultz's assets and overseeing various New York prostitution rings. If he had any time left at all for muscling in on the running of

Thelma Todd's café, chances are he would not have done it in person; his demands would have been relayed by his West Coast associates.

As suspicion of Luciano has grown over the years, another, more likely suspect has been overlooked entirely. This particular mobster would have had far more reason to target Thelma's restaurant, and he was most certainly in the Los Angeles area during the mid-1930s.

Anthony Cornero Stralla, better known as Tony Cornero, was born in Italy and immigrated to California when he was just a child. In and out of trouble from his early teens, he was forever on the lookout for a good way of making money. When Prohibition came, he needed to look no further, and before long he had become a notorious rumrunner, bringing vast amounts of illegal alcohol into the country. Together with his brothers, Frank and Louis, Tony supplied nightclubs with whisky obtained from Canada. He became rich very quickly and even enrolled his sister in the operation by having her help to unload booze onto dark, deserted beaches around the Los Angeles area.

The Corneros caught the attention of federal officers, who observed them for years and arrested one family member or another at various times. Tony made the biggest headlines, however, when he managed to escape federal agents by jumping from a train. To avoid capture he headed first to Europe and then to Mexico. He lived on the run for several years until finally returning to the States. There he turned himself in and was sent to McNeil Island Penitentiary in Washington State.

By 1931, Tony's brothers had announced their intention to open a casino in Nevada, where gambling had just been legalized. Their establishment was to be called the Meadows, and Frank and Louis hoped it would appeal to builders currently working on the Hoover Dam. The brothers began construction in May 1931, bragging that the Meadows would be elaborate, built around a glamorous lobby and waiting room. The designer estimated that it would be "the finest thing in the entire state of Nevada."

Tony heard about the project, and as soon as he was released from prison, he decided to help his brothers with their enterprise. However, from the start it became famous for the wrong reasons. Shortly after construction finished a small fire broke out; it was rumored (though never proved) to have been started by rival gangsters. In November 1931, Frank was arrested on suspicion of conspiracy to violate Prohibition, then a month after that, Louis announced he was suing actress Clara Bow, whom he said was refusing to pay a gambling debt incurred in September of that year. Clara denied owing the $1,100 demanded of her and said she really owed only $69.50. The matter was later settled, but not before it made embarrassing headlines.

The casino was meant to be a place for the local builders to hang out after a busy day at work, but it did not work out that way. Instead of enjoying the location, the workers would often visit just once, declare it too grand for their liking, and then head off to other, less formal venues down the road. In March 1932, just months after opening the business, Louis and Frank decided to step away, leasing the building to several associates. Frank stayed on for a short while after they took over; Louis headed off to San Francisco, while Tony went back to Los Angeles.

The casino limped on for a time but eventually closed as the Meadows in late 1935, though it was apparently still in Frank's name when he was killed in a car crash in 1941. By this time the building had become a rundown boardinghouse and brothel. Its sad existence eventually ended later in the 1940s when a neon light somehow broke from its hinges and plunged into the building, starting a fire and burning the whole place to the ground.

While the Nevada business had been something of a nonstarter, the experience of running a casino gave Tony a taste for what he might be able to achieve. There was only one problem: he was now based in Los Angeles, and gambling in California was illegal. He laid low for a while, but when an article in the *Los Angeles Times* claimed that he was now aiming to get into a legitimate business, it seemed too good to be true. By 1934, his own wife was complaining about his unpredictable behavior, claiming that his business dealings were keeping him out of the house until all hours of the night. She never discussed what those interests consisted of, but given his track record it is safe to assume that he wasn't working as a florist.

By 1935, to get around the state's tight no-gambling laws, a variety of gaming ships were being operated off the coast of Long Beach in what were considered international waters. Water taxis would take revelers to and from the ships, and they'd party the night away before being taken back to shore, lighter on cash and loaded up with alcohol. The ships were making millions just out of the reach of law enforcement, and by August 1935 gangsters had targeted the gaming ship *Monte Carlo*, keen to get in on the operation. The authorities were of course incensed and tried every possible way to get the ships closed down. Police arrested a number of so-called pirates, and they were eager to speak with one other: Tony Cornero's brother Frank.

By October, authorities began arresting not only the taxi boat operators but the parking lot attendants too. It was a bad time to get into the gambling ship business, and Tony was smart enough to know that if he wanted to go that route, he would need to bide his time. It is a distinct possibility that in the meantime, he turned his attentions to other illegal gambling opportunities. If, as has been reported over the years, Tony's rivals would not allow him access to their gaming businesses in the heart of Hollywood, he would have looked for premises elsewhere—probably somewhere quiet with no immediate gangster association.

Thelma's Sidewalk Café building would have been a perfect place: it was out on the beach, far away from central Los Angeles, and under the cover of darkness, it was a discreet place for people to meet up. What's more, when Tony saw the place for the first time, he would surely have been struck by a bizarre coincidence: the building was almost identical to, and somewhat grander than, the Meadows in Nevada.

There is indeed evidence that Tony was familiar with the building. In 1963, an intriguing article appeared in the *Los Angeles Times* stating that during the mid-1920s, Tony's brother Frank had been quietly kidnapped by other gangsters and a $300,000 ransom placed on his head. Tony arranged to meet the men to hand over the money, and the place chosen to take care of such business was the site of Thelma Todd's café.

The reported date of the episode—circa Christmas 1925—is incorrect, as the building was not finished at that point. By the time it had opened to the public, Tony was out of the country and was then sent to prison until the early 1930s. The episode therefore, must have happened some time later, after the brothers returned to Los Angeles in the mid-1930s and before Frank's death in 1941.

Even a mobster like Cornero would not have been reckless enough to hand over a vast amount of money to fellow gangsters in a location with which he was not familiar. Thus, he must have known the place well and felt confident and at ease there.

If Tony Cornero was the gangster behind the infamous planned takeover, the fact that Thelma was not an easy woman to control or manipulate would not have sat well with him. In many ways Tony was exactly the sort of person people think of when they imagine a 1930s gangster: suave, mischievous, ready to jump off a moving train at a moment's notice. . . . But most of all he was a man used to getting his own way at all times. He may not have been as volatile as the most infamous gangsters, but Cornero liked people to say yes; he most certainly did not appreciate being told no.

Years later, when authorities targeted his gambling ship business, the hood was defiant. He told them that it made no difference to him what they thought about his illegal activities; they could say no to him a million times over and he would still remain in business. Governor Earl Warren told reporters that the man had made threats, displaying "the defiance that lawless elements have for law and order." During his rumrunning years, Tony had been rumored to get into gunfights with rivals on deserted highways. In 1946 it would be claimed that his gambling ship the *Rex* had a special padded room known as the "law enforcement room," where people were taken for "a thorough working over" after being beaten up on shore. Cornero may not have been impulsively violent, but he was certainly willing to resort to force when others displeased him.

Clearly, some sort of threat was hanging over Thelma in the last few months of her life. Her lawyer, A. Ronald Button, told police she had been troubled deeply. In the past, the relationship between Button and his client had been purely business, but she had begun dropping into his office to chat with him about all kinds of day-to-day matters. He got the feeling she was withholding information—that something was worrying her but she just didn't have the nerve to say what it was.

Then, out of the silence, came a confession: she was very concerned about a group of gangsters who were trying to open a gambling establishment in her café. "She told me she was opposed to gambling and would have nothing to do with it," he told police. "Whether the gamblers ever made a deal I do not know."

Was Cornero the mobster so eager to get into Thelma's business? We will probably never know for sure. But the circumstantial evidence is compelling: he was a dangerous gangster, apparently familiar with Thelma's property, who was searching for a new gaming operation at the same time that the actress was living in fear of gangsters doing just that.

16

A CHANGE IS COMING

While the gangster problems were foremost in her mind, Thelma was also thinking seriously about her acting career. She was gaining confidence in herself: she received word that producer Joseph M. Schenck was interested in signing her to a long-term deal, she fired her business manager and assumed complete control over her own contracts, and she insisted that she receive first billing after Laurel and Hardy in any future films she made with them. But if she had her way, there would not be many more of those—she was planning to make just a few more shorts with Hal Roach before dedicating her time to features.

She was sick of comedy shorts, she confessed to a reporter from the English newspaper the *Daily Express*. She was bored, she said, and wanted a role that she could really get her teeth into. "I wish I could get back to Elstree [Studios]," she told him. "There I would get in another good picture. It is just too bad here, once you get small parts in short comedies." She wanted to be taken seriously as an actress, to play great character parts, and have a real future in the craft she had chosen, but still she kept getting offered the same kinds of roles. "Always I must be the other woman," she said. "I'm a bit tired of always losing my man, or breaking up happy homes, or causing sweet things to end it all."

Many fans agreed with Thelma's frustrations, and by 1935 they had started writing to fan magazines to show their displeasure at the way she was being treated. "Why doesn't Hollywood give Thelma Todd a chance for real stardom?" asked fan Lorne Waddell. "Why is she put in comedies with ZaSu Pitts or Patsy Kelly? She should be cast in a real picture. She well deserves the chance to get some honest-to-goodness praise."

"I'll tell you why someone doesn't give Thelma a chance," answered another fan. "Producers are too busy looking for new talent really to discover the old! I don't mean old in years either, but old in experience on the screen, which ought to make one more in demand if anything."

On December 11, Thelma met ZaSu Pitts and her husband for lunch at Perino's Restaurant, and then the two women went shopping for Christmas presents. ZaSu ordered her turkey for the big day, while Thelma bought wrapping paper and tags. This, her friends said, was an indication that the actress certainly planned to be alive for the festive season. ZaSu told reporters that she had never seen her happier in her life.

However, at one point in the afternoon Thelma turned a little melancholy. She and ZaSu visited the Sunset Boulevard shop of hatmaker Helen Ainsworth, where Thelma ordered a hat. It was scheduled to be delivered the following week, and the actress told Ainsworth that instead of paying her when it arrived, she would do it there and then. "I may be broke by the first of the year," she said, before adding that many changes were coming into her life. This comment was overheard by Ainsworth's assistant, Robert Galer.

Continuing the conversation with her hatmaker, Thelma said she had recently been seeing a psychoanalyst, who told her she wasn't making the right use of her talents. "And he hit the nail right on the head," she said. "I'm pulling out of here if you know what I mean." After her death, reporters jumped on these statements—especially the one about her going broke. They decided that Thelma must have known something was going to happen to her, though Ainsworth insisted that she was sure all her client meant was that she might be short of cash after finishing her Christmas shopping.

ZaSu, too, was unconcerned by any brief flashes of depressed self-reflection; she later told the grand jury that her friend hadn't given her any cause to think she was contemplating death. She certainly seemed in good spirits when ZaSu's thirteen-year-old son, Don Gallery, spent time with a playful Thelma that same week, throwing a ball on the beach outside the Sidewalk Café. Aunt Thelma, as he called her, was always full of fun, and whenever she visited ZaSu she made sure to spend time with Don and his sister too. "We were all so silly together," he remembered. "She'd take us to the pier or to the beach to throw baseballs at milk bottles."

Christmas was Thelma's favorite time of the year, and in the weeks leading up to mid-December, she had carried out her custom of discreetly going around the studio and finding out what everyone wanted as a gift. Armed with this information, the actress then went out and bought cards and packages for everyone she knew. The cards and some of the gifts she mailed around December 13, while other packages were found lined up against her apartment wall after her death.

Thelma may have been trying to keep upbeat, but circumstances were still conspiring to cast a pall over her troubled final year. Sometime in mid-December, the actress was attacked by a man she knew while she tidied up the café. The hour was late and almost everyone had gone home when the actress got into an argument that grew increasingly violent. All of a sudden, the man she was arguing with lashed out and punched or slapped Thelma in the face, and she went flying across the table. More blows landed before a waiter intervened and eventually broke up the fracas.

Police never publicly identified Thelma's attacker, but after her death officers did say that he was "a central figure in the current investigation." It was widely believed to have been Roland West. He denied all knowledge of the incident. "It's ridiculous like most of the mysteries here," he said.

The weekend after the attack, on Saturday, December 14, Thelma and her mother had plans to go into the city and finish up any remaining gift shopping. That morning, Alice was driven to the café by Mae Whitehead, who parked her car at the back of the building, delivered Alice, and then walked up to the garage several blocks away to collect Thelma's car. That done, the actress instructed her maid to telephone Martha Ford's home and accept an invitation to a party the next day, adding that she should tell her Thelma intended to bring a guest. She and her mother then left for their trip, stopping on the way at the dentist, where the actress had a temporary cap placed on a tooth.

Once mother and daughter returned to the café around 6 PM, Thelma spoke to Mae, who showed her some shoes she had sent away to be dyed blue. She was planning to wear them at a party being held by Stanley and Ida Lupino in her honor that evening at the Cafe Trocadero, and the actress said the footwear was just what she wanted. She then went upstairs briefly to see how the plans were coming for the new cocktail bar at Joya's and then to lie down on her couch to speak to her mother for a while. Later, newspapers would claim that Roland West walked in on the two women at this point, just in time to see them both crying as they spoke. However, Alice denied this, saying they were merely having a conversation and no tears were involved.

With the help of Mae, Thelma dressed in a blue sparkly evening gown and long mink coat, with clasps in her hair, a diamond pin in the shape of a knot, and several expensive rings. Her mother watched the proceedings, chatting to the actress as she did so. Mae asked if the actress was planning on taking her large bundle of house keys to the party. Thelma did not wish to be weighed down, so the maid separated out the key to the side door of the building. She put the single key into a white coin purse along with thirty-five cents, placed the purse into the bag Thelma was using that evening, and then told her boss what she had done.

When she was ready, Thelma asked Roland West if he would like to go to the party with her. He assured her that he couldn't—it was Saturday night and the restaurant would be far too busy to have both of them take a night off. He then escorted the actress and her mother down to chauffeur Ernest Peters's car and told her to be in by 2 AM. Thelma was said to have retorted that she'd be in by 2:05 AM, and the two went back and forth for a few minutes, in what West described as a laughing manner. "Was it all in good spirits?" he was asked during the inquest. "As far as I was concerned, it was laughing," he replied. "I told her, anytime you have to stay out later than two go to your mother's," West said. "That will save you that half hour of sleep. You must have your rest because your work depends on you."

17

FAREWELL

*A*fter the actress bid Roland West good-bye, driver Ernest Peters closed the car door and drove Thelma Todd and her mother toward Hollywood. The idea was for Thelma to be dropped off at the Trocadero in time for her party, and then Peters would take Alice Todd on a short shopping trip before dropping her home.

As they headed up Wilshire Boulevard, the actress asked her driver to pull over at a nearby flower shop to see if they stocked camellias. Once Peters confirmed that they did, Thelma requested he buy one for her dress. While the driver was in the store, Thelma and her mother chatted about their day and debated whether the actress should accompany her mother home or go directly to the party. By the time Peters returned to the car with the flower, it had been decided that Thelma would stick to her original plans, and they headed toward the Trocadero, arriving at 8:25 PM.

The Troc, as it was known to regulars, was located at 8610 Sunset Boulevard and had seen its fair share of glitz, glamour, and scandal long before Thelma Todd pulled up outside. Originally called La Boheme, it had closed in 1931 after a gun battle but was later purchased by Billy Wilkerson, owner of the *Hollywood Reporter*. He renamed it Cafe Trocadero and celebrated its reopening in September 1934 with a glitzy party.

Wilkerson loved the attention of the famous folk who piled through the Troc's doors and eagerly greeted luminaries such as Lana Turner,

Robert Taylor, Fred Astaire, Jean Harlow, Clark Gable, Bing Crosby, and William Powell. In fact, so in awe was Wilkerson that when Norma Shearer complained about lack of privacy, he was said to have installed a downstairs bar called Little Troc on Sunset, where stars could gather without the risk of newspaper columnists spying on their conversations.

Still, there was a darker element to the Cafe Trocadero, in the form of the notorious gangsters who enjoyed hanging out there. There was a back room that held Saturday-night gambling parties for exclusive guests such as studio heads Sam Goldwyn and Irving Thalberg. Were these gaming rooms run by the gangsters who roamed the Troc's halls? It is certainly a possibility—especially since when Billy Wilkerson sold the Trocadero just a few years later, it was Bugsy Siegel and Mickey Cohen who quickly bought the establishment.

Outside the Troc on the evening of Saturday, December 14, 1935, Thelma waved good-bye to her mother and made her way through the front door and into the cocktail room. There, waiting for her, was a group of approximately twenty guests, including her friend Harvey Priester, along with hosts Stanley Lupino and his daughter, Ida. Everyone seemed ecstatic to see her, and they all enjoyed a cocktail before moving upstairs at approximately 10:15 PM to the cream and gold dining room.

Sitting with her friends, Thelma seemed in good spirits as she dug into a meal of seafood cocktail, turtle soup, filet mignon, and salad. She declined dessert but did accept a glass of champagne and an after-dinner brandy, which guests later observed had no effect on her behavior. If she became drunk or even tipsy, others were not aware of it.

Actor and dance instructor Arthur Prince, who sat with Thelma for some of the evening, described the actress as a very happy and witty woman, who seemed "in particularly fine fettle." Both Prince and Stanley Lupino said she was the life and soul of the party. "There was nothing in her manner to indicate that anything was worrying her," Lupino later told detectives. This was also confirmed by party guest Fred Keating, who said that she seemed very happy: "I was struck by her charm. She seemed more vivacious than when I knew her before."

However, Thelma's mood did threaten to sour somewhat when she saw ex-husband Pat De Cicco, who was with his current squeeze, actress Margaret Lindsay. Thelma had bumped into De Cicco unexpectedly when she was shopping a day or two before, and according to her ex, it had been the first time in a year that the two had seen each other. He later told detectives that they spoke briefly, said their good-byes, and then got on with their day.

Thelma wasn't the only person De Cicco had bumped into that day, as shortly afterward he saw Ida Lupino, who mentioned the party she was giving at the Troc. De Cicco jokingly asked where his invitation was, so the young actress told him that he'd be more than welcome to come, so long as he was aware the party was actually for his ex-wife. That was fine, he said; the two were on speaking terms, and seeing her at the party would not be in the least bit awkward or difficult. "I'll be glad to come," he told Ida; he even hinted that he'd like to be seated at the main table, near Thelma.

What happened after he ran into Ida is something of a mystery. According to De Cicco, he later discovered that his girlfriend, Margaret Lindsay, would be in town and decided to go out with her instead. He claimed to have phoned Ida to give her the news, though the message seems to have gone astray, and she denied ever hearing from him. However, even though De Cicco no longer wished to be a guest at Ida's party, it didn't stop him taking Lindsay to the Trocadero, where he knew that the party was going to be in full swing.

When Thelma entered the downstairs part of the club, her ex and his girlfriend were upstairs. "Pat learned that Miss Todd was below in the cocktail room," Lindsay later told investigators, "and he said he'd rather not see her, so we didn't go down there." When the actress finally did come upstairs with her party, she was quite surprised to see De Cicco and Lindsay already there.

Ida would later say that Thelma was furious to see her ex with his new girlfriend and had stern words with him as a result. However, Harvey Priester, who spent a lot of time with her throughout the evening, denied that she was in any way concerned. Priester also said that he had not noticed the two together at all, which was backed up by Margaret Lindsay, who told the grand jury that Thelma spoke to her ex-husband only as she danced past their table, stopping briefly to ask if he had informed Ida of his decision not to join their party. He said that he had, and that he would talk to her again the next day.

Sometime during the evening, Ida slipped away with Thelma for some girl talk in the ladies' room. According to the young actress, Thelma asked if she had a good love life. Ida explained to the actress that since she was so busy at the studio, she just didn't have any time for boyfriends, to which Thelma replied, "I'm in the midst of the most marvelous romance I've ever had, with a businessman from San Francisco who is too grand for words."

Ida raised her eyebrows and asked if that meant she had to travel all the way to San Francisco to conduct this wonderful relationship. Thelma replied that yes, she most certainly did, though did not divulge any further details. This confession is intriguing and puzzling. Though Thelma did visit San Francisco occasionally, her friends would later tell reporters, the police, and the coroner that they had no idea who this mysterious man could possibly be. ZaSu Pitts, meanwhile, did remember her being involved with someone from the city at one point in the past but could not identify him by name.

After Thelma's death, police did some initial investigation into who the mysterious person could be. Claude Peters, chief special agent of the Southern California Telephone Co., was asked to scour telephone records and check lines. He looked at every angle, including calls to and from the Trocadero, other restaurants Thelma was known to visit, and the Sidewalk Café itself. It was thought that the romance would be a sensitive subject between her and rumored lover West, and so the actress may have made calls from various other locations, away from her usual haunts. However, despite looking at every option available to him, Peters came up with nothing. In the decades since, the identity of Thelma's supposed mystery man has never been determined.

By the time Ida and Thelma returned to the dining room, Stanley Lupino found the actress to be in a most agreeable mood. He asked her to dance, and while they made their way across the floor, Thelma told him of her plans to make another movie in England. She had acquired a property, she said, and was more than willing to bring him on board the project. Lupino was intrigued, and afterward they sat and discussed the film for quite some time, both excited about the possibility of working together again. They became so engrossed in conversation that the minutes soon turned to hours. Before she knew it, Thelma's curfew of 2 AM was looming large.

Around 1:50 AM, the actress went over to visit with another friend, legendary theater owner Sid Grauman, and during their conversation she was apparently handed a note by a waiter. Later nobody could tell police what this letter had said or who it was from, but given the hour, it is a distinct possibility that it came from Roland West, reminding Thelma that the time had come for her to return to the apartment. Ida Lupino commented that on reading the note, the actress became furious, and later in the ladies' room she was pacing up and down, muttering about "him."

Arthur Prince remembered that Thelma was in a positive mood earlier in the evening, but by the time she was handed the note, it had changed. "When she came back she was totally different. All her gaiety had evaporated. She seemed terribly depressed," he said. However, this is contradicted by Harvey Priester, who came over to her table to say good-bye. He asked the actress how she would be getting home, and she told him that Ernest Peters would be waiting for her outside. Her friend then bid Thelma farewell, noting that she still seemed to be in the same good spirits she'd been in all evening.

By now, Thelma was talking to her friends the Skouras brothers and asked Sid Grauman to telephone West and relay the message that she would be leaving soon. He did as he was asked at around 1:55 AM. West later recalled that he was in the cocktail lounge of the Sidewalk Café when he was called to the phone, and after Grauman gave him the message, the theater owner chatted sociably with West about plans to visit the café and to bring his mother along with him.

In spite of the fact that Thelma said she would be leaving soon, she then decided to return to Stanley Lupino to continue their conversation about the British movie project. He later recalled, "[The Sidewalk Café] closed about 2 o'clock and Miss Todd and I were so interested in discussing the story that we must have sat there until about 3 o'clock when she said she felt tired and that she wanted to go home." Despite the fact that the band had already stopped playing, Thelma had one more dance—a tango with Arthur Prince—and he later commented that she seemed to like it very much. Afterward Prince's wife accompanied Thelma into the checkroom to collect her coat.

While there, the actress suddenly turned and looked at her very seriously. "Don't let Hollywood change you," she told the startled woman. "Stay just the same and don't take any stock in what people tell you. Go your own way." This made no sense at all to Mrs. Prince, as it wasn't part of any previous conversation they'd had during the evening. The comment played on her mind for some time afterward, and she later shared her concerns with her husband.

Thelma said good-bye to her friends before Arthur Prince accompanied her out to the car, noting that she suddenly seemed to perk up as she talked about the tango they had shared just moments before. "The irony," he later said, "was that I ushered the dear soul out with a dance." Driver Ernest Peters was there to greet her. After bidding Prince good-bye with a dramatic farewell salute, Thelma climbed into the vehicle. The engine roared into action, and at 3:15 AM, the chauffeur drove Thelma Todd into the night.

In the back of the car, the actress sat quietly, looking out of the window and watching Hollywood disappear behind her. Peters noted just how quiet his passenger was. "She was unusually silent," he told police later. "I have driven her many times during the past three years and we generally talked about automobiles, her film work, or her café. Saturday night she had nothing to say. I thought it was strange."

"Was she good-natured or talk to you at all?" asked the coroner several days later.

"Never spoke to me from the time she got in the car when she said, 'We will go home,' until she got out."

What is interesting to note is that while Thelma was silent on this particular journey, on a previous drive she had told Peters to make sure he was going as fast as he could. He later told police that the actress was scared she might be slain or kidnapped by gangsters. "She had told me to drive at top speed and not to make boulevard stops. I drove between 65 and 70 miles an hour," he said.

As the car pulled up at the front of the imposing Sidewalk Café building at 3:45 AM, Peters went to the passenger door to let his famous passenger out. As she exited the vehicle, Thelma stalled for time. "I don't think I've left anything," she said, and Peters looked around the car to make sure.

"No, there's nothing there," he replied.

"Send me the bill," requested Thelma. "I believe I owe you some money."

"That is all right, don't worry about it," replied Peters, as he closed the door and started to accompany the actress toward the steps leading to her apartment. What happened next shocked him. Thelma turned and stopped Peters from coming any farther with her.

"She told me I needn't escort her up to her apartment above [the café]," he later said. This surprised the driver, as in the five times he had driven her that year, she had always asked him to walk her right to the side door. It was a custom for them, but Thelma was adamant that on that particular evening, she would go alone.

"No, never mind, not tonight," she told him. "I'll look after myself." She then bade him good night and headed off toward the apartment.

Peters wasn't happy about leaving her, but it wasn't his place to argue. He noted that there was not a soul outside the building and said later that if there had been, he would have insisted on going with her to the door. However, while the café itself seemed in darkness, he was unsure about her residence above it. When asked by the coroner if he could see the windows of the apartment, he replied, "No, I could not. Not from where I stopped the car. There were no lights in the building in any way."

"If there were lights in the apartment, could you have seen them?" asked the coroner.

"I hardly think so," he replied. "Because I am on the off-side and the top of the car would obscure my view."

As everything seemed to be perfectly quiet, Peters got back into the car and proceeded to turn it around onto Roosevelt Highway, stopping briefly to watch the actress walk along the parking area toward the side of the building.

"There is an incline that goes up to the right opposite my car where I let her out," he said. "Then she had to turn around and revert right back on an incline and when I left her she had just turned the corner and her back was towards me and I was just moving at the time and looking at her and then I drove away." This small, shadowy glimpse was to become the last confirmed sighting of Thelma Todd alive.

Thirty hours later she was found dead in the front seat of her car by Mae Whitehead. But how did she get there, and what happened between the stormy overnight hours of Sunday, December 15, and the bright, crisp morning of Monday, December 16? The answer has been a mystery for the past eighty years.

18

THE DISCOVERY

The first police officer to arrive at the Sidewalk Café on the morning of December 16 was Captain Bruce F. Clark, who greeted manager Rudy Schafer shortly before midday and followed him to the garage, several blocks up the hillside. There he saw the grim reality that Thelma Todd, international film star, was slumped in her car, completely motionless.

Clark later told the coroner's inquest that by the time he saw her, she was "lying in the front seat of the car. She appeared to have been sitting about the middle of the seat, with her head over toward the driver's door, and her feet were on the floor, near the pedals—underneath the pedals, which would indicate that she had been sitting behind the wheel." She was dressed exactly as she had been on the evening of December 14: sheer blue dress, blue sandals, mink coat, clips in her hair, and thin hose on her legs.

The police officer felt for any signs of life and discovered that rigor mortis had set in. She had obviously been dead for quite some time. He noted that there were no signs of struggle: no torn clothes or marks on what he could see of her body. There was, however, blood around her nose and mouth, but whereas Schafer had said he saw a lot when he was first called to the garage, the officer noted just a speck. This was later explained by Roland West, who said he wiped her mouth with his handkerchief. Clark looked for a suicide note—very carefully, he insisted—but he didn't find one.

The officer immediately discounted the possibility that the actress had been killed in a robbery with the discovery that her jewelry was still accounted for: her wedding band set with diamonds (which she continued to wear despite being divorced), a square-cut diamond on her left hand, a blue cabochon on her right, an expensive diamond watch on her wrist, and two custom brooches on the cape of her coat. The camellia that her driver had bought on the way to the Trocadero was held onto her dress with her bow-shaped brooch, but the petals were withered. Her bag was found open next to her, also with no signs of interference. It contained a cigarette case, lipstick, four handkerchiefs, and the coin purse housing the key to the side door.

Clark phoned Captain Wallis of the homicide squad and was told not to disturb anything until he arrived. The investigator then phoned the Todd and Leslie Mortuary, the employees of which arrived and fought their way through the crowd gathering outside the garage. By this time various other officers had arrived, and onlookers included Harvey Priester, Mae Whitehead, and, surprisingly, Pat De Cicco. Photographs of the event show the body being taken out of the car, a white sheet protecting Thelma, and Roland West next to the stretcher supervising the proceedings.

Once the body had gone, the investigation continued. Officers found dust on the back of the car seat, which indicated that there was most likely no kind of struggle in the car. Similarly, no weapons were found to suggest murder. "I haven't been able to find anything that would indicate anything out of line at all," Clark told the coroner. "I looked casually; I noticed the ignition was on, and I looked and saw there was gas in the car. The officers drained out a gallon of gas, and there was still enough gas in the car to drive it down the road and back. . . . It threw off quite a bit of fumes."

Later tests by investigators revealed that at the time of Thelma's death, the engine would have choked off in approximately forty-six minutes due to a lack of oxygen in the garage. During the coroner's inquest, car salesman Robert H. Cooper gave his views on the state of the car's engine: "[Thelma's] car had what we call a blow-by in the motor; that is an excess amount of oil being used. . . . The blow-by condition in an automobile, it will run smoother than if you are running it otherwise. If you are idling it, that blow-by oil is up on the top of the cylinders, and as the compression comes down it forces oil wherever it will go, throws it over the breather and sometimes comes through the floorboard of the car and also gets up in the plugs, and there is a possibility in a car that has blow-by, when you idle [it] will stop because the plugs are being fouled."

"In other words," said the coroner, "If it is running idle it will stop or the engine die quicker than in another car without that trouble?"

"Oh yes, because if the blow-by is bad enough the oil will get around the plugs, right where the plug fits it."

Thelma's body arrived at the morgue at 3:45 PM on December 16. Deputy coroner Russel Monroe noted the wilted and faded camellia flower. All of Thelma's jewelry was listed, removed, and eventually given to her good friend Harvey Priester, who in turn handed it over to Alice Todd.

According to paperwork, the autopsy was conducted by Dr. A. F. Wagner on December 17. He noted that the exterior of the actress's body showed no signs of violence. There was a red discoloration of her skin, however, and her brain and other organs showed a "scarlet red color of the blood." This was as a result of her blood having 75 to 80 percent carbon monoxide saturation—which proved that regardless of the mysterious circumstances surrounding Thelma's death, she had been killed as a result of carbon monoxide poisoning.

Later, Dr. Wagner gave a full explanation of how the poisonous gas would have affected Thelma's body: "The poison is drawn in, a little of it, by each breath, and it accumulates in the body until finally the blood is practically saturated. . . . The effect is the same as asphyxiation. It is an internal or blood asphyxiation. Besides keeping the oxygen out, it also keeps the oxygen from the tissues. The carbon monoxide takes the place of the oxygen in the hemoglobin of the blood, so the final result is asphyxiation. Carbon monoxide retains its hold upon the hemoglobin, which the carbon dioxide does not do. That is given off the moment it comes in contact with the water." The doctor explained that the first thing to be affected by such poisoning would be the blood and the brain. "All the tissues of the body, however, are filled with blood and therefore become red."

The autopsy revealed that a discoloration found on her lower lip had not penetrated the skin. It was thought to be the result of her falling forward onto the steering wheel, dislodging her temporary tooth as she did so. "Inside the lip and beneath that there was no bruise at all. It must have been due to the lip coming in contact with a hard object." The small amount of blood around her nose and mouth could have been caused by the steering wheel too, though Dr. Wagner had another possible explanation: "Most cases, especially after they have been dead any length of time . . . the mucous membrane congests and they bubble up a little swath that is blood stained, and [carbon monoxide] cases do the same thing, but when these cases do it, that swath is usually fairly red, inasmuch as that blood has come out before they were fully saturated with the gas. The blood that was seen around this case had no significance other than just the poisoning of the gas. It did not mean that it was due to any bruise or any fall or any violence at all."

Meanwhile, tests of Thelma's brain revealed an alcohol level of 0.13 percent, though coroner Frank A. Nance divulged that it had probably been higher; her body would have eliminated some of the alcohol between when she was at the party and the point of death. "There was an indication of sufficient alcohol to have stupefied the woman," he said, before adding that the effect of alcohol would have increased the heart action, thereby quickening the rate at which the carbon monoxide was pumped through her blood.

The coroner's examination also shed some light on a rumor that began to spread in the days after Thelma's death: that she had died of a massive heart attack. It was not an unreasonable supposition, as her father had died of a heart attack and at least one doctor had diagnosed her with a heart murmur. And after her death, various people came forward to claim that the actress had suffered from a permanent heart ailment.

On the same day as the autopsy, West's estranged wife, Jewel Carmen, was giving a statement to police about that very subject. According to her, one day during the filming of *Corsair*, Thelma was bathing in the ocean at Catalina when she suddenly fainted. "She ascribed it to the condition of her heart," Carmen said. She recalled asking Thelma why she continued to smoke and drink if she had such a condition, to which the actress replied, "The physicians have given me five or six years to live, so I might as well have fun when I can." Thelma also supposedly explained that as a result of the condition, she was frequently turned down for life insurance.

But the autopsy actually found that her vital organs were free of organic disease and considered to be "perfectly normal." The coroner made special note that the heart was free from any chronic ailment, effectively ruling out the heart attack theory. This was consistent with the statement from Thelma's own physician, Dr. Edwin Larson, who had examined the actress ten days before her death. "She was in perfect health," he said. "She had no indications of heart disease and never had any."

Thelma herself never said anything publicly about her heart or her life expectancy, and many interviews show that she was making plans for her eventual retirement. As the autopsy showed no heart deformities, we can assume that either Jewel Carmen's recollection was inaccurate or the doctor's prognosis was somehow mistaken. However, the mystery of Thelma's health was never fully cleared up, as no explanation was provided for the fact that she was sometimes prone to fainting spells.

Dr. Wagner found that Thelma's stomach was approximately half full. He'd explain at the inquest that in normal circumstances, it empties in six or seven hours—though most people were not considered "normal." He added that a mixture of things such as excitement and alcohol ingestion could have an effect on how long it took the food to go through the normal channels. Taking everything into account, he figured Thelma had been dead anywhere from twelve to thirty hours. However, he then added that the likely time of death was somewhere between 6 and 8 AM on the morning of December 15, 1935.

This was all rather straightforward, until word came later that when Wagner examined the stomach, he found beans and peas, which had only just started digesting at the time of death. The revelation was surprising, not least because Thelma was not seen to have eaten the vegetables at the Trocadero. This new development prompted grand jury foreman George Rochester to tell the court, "Either Miss Todd came back to the table at the last moment and ordered peas and beans, or she stopped somewhere on the way home and ate the vegetables, or the entire theory that she died Sunday morning is wrong."

Since all other evidence pointed to the time of death being correct, how did Thelma have peas and beans in her stomach without being seen to eat them? According to Harvey Priester, the answer was simple: food was being eaten all evening in an unorganized manner. "Some people kept on eating. They would dance, finish dinners at different times. I would say some were still eating at twelve o'clock." There were also many people moving in a sociable manner from one table to the next. Thelma could have quite easily have stopped to grab some beans and peas at some point during the evening without anyone paying any attention to it at all.

On the day Thelma's body was discovered, Pat De Cicco telephoned A. Roland Button, who was his lawyer as well as his ex-wife's, and asked if it was OK for him to leave California. He told Button that he wished to visit his mother in Smithtown, New York, for the holiday season and had bought a ticket just days before the death. The lawyer told De Cicco to continue with his plans, and on December 17 he headed for the airport, closely followed by a number of reporters. Cornering him in the lounge just fifteen minutes before the plane was due to take off, they asked De Cicco how he thought Thelma had died. He shrugged and assured them that after seeing her body for himself, he felt sure she must have died from natural causes—though in reality, of course, carbon monoxide poisoning is anything but "natural."

Another reporter asked about his ex-wife's funeral, to which De Cicco replied, "I have offered my services to Thelma's mother, but there appeared to be nothing further I could do." When asked why he wasn't staying for the coroner's inquest, he said he was willing to postpone his trip, but in the absence of any official word, he was sticking to his original plans. He then added that he was under the impression that the inquest had already been held. Since it was only one day after the body had been found, that would have been very quick planning indeed.

Pat boarded the plane and headed to New York City, where he booked himself into the Hotel Delmonico ahead of his trip to Smithtown. Reporters soon found him there and descended on the hotel for a more thorough interrogation. They asked again how he thought his ex-wife had died. This time he vacillated between saying he had no theory at all and that the whole situation was "confusing" to insisting that it was an accident and the investigation was based only on politicians wishing to further their careers.

By the time De Cicco finally got called to give evidence to the grand jury about the death, he was so sparse with details that the foreman had no option but to declare him no use at all and send him on his way.

Meanwhile, Alice Todd tearfully sent a telegram to her family back in Massachusetts telling them the dreadful news: "Thelma passed away suddenly. Details later. Please notify rest." It came as a blow to everyone who had known her as a child. At first they didn't believe it, thinking maybe it was a sick prank by someone pretending to be Alice, but when reporters knocked at their door, it confirmed their fears. The family released a statement saying, "She was such a fine girl, a favorite with everybody who always had a pleasant word for her. It is a terrible blow, like a bolt of lightning." Just days before she passed away, Thelma had packaged up the Christmas presents for her Lawrence family and posted them along with several cards. Her final note was poignant: "Thought I'd be handing packages to you this holiday, instead of mailing them, but things didn't work quite as I expected them."

Tributes began to pour in from people Thelma had worked with over the years, including Patsy Kelly, who also refused to believe it when reporters first telephoned her with the news. "She has so much to live for," she told the caller. "Thelma's just kidding us." When the news was confirmed, Patsy collapsed, convinced that bad luck somehow followed her. She told friends that she seemed to put a curse on everyone she came into contact with, and from that moment on, she would find it difficult to visit the projection room where she had spent many happy hours with Thelma. The joyful memories were just too traumatic.

Another costar, Charley Chase, was devastated to hear of the actress's passing and promptly burst into tears when he received a Christmas card from her a few days later. He had very much enjoyed his shorts with Thelma, and although she had since been teamed up with ZaSu and Patsy, he still harbored the dream that they could one day become a permanent team.

Another tribute came from Thelma's boss, Hal Roach, who announced that she had just signed another contract to make more shorts at the studio and that he was "shocked beyond words." He then said that she had been a favorite member of the studio for the whole time she had worked there, that she showed support for everyone regardless of that person's job, and that she had always appeared to be happy in her work. In tribute to the fallen star, the Hal Roach studio closed for the day as soon as the news of her death was announced.

19

DEATH ACCORDING TO WEST

A t 9:30 AM on December 18, the coroner's inquest into Thelma Todd's death began at the Hall of Justice in Los Angeles. Notification was sent to nine prospective jurors to attend, "or answer the contrary at your peril," and key witnesses were subpoenaed. These included people Thelma knew personally—Harvey Priester, Roland West, Mae Whitehead, driver Ernest Peters, bartender Bob Anderson, and several others—as well as the autopsy surgeon and a variety of policemen. All of the attendees crammed into the small room, hustling for position alongside court reporters, photographers, and general staff.

Quotes and information from the witnesses have been used throughout this book, but one person's testimony was so profound and conflicting that it deserves particular scrutiny: that of self-proclaimed best friend Roland West.

According to the director, on the evening of the party he took Thelma's dog out for a walk shortly after receiving Sid Grauman's phone call at the Sidewalk Café at 2 AM. When he returned, he went into the building through the side door and bolted it from the inside, not knowing that Thelma had intended to come in through that door after the party. "It was not the customary way for her to come in. She came in the other doors as much as the side door. She never came in that door on Saturday nights, because it was always bolted when the maid left." But Mae

Whitehead had given her boss only the key to that door, so it would seem that the maid (and indeed Thelma herself) was not aware of any such arrangement. Added to that, Ernest Peters said he always walked Thelma to the side door; he had never known her to use any other entrance at all.

Once the door was bolted, West said, he readied himself for bed, took the dog into his room, and retired, falling asleep sometime before 3 AM. Around 3:30 AM, West claimed, he heard the dog whining. "He never whines," he said, and yet in the very next breath, he revealed that the dog "has a habit of whining when he gets uncovered." A few moments later he added that the dog was also in the habit of whining when he heard his mistress return home. "When he whines I knew he would know her," West said. He looked over and noted that the dog was still covered with his blanket, before checking the table clock in his room and seeing the time was exactly 3:30 AM. Strangely, West made a point of adding, "Whether that clock was right or not I don't know."

West then told the coroner that he lay for a few moments before hearing what he thought was running water coming from Thelma's room. It ran for a while and then stopped. West later asked Rudy Schafer about this and was told that it could have been the noise from an electrical device that pumped water periodically through the café's decorative fountain. He called Thelma's name to see if she was home. When he received no answer, he then went back to sleep. "You didn't get up?" asked the coroner. "No," replied West. However, after a short intermission he was once again asked what happened when he woke up at 3:30 AM. This time he replied, "I got up and examined the dog to see if he was uncovered— he always whines when he is uncovered—and I covered him up." But when questioned several hours before this, West had been adamant that he did not get up, that the dog was still covered with this blanket. Was this a lapse of memory from one hour to the next?

Despite having a clock in his bedroom, West could not give a precise time for when he rose the next morning. "I think I got up between nine and eleven; I think that was Sunday, nine and eleven," he told the coroner.

He knocked on Thelma's door. When he received no answer, he entered and discovered that she wasn't there—nor anywhere else, for that matter. He did, however, see that there was an impression on a big couch in what he called the lady's boudoir, so he decided that Thelma must have slept there and then left early to go visit her mother. No other inspection was made, he said, and instead he took delivery of the newspaper and went back to his room to read. When asked what happened next, he gave a rambling reply: "I finished my paper, my newspaper, and then I rung for breakfast, because when I didn't have the servants at the house—that is why I always lived down there: we have servants and have everything there, and I had my breakfast after I read the newspaper."

During further questioning, West said that he had known Thelma must have worn an evening dress when she left the building that morning. "I couldn't see any other way she could have any clothes if she went to her mother's," he said. Why would she have no clothes if she had been in the building that morning? Maybe West thought she didn't have access to her wardrobe for some reason, or maybe he was by then thinking that she must have gone directly to her mother's from the party. Without investigating it further, however, there really wasn't any reason for him to believe she hadn't returned home, changed her clothes, and then left again.

Sometime between 12 PM and 1 PM, West said he headed down to the café and asked bartender Bob Anderson what car Thelma had used that day. The young man was behind the bar at the time and told him he had been so busy that there hadn't been time to go up to the garage and check. Later, waiter James Malin would tell police that the morning had been busy with riding parties coming into the café for breakfast, and the establishment had been full for most of the day and especially that evening.

After West asked Anderson about Thelma's car, he greeted salesman Robert H. Cooper, who had come to discuss a vehicle West was purchasing for his estranged wife's Christmas present. He sat in the bar talking with Cooper for the next two hours, before his mother arrived and he took her up to the apartment. She asked where Thelma was, and West explained that she had gone to her mother's house—but at no point did he actually make any solid inquiries to see if that was true.

After his mother left, West claimed that he was very tired, "nervous for some reason, I don't know why." He lay down before receiving a phone call from one of the Skouras brothers, telling him that Thelma had bet him that he wouldn't bring his family of eleven to the café for dinner that night. Skouras was told that she wasn't in but that they were expecting her any minute. West then called the restaurant manager to instruct him to prepare a table, and then at 7 PM he took a phone call from a George Baker, who asked him to pass on a message to Thelma that Martha Ford, wife of actor Wallace Ford, wanted her to call. He told the caller that Thelma would be at the café "in a little while" and that he would pass on the message.

By the time West returned to the café, the Skouras family had arrived, and they spoke to West about Thelma, expressing their disbelief that the actress wasn't at the café to greet them. Roland agreed and then went about his business, confident—according to him—that Thelma would be back at the café before the family left.

At this point in the questioning, the coroner asked West if he had made any attempt to call Mrs. Ford, who he knew was hosting a party Thelma was meant to go to that afternoon. "No, no," he replied, before then stating that at no time that day did he leave the building, that he made no inquiries regarding the whereabouts of the woman he claimed was his best friend, and that he made no further attempts to find out what car she had used that day. He then said that at midnight he took the dog out for a walk and then retired to bed, despite not hearing anything from or about Thelma for the entire day.

If we are to believe his story, the mystery of where she had gone must have been playing on West's mind, as he said he could not sleep until his body finally gave way to exhaustion at around 5 AM. Then the next thing he knew, the house phone was ringing, and the news of his lover's demise was about to become world news.

After seeing Thelma's body in the garage and adding everything up in his mind, what did West believe could have happened to the actress, from when she disappeared in the early hours of Sunday morning through to when they found her on Monday? According to him, Thelma may have tried to get in the side door, realized it was locked, and didn't want to wake him up. Instead she went up to the garage either by walking up 271 hillside steps or trekking through the dark adjoining streets. There, he speculated, she decided to either wait until the porters came to work at 6 AM or else drive to her mother's house.

Since the keys were always in the ignition and the garage was not locked, this seemed to West to be a logical scenario: "And say she went there at three thirty or four, she may have got chilled and started the car and may have thought she would drive down to her mother's, started the car and warmed it up and then open the doors." His reasoning was garbled, but West certainly seemed convinced that regardless of where she intended to go, Thelma had switched on the engine of the car with the garage doors closed, without considering the dangers involved, and accidentally succumbed to carbon monoxide poisoning.

As West continued his testimony, the confusing array of holes and contradictions only grew. When asked about the distance Thelma would've had to travel between the café and the garage, West told the coroner, "There are two ways to get to the garage, one steps and one a walkway. Miss Todd used to take the steps. She never wanted to walk, but if we ever came home and knew there was no one to take the car up, sometimes she would take the steps and I would take the walk down." Then a little later he was asked if she was accustomed to exercise, to which West replied, "She never walked; you never could get her to walk." So was she absolutely averse to walking, would she sometimes—albeit begrudgingly—walk down the steps?

He was also asked whether he knew Pat De Cicco, to which West replied that he did not, except for knowing the two had been divorced. He was then asked if he had ever talked about him with Thelma, and he said he had not. Yet just four questions later, the coroner asked once again whether he had discussed De Cicco with her, and he then replied,

"Oh, I talked to her about him, yes; I knew her before she married him, and afterwards."

He evinced more uncertainty when he told the court that the café's treasurer, seventy-year-old Charles Harry Smith, lived in the apartment above the garage where Thelma was found, and on the night of the disappearance had not heard the sound of a running engine in the garage below. The coroner was willing to believe that maybe the lack of noise was because of the howling wind outside, so he asked West what he thought about that. West assured the court that the wind could not disguise the noise: "When you start [the car] you could hear it all over, twelve cylinders, very loud." He added that the vehicle made more noise than the breaking of a pane of glass and that it could "waken anyone."

West then changed his mind and told the court that bartender Bob Anderson had once explained to him that the engine *could* be started very quietly, and that it only started loudly because Anderson was "a young fellow and he likes noise." This was backed up by Bob himself, who later took to the stand and explained that he always believed there wasn't much noise associated with the car, and that when idling, it was very quiet indeed. "The only time it would make a loud noise would be if you opened the motor wide when you started," he explained. "It was very easy to start the car without any noise—starts very quietly." He went on to say that had Thelma wanted to avoid waking anyone up with the noise, she most certainly would have been able to.

Charles Harry Smith told detectives that he had read until 3:30 AM, gone to sleep for three or four hours, then woke up for a glass of hot water. He went back to sleep until 11:45 AM, before readying himself for a day's work at the café. He admitted that he had heard no unusual sounds, before adding that because the wind was blowing and the waves pounding "with unusual violence," he may have been prevented from hearing anything going on below him. When detectives went to the garage themselves, they discovered that the engine could be heard only faintly in the apartment when it was started or revved. At other times the engine was not audible at all.

Amid all his misstatements and contradictions, Roland West was obviously keen to have everyone believe his version of events: that he had not seen Thelma and had no idea where she had gone, until he discovered that she had perished in a tragic accident. His assertions to that effect were often accompanied by a large smile or the wiping of a tear, and spectators sat riveted, waiting to hear what he would say or do next. Beneath the demeanor of the grieving loved one, however, was behavior that did not seem to have Thelma's best interests at heart. At no point during the Sunday she was missing did West ever make more than a cursory attempt to find out where the actress had gone. He made no phone calls, no attempt to contact her mother even though he thought Thelma might have gone to see her, and he expressed no worries over her absence even when the Skouras brothers came to the café expecting to see her.

There are a handful of reasons why West would not have pursued her disappearance further. Either he simply wasn't worried or didn't care where Thelma had gone—or he knew only too well that she was lying dead in the garage but could not bring himself to raise the alarm.

20

THE CASE IS CLOSED

The coroner wrapped up the inquest by giving a short speech to the jury: "All right, that is all the evidence we have for you at this time, gentlemen. Please retire to the jury room with the clerk and deliberate upon the evidence that has been presented to you and determine how, when, and where the deceased came to her death and whether her death was homicidal, suicidal, accidental, or natural. Now, please retire with the clerk."

While the jury deliberated, Thelma's loved ones (and in particular Harvey Priester) were organizing the funeral. Before the final, private send-off, she lay in state at Pierce Brothers Mortuary, where it was estimated that ten thousand fans—mostly women—filed past to pay their final regards. They came from all over town, with some riding on many buses and trams for one last look. Two elderly women were asked why they had come, and they told reporters that Thelma had given them much happiness over the years. "I'm so sorry she was called so early in life," said one.

Thelma was dressed in blue satin pajamas, which were to have been a Christmas present from a friend. She was surrounded with flowers placed by her friends and family, and a beautiful portrait said to have been Harvey Priester's personal favorite was close by. One wreath of white roses and lilies had a card reading simply, ALISON. The card was from Roland

West, and the name was that of the alter ego he had given Thelma during the making of *Corsair*.

———— ∞∞∞ ————

Shortly before her daughter's funeral, Alice Todd gave an interview to columnist Edwin Schallert. She began by telling the reporter how she firmly believed Thelma's death was an accident—that she was far too happy to commit suicide, and murder was not an option because her daughter had no enemies at all. This was a turnaround from her initial assertion that "my daughter was murdered" and showed either naïveté on her part or an unwillingness to accept what was going on right in front of her eyes. Though she may have convinced herself that there were no bad guys in Thelma's life, everyone knew that was not true, because she had been plagued by death threats, a burglary, and gangsters for the better part of a year.

As the interview continued, Alice told Schallert that not a day had passed when she and Thelma weren't together—that she was number one in her life and vice versa. She also described Thelma's habit of telephoning her every morning, so she must have been dead by early Sunday or she'd have been in touch. "She would never let a whole day pass without communicating with me," she said. This is an interesting comment, because if she was so used to speaking to her every day, did Alice not think it odd when that Sunday brought no communication at all? The matter wasn't addressed in the article, yet she surely must have thought it was strange.

The rest of the interview related Alice's theory of Thelma's final hours, which was almost word-for-word the same as Roland West's. The two had certainly spent a lot of time together in the days after the death, and it seems clear that if Alice had any initial theories about what had happened to her daughter, they were soon dispelled and replaced by Roland West's version of the truth. Her thoughts and his were just too similar for them not to have had an in-depth discussion about the whole matter.

———— ∞∞∞ ————

Thelma's funeral took place at Forest Lawn cemetery in Glendale, California, on December 19. It was attended by a mixture of close friends and family, all there by invitation only. Patsy Kelly, Sally Eilers, Laurel and Hardy, Minna Gombell, Martha Ford, Mae Whitehead, ZaSu Pitts, Lois Wilson, Joseph M. Schenck, and around two hundred others all came to say good-bye. No chair was left empty, and outside five hundred fans gathered, some whispering and making remarks about what could possibly have happened to take the blonde comedienne away so soon.

Inside the chapel, Harvey Priester showed friends and family to their seats, and then the Reverend Harold Proppe of the First Baptist Church conducted the ceremony. Because Thelma attended his services regularly, his sermon was exceptionally personal and touching. First he stated that life comes complete with mysteries and unexpected events, before adding, "In her going, I have lost a great personal friend, and the motion picture industry has lost a marvelous actress." He also paid tribute to Thelma's genuine nature, describing her as sweet, honest, sincere, congenial, and a friend to all. Afterward the congregation filed past her coffin, some plucking flowers as they did so, all lost in their own memories of their friend, family member, or lover.

The day after the funeral, Alice Todd was at home when she received a letter that had been forwarded unopened by staff at the Sidewalk Café. Tearing it open, she was shocked and scared to discover a threatening note. "Now Mrs. Todd," it said, "We will give you one week to contact us in the Times in the personal column or you will go next. We got her because she double crossed us and we will get you too. Call me Ace and give me your telephone number. No funny work. No cops. Ace."

The letter was so sickening that Alice immediately gave it to her neighbor to read before handing it back to staff at the café. The names have been blanked out in FBI documents, but the people she gave it to were most likely Roland West and Rudy Schafer. The FBI was informed and an investigation took place, though it was clear that the letter could not have come from the original Ace, as he was now in custody. It would seem that no other details of the sender were found, and the sender was likely a crank, though the threatening words were enough to ensure Alice's future silence.

On the very same day, the investigation took another sinister turn. In an FBI file related to Thelma's death, an agent wrote the following: "Information was furnished [to] this office to the effect that two letters had been received by Miss Todd within a few days prior to her death, demanding payment of gambling debts under threat of death. [*Redacted*] emphatically denied that any such letters had been received by victim and advised that the only letters received were [the extortion letters from the Ace]."

The coroner's inquest returned with a verdict of accidental death but urged further investigation to be carried out by a grand jury. Deputy District Attorney George Johnson seemed to relish the idea of opening the investigation; on December 23 he told reporters that he was going to consider the possibility of murder and could not discount jealousy or unrequited love as potential motives. For Thelma's friends and family, Christmas was effectively canceled, as the likes of Alice Todd, Roland West, Helen Ainsworth, Ida Lupino, Catherine Hunter, and Jewel Carmen were all called to testify in the days ahead.

Unfortunately, the grand jury investigation was a disappointment for many, as it revealed little more than the original coroner's inquest. One potentially worthwhile witness was Earl H. Carter, the night watchman who patrolled the vicinity of West's garage. For days after the death, rumors circulated that he had seen "strange and unusual things" that night, but by the time he took to the stand, he denied having seen anything at all.

Next up was Thelma's mother, who was still reeling from the death of her daughter and the threatening note. The jury hoped she would be able to clear up rumors in the press that Thelma kept a secret diary in a rented safe deposit box. Despite being on the stand for hours, Alice was so upset she could hardly relay any information at all, and many of the questions went unanswered. However, she did manage to reiterate her and West's belief that her daughter died accidentally. When asked about her initial statement that Thelma had been murdered, she denied having made it. She then left on the arm of Harvey Priester, weeping and sobbing as she did, while the jury begrudgingly accepted the fact that she could offer no new information.

The investigation rumbled on into the New Year, with potential witnesses coming and going in quick succession. Perhaps the most eventful moment for the jurors came on January 3, when they visited the Sidewalk Café. Roland West gave them a tour of the building, which included the Tower Room, where the rumored gambling parties were said to have taken place. During the tour of the café, West even saw fit to joke about tourists who kept turning up to steal items with Thelma's name on them. He even delighted in showing exactly what pieces of memorabilia went missing most—sugar cubes with a photo of the actress on the wrapper—before taking the jurors up to the garage and pointing out where her body had been found. The press made no mention of the director seeming upset or downcast during the tour, and photos show him fairly animated as he showed them around.

The newspaper coverage of the case began to dwindle, and public interest started to wane. The grand jury announced that it was willing to keep the case open for months to get to the bottom of how Thelma passed away, but jurors were becoming frustrated. Foreman George Rochester denied any tensions, but on January 8 there was something of a revolt in the jury room, when two jurors stated that they were fed up with the case. This episode threatened the end of the inquiry, and Alice Todd deemed the whole situation "unbearable." She then took a shot in the attorney general's direction by announcing that the investigation was being conducted "only for the purpose of a lot of cheap politicians trying to get jobs."

After the revolt and the disparaging comments, the grand jury quietly started to wind down the investigation. By this time the newspapers had moved on to other stories, and the outcome of the investigation was virtually ignored. However, the jury's conclusions were revealed in late March after police in Ogden, Utah, received an anonymous tip that a forty-five-year-old man had slain Thelma and was currently staying in a local hotel with a mysterious woman. Utah police put the man under surveillance and sent a telegram to officers in Los Angeles, telling them of the latest revelation.

Though the lead would likely have turned out to be false, L.A. homicide squad surprised everyone by not even following up on it. Police chief James E. Davis replied via telegram to say not only that the man was not a suspect but that the actress had not even been murdered. Homicide captain Hubert J. Wallis added the investigators' thoughts on the person who had tipped off the Utah police: "Obviously a crackpot," he said. "Miss Todd committed suicide. The case is closed."

21

THE MYSTERIOUS SIGHTINGS

*I*t was a shock that investigators were so eager to close the case, but their impatience with far-fetched leads was understandable. In the days and weeks following the death, a number of people had come forward to say that they'd seen Thelma after the time of death determined by the autopsy. These stories caused shockwaves in the newspapers and confusion to the officers covering the case, but more than anything, they all turned out to be a gigantic waste of police time.

The first person to come forward to claim she had heard from the actress was Wallace Ford's wife Martha, hostess of the party Thelma had been invited to on December 15. She told the investigators that during the anniversary celebration, Thelma had called to say she would be arriving soon and would be bringing a mysterious guest. When she did not turn up, Mrs. Ford asked a relative to call the actress's apartment and discovered from Roland West that she was not there but he expected her back soon.

Mrs. Ford was adamant that she had spoken to Thelma that day, but police believed the conversation was just a case of a joke gone wrong—that one of the guests could see her growing impatient for Thelma's arrival and thought she would wind her up by making a call pretending to be the absent actress. This seems reasonable, but another explanation is simply a case of mistaken identity. When Mrs. Ford answered the telephone, she originally thought she was speaking to a friend named Velma before coming to believe that it was Thelma after all. If the caller was actually this Velma, she may eventually have arrived with her guest, only to go unnoticed as the hostess mistakenly awaited Thelma's arrival.

Many more reports of mysterious sightings came in each day from members of the public, who supposedly saw her driving her car, visiting a cigar shop or a drugstore, or even buying a Christmas tree on the day she was actually lying dead in Roland West's garage. Whether these tipsters were simply mistaken or desperate for their five minutes of fame, their calls became such an inconvenience that police saw the need to release a statement saying that following up each lead was causing a real backlog. District Attorney George Johnson added that people seeing Thelma throughout Sunday were merely publicity-seeking and in it for what they could get.

However, one story the authorities did take seriously was from Jewel Carmen, Mrs. Roland West herself, who threw her theory into the now-overflowing pot.

At first when questioned, the actress told police she had been out of town and knew absolutely nothing about Thelma's death. Then, quite suddenly, she changed her mind and called the officers back to her home for a dramatic interview. "I was evasive when I first talked to you last night," she told the puzzled officers. "I now want to tell you everything I know."

The woman went on to claim that she had been driving at approximately 11 PM on Sunday when a car came up beside her on Sunset Boulevard, with Thelma on the passenger's side and a "man of dark complexion" sitting next to her in the driver's seat. According to Carmen, the couple was in Thelma's Lincoln phaeton, the very one she would be found dead in almost twelve hours later. "I hurried my own car and drove as close as possible. Sitting next to the driver was Thelma Todd. I recognized her from a smart hat I knew she wore and also her blonde curls."

Carmen's claim was awfully convenient. The woman whose husband had fallen in love with Thelma just happened to come upon her just hours before she was discovered dead. And she was able to identify the actress by her hat, her curls, and her car despite the fact that it was 11 PM.

To get to the bottom of her story, reporters knocked on Jewel Carmen's door for days on end, and she eventually withdrew, claiming she was in a state of collapse. She asked a friend to release a statement saying she must have been mistaken about the sighting. However, rumors rumbled on for the entire investigation, but they were eventually officially ruled out, not just because the autopsy had found that Thelma was already dead by the time of the sighting but also because Carmen was sure the actress was wearing a hat. On the day of her discovery, no hat was anywhere to be seen and her head was bare, exactly as it had been when she was last seen at the party on Saturday night.

Why did Jewel Carmen feel the need to report such a sighting? We can never know for sure. But maybe with all the talk about Roland West's fling with Thelma, she just wanted everyone to know that she was still around—that she was still very much "the scorned wife." And if nothing else, her miraculous sighting afforded her a lot of attention. Eighty years and counting after Thelma Todd's death, it remains one of the only things Carmen is remembered for.

The final mysterious appearance is one that was said to have taken place December 8, when Thelma was still alive. This sighting was written down in a letter and sent to the police the day after her body was found, by a young person—generally thought to be a woman—who was leaving Los Angeles and heading up the coast to San Francisco in search of work. According to the woman, she was trying to hitch a ride when Thelma stopped and offered her a lift, telling her she was only going a short distance but would take her as far as she was going. The two began talking and the woman explained to Thelma that she had been unable to find work. "Everyone has their troubles, haven't they?" replied the actress. She then went on to say she had problems too—only hers were worse.

During the short journey, Thelma said she was in partnership with a man whom she had given money to. He would not give the money back; he was frightening her and had done so several times. "I guess I need what you have—courage," Thelma said, before the woman replied that she was sure the man was merely bluffing. The conversation ended when they pulled into the parking area of the Sidewalk Café and Thelma told the woman that if she didn't find employment in Frisco, she should come back and find her. "I expect to make some changes," she said. "Perhaps I can do something for you."

When police received the letter, they released it to the newspapers, but they didn't seem to take the information seriously. However, various aspects of the story show that it may have been dismissed too quickly.

First, the woman describes Thelma as saying she had given money to a man who would not give it back. This was at least partly true, as it was revealed during the investigation that she had invested money several times over recent years, not through lawyer A. Ronald Button but through Roland West. Button testified that while he didn't handle any of the projects himself, he was aware of several annuities, and West admitted that he had been handling Thelma's investments for the past two years.

According to the letter, Thelma had been having arguments with the man in question, and he was frightening her. Roland West told the coroner that he never had any arguments with Thelma in his entire life and yet later admitted to the grand jury that they did occasionally argue about the investments. They argued, he said, but never rowed or quarreled—what he considered the difference was not apparent. His answers to questions from the jury and the waiting reporters were contradictory, to say the least. "No one could row with Thelma Todd or strike her and get away with it," he said. "I know I never did. We have argued, but never in anger." He then went on to explain that the two would bicker if he wanted her to do something, though if she didn't want to do what he requested, she wouldn't do it.

Finally, the letter-writer said that Thelma had told her to come back if she couldn't find work, because she was planning some changes. Change was exactly what she talked about with Helen Ainsworth during the shopping trip just days before her death.

Although the rest of the mysterious sightings could easily be dismissed, perhaps this note was actually a vital missing link in the investigation.

22

THE THEORIES

*P*iecing together information about Thelma Todd's death is like putting together a five-thousand-piece jigsaw puzzle of the sky at night—one encounters many false links, wrong turns, and moments of sheer confusion. In the end, however, there are only three ways that she could have died: accidental death, suicide, and murder.

Accidental Death

One of the main theories surrounding Thelma's death, championed by Roland West, is that when she returned from the Trocadero party, she found herself locked out of her apartment. Unable to wake up West, she sought shelter elsewhere, walking the 271 steps up the hillside to get to the garage. Once there, she must have started the engine of her car, perhaps to turn on the heater. The garage filled with deadly gas, and she lost consciousness and quickly passed away. Over the years, this has become one of the most popular theories of the case. But while it is a convenient explanation, it is full of holes that call it into question.

During the grand jurors' visit to the café, one of the first things they did was to check the side door that Thelma was allegedly locked out of. What they saw quickly convinced them that she could not have made any significant effort to get into the house that evening. The door was quite close to Roland West's bedroom, and it was made from what appeared to be a large metal sheet. Had Thelma decided to knock, she would almost certainly have made enough noise to wake the sleeping West. One juror was overheard telling another, "It's impossible to believe he didn't hear her, if she found herself locked out and rattled this door."

Despite this, let us give West the benefit of the doubt and imagine that he was sleeping so soundly that he didn't hear her that evening. During the inquest he told the coroner that she had been locked out and unable to rouse him once before. She had not, however, gone traipsing up 271 steps on that particular night. Instead she rapped on the window, and when West still couldn't be woken up, he said, Thelma decided to break the pane to get his attention. West explained that he had been dreaming about breaking glass and then woke up to hear Thelma's voice, telling him that she was locked out. "You could not keep Miss Todd out of any place she wanted to get in," he told the coroner.

West probably would not have been pleased to be woken up in such a manner, and perhaps he complained bitterly, not only because of the disturbance but also because of the time, effort, and money required to sort out the broken window. Perhaps in the early hours of December 15, 1935, Thelma decided not to risk a repeat performance, for fear of what West would say or do.

Even so, she would have had other options than to walk up treacherous hillside steps alone and in the dark to find shelter. By the time Thelma realized she was locked out of the apartment, it would have been approximately 4 AM and the sun would be up in less than three hours. She was attired in an evening dress, high-heeled sandals, and a fur coat. The wind was howling and it was cold, but nevertheless the night was dry. The Sidewalk Café building was surrounded by various nooks and crannies that would likely have been accessible to Thelma that evening had she wanted to wait it out: outside staircases, alleys, and archways all could have offered some protection for the few hours left before staff arrived.

However, perhaps she did not feel particularly safe sitting out in the open. That is perfectly understandable. She was, after all, a recognizable figure who may have felt self-conscious about hanging around a public area while wearing an evening dress. The thought of someone seeing her huddled on an open staircase or against a wall in the middle of the night was probably not something she particularly relished.

But would retreating to the garage have been a preferable option? To get there, Thelma would have had to either climb up the 271 steps or walk through the dark hillside streets, in high heels and a heavy fur coat. Although Alice Todd told reporter Edwin Schallert that her daughter could outwalk anyone if she wanted to, this was surely an exaggeration, because she also admitted that Thelma did not like to walk because of two ankle injuries: one from a skiing accident and another suffered during a film shoot.

When questioned by the coroner, Roland West admitted that the distance from the café building to the garage was "a climb for anyone." The coroner then told him, "If one has been at a dancing party and exercising that way, several hours in the evening, and has to climb a hill, that would be rather fatiguing for one not used to exercising."

"The chauffeur told me she was very tired when she got out of the car," West replied. "He had never seen her that way, so she must have been tired before she even started to climb." Later, when jurors experienced the walk for themselves, many complained bitterly that they were absolutely exhausted by the time they reached the top. At least one was heard telling another that he truly believed Thelma could not have made the climb.

Thelma's footwear consisted of high-heeled sandals, designed for partying, not for an outdoor walk. When Captain Bruce Clark first saw them he said they looked as though she had walked some distance on concrete. That he immediately came to such a conclusion, knowing nothing at all about how she arrived at the garage, is intriguing. However, photographs of the brand-new sandals seem to show wear and tear consistent with a night on a dance floor, not a trek up a hillside. When a policewoman made the same trip in high heels just days later, hers were considerably more scuffed than Thelma's, and they had not been used to dance the night away beforehand. In addition, no mention was made during the autopsy about her feet being scuffed or unclean, and no mention was made of her thin hosiery being dirty, snagged, or torn in any way, as they surely would have been had she taken her footwear off before embarking on her journey.

And despite the howling wind she would have faced during the climb, when Thelma's body was found on Monday morning, her hair was immaculate, in exactly the same style as it had been when she left on Saturday evening. Even her hair clips were still in place. Photographs of the body at the time of discovery show glossy smooth hair at the top of her head, going down into tight curls at the nape of her neck. Even with the firmest of lacquer, had she taken the long walk from café to garage, her hair would at least be a little disheveled. It would also be dull and lifeless, with dust blown from the hill, and yet the photographs do not show such a thing. In fact, so perfect is Thelma's appearance that one may be forgiven for thinking she was merely sleeping—certainly, that is what Mae Whitehead thought when she made her devastating discovery.

Let's put aside the facts that her shoes were not particularly scuffed and her hair was not windswept. According to the accidental death theory, Thelma entered the dark garage and sat in the car, but even though she was wearing a heavy fur coat, she still wasn't warm enough. She therefore made the fatal decision to turn on the car engine to blast the heater and warm herself up. After the discovery of her body, Alice Todd and Roland West both said that it was perfectly acceptable to believe that Thelma would start the car and not think anything about the dangers involved. She probably had no idea about carbon monoxide or the fact that it could kill, they said. This theory is difficult to believe, for many reasons.

During the 1930s, carbon monoxide poisoning was a frequent subject of discussion in the newspapers; there were regular reports of people passing away as a result of faulty heaters or because they had turned on the engine of their car to keep warm in a closed garage. With so many deaths attributable to the invisible gas, the media also devoted itself to prevention: at least one educational film was produced, and every winter there were reports on how people could protect themselves. The Automobile Club of Southern California regularly issued warnings about the dangers of warming up cars in the winter months and urged motorists to make sure they never sat in a closed garage with the engine running. The main focus of the warnings was always that *death will result*.

Just over a month after Thelma's passing, the surgeon responsible for overseeing her autopsy posted his own warning in the *Los Angeles Times*, saying that the actress's death had shown that "too many people are woefully ignorant of the deadly nature of this gas." The numerous deaths every year made it clear that many people did not know about the dangers. But could Thelma have been one of those people? After everything the media had done to raise awareness, is it possible that she was still unaware of the problem?

It seems unlikely. Thelma was, after all, known to be very intelligent; she was, as actress Dorothy Gulliver once said, "the smartest dumb blonde I ever knew." The former schoolteacher had a reputation across Hollywood for being knowledgeable about all kinds of subjects, including physics. She negotiated her own contracts and spoke several languages, including Russian and Spanish. Actress Neva Carr-Glyn later called Thelma a woman of remarkable intelligence, who never forgot a face or name.

She also now ran a restaurant and would have been expected to know something about the attendant health and safety issues, including heaters, gas, and the dangers posed by both. The café's bartender confirmed to the coroner that he knew about these dangers, so it would be sensible to imagine that others involved with the café were aware of them too— particularly someone like Thelma, who said on several occasions that she played a major part in every aspect of the business.

Perhaps most telling, in 1932 Thelma gave an exclusive interview to David Ingram from the *Boston Daily Record*. During the conversation the actress told him that while she had several servants in her home, she did not have use for a regular chauffeur, because one of her biggest hobbies was driving and repairing cars. "I have a Cadillac, a Lincoln, and a Packard," she said. "I look after them myself, cleaning the motors and everything." Is it plausible that a woman who cared for and repaired her own cars would be unaware of the dangers of exhaust fumes?

By the time the grand jurors left the Sidewalk Café on January 3, 1936, most had come to the conclusion that the theory of accidental death was bogus. Foreman George Rochester released a statement to the press that said, "It is apparent Miss Todd did not die accidentally. We are not convinced what the motive for her death was, but it is obvious certain witnesses either have concealed what they knew or have given false evidence."

Suicide

The previous year had been tough for Thelma, but could the actress have been so depressed about her circumstances that she wished to end her own life, as the grand jury concluded? It is true that she suffered bouts of anxiety, and she had been particularly stressed by the extortion attempts and phantom callers. Associates recalled her expressing worries about the influence of gangsters in her establishment and even confessing thoughts of death. But the actress had always endured difficult times, from the deaths of her brother and father to divorce, heartbreak, and ill health, and yet there's no indication that she ever tried to commit suicide.

Indeed, the idea that she would have taken her own life deliberately does not seem to fit the Thelma her friends and colleagues knew. While some of Roland West's inquest testimony was questionable, his view of his lover's personality agrees with the general consensus that the actress was not suicidal. He described her as an "individual with the strength of any man in this room." He also said that she had everything a man had, in terms of money and "plenty of everything. . . . She was finishing a Roach contract and Mr. Schenck told her in front of me that as soon as she was finished he was ready to sign her up. She has her mother she was taking care of, and has her café, and has everything in fact."

Rudy Schafer was surprised to hear of the suicide theory. When asked if Thelma could have taken her own life, he replied, "No. She was planning on opening our upstairs part of our business down there, and she was just as occupied in it and making plans for the future, just like the rest of us were, naturally." In the same vein, Harvey Priester said he knew no reason at all why Thelma would have committed suicide, describing his friend as "full of life and full of laughter." He added, "She certainly was [looking to the future], because she had bought her Christmas tree and packages and gifts and always enjoyed Christmas and liked that best of all." Mae Whitehead said almost the same thing: her boss was "happy and cheerful" and had no reason to want to end her life, and she had made plans for the future and done all of her Christmas shopping. And Patsy Kelly insisted that her friend was far too considerate to ever take her own life. Thelma would never hurt her mother so deeply, she said, particularly just before Christmas.

But if Thelma had become suicidal without her friends' knowledge, the question becomes: what triggered the change? One possibility is that the actress became so scared of the gangsters threatening her business that perhaps she felt it was preferable to take her own life instead of letting them take it for her. However, once again, this goes against Thelma's reputation as a tough lady who spoke her mind and stuck to her guns, a woman who did not back down over what she believed in. Furthermore, why would she pick that particular night to commit suicide, after she had been tormented for almost a year by anonymous letters and mafia threats? She had spent the night not fretting over gangsters but partying until the early hours and making plans for the future. It hardly seems like the moment when she would decide to end it all—unless, of course, something else happened that night to make her feel she had no other option.

Another theory is that the events of the party were actually what sent Thelma into a suicidal spiral—namely, the sight of her ex-husband with another woman. However, since she had not shown any interest in her husband in more than a year and had since been romantically linked to several others, including Roland West and Harvey Priester, it would seem out of character for her to kill herself over the realization that De Cicco was seeing other people too.

Finally, there is the fact that no suicide note was ever found—or, at the very least, none was brought forward as evidence. This was a lady who was never stuck for words, who wrote letters to friends, fans, and relatives on a regular basis and had actually written and mailed all of her Christmas cards and letters in the days leading up to her death. If Thelma had chosen to end her own life, certainly she would have not gone quietly; she would have left some kind of explanation. So unless the note was removed or destroyed by someone trying to protect her reputation—or perhaps the reputation of some other party mentioned in the letter—the evidence indicates that no note was ever found near the actress's body.

Though the events of 1935 had ensured that Thelma was not as carefree as she had been in other years of her life, there is no evidence that she was seriously thinking of killing herself, nor that she had made any past attempts to do so.

Murder

The idea that Thelma was murdered has stronger support, including from friend ZaSu Pitts, who told her son, Don Gallery, that she believed Roland West was associated with gangsters and had been pressuring Thelma to open a casino inside the café. She was not the only one close to Thelma who felt that way. Mae Whitehead found herself at the center of the investigation into Thelma's death and was frightened that because she had found her employer's body, she might be considered a suspect. In the years after the tragedy, she confided to her son and granddaughter that she believed the mob had something to do with Thelma's death because of her refusal to allow professional gambling in the café.

In the 1980s, writer Jim Brubaker and his wife, Joyce, spent some years researching Thelma's life for a screenplay. In 1986, Jim spoke to retired police officers who had been involved in the investigation and read some of the files associated with the case. According to Jim, all of the police he spoke to believed that Thelma had been murdered and that it had something to do with the gambling issues at the café. Furthermore, he said, the police were sure Roland West was instrumental in some way—either by withholding information from investigators or by actively participating in the crime itself. Brubaker also found the police to be convinced that her death had been preceded by a meeting with the gangsters at the Sidewalk Café.

These comments may be hearsay, but they are strikingly similar to ones made by the police at the time. Shortly after Thelma's death, district attorney investigator Tom Cavett released a statement saying he was aware that a gambling establishment was to be opened at the Sidewalk Café in the very near future, possibly as early as New Year's Eve. Investigators did not know who was backing it or whether it had any connection with the death, but Cavett told reporters that he would be attempting to look into the matter further.

ZaSu Pitts told her son that she believed Thelma's death came as a result of one of West's associates taking her up to the garage and leaving her there to die. But how could they have gotten her there without creating a lot of noise and drama in the process? During Brubaker's research, the officers said they believed that in the meeting prior to Thelma's death, gangsters gagged her in some way to quiet her down. This action, officers suggested, ultimately rendered the actress unconscious and enabled them to get her to the garage very easily. Again, while officers may have shared this theory with Brubaker in the 1980s, their memories tie in with what was announced at the beginning of the initial investigation. During the days following her death, newspapers reported that the police were investigating the possibility that Thelma could have been put into a stupor and then placed into the garage to die. This would effectively create a perfect crime, since everything found in the garage could be explained away.

These stories gathered momentum in the lead-up to Christmas Day 1935, when a person from the coroner's office phoned newspapers and said that a laceration or swelling was found at the back of Thelma's throat. It was further revealed that this injury would indicate that something— possibly a pipe or bottle—had been thrust into her mouth shortly before death.

Autopsy surgeon A. F. Wagner denied the reports, but at the same time District Attorney George Johnson said he wouldn't discount them. He did add, however, that if she had been dead the number of hours she was supposed to be, he could see how her throat would be affected.

Mortician Katy King thinks this could be the case: "The swelling could be attributed to the natural decomposition process. The first places that start to swell are usually from the waist up. . . . I think it is possible that it was natural decomposition, especially being found in a car inside a garage, as temperature can have a huge factor in the rate of decomposition." Katy also believes that if she had been gagged with a bottle as indicated in some of the accounts, there would probably be more damage to the mouth than just the loss of the cap on one of Thelma's teeth and the slight discoloration of her lip.

Nevertheless, the report does confirm that investigators were still considering the possibility that Thelma had been gagged. And the improbability of a bottle being used as a gag does not preclude her from having been gagged in a more conventional way and passing out—particularly given her history of fainting spells.

The belief that Thelma could have been murdered grew stronger still when on December 20, 1935, it was reported that the waiter in charge of the Todd/Lupino party at the Trocadero had been threatened with kidnapping since the actress's death. He had received a postcard with the words "Withhold testimony or kidnap trip" early in the day, and then later his car was stopped by two men shouting threats at him as he made his way home. "He knows nothing about the case and has nothing to conceal," said Police Captain Blaine Seed, and investigators never did find out who made the threats.

The story drew curiosity, and it wasn't long before grand jury foreman George Rochester announced that he now believed that Thelma had been the victim of a homicide. How did he think she died? The answer was murder by monoxide.

23

THE DEATH OF THELMA TODD

We will never know exactly how Thelma Todd died, since eighty years have come and gone and the people connected to the case have long since passed away themselves. However, considering everything we do know, the idea of foul play is high on the list of possibilities. One distinctly plausible theory follows.

After the Trocadero party, Thelma Todd returned to the Sidewalk Café, where she was not locked out of her apartment as Roland West encouraged everyone to believe. Instead, she entered the living quarters by the side door as usual and was greeted by West and several gangsters, who were determined that the future of the gambling room would be resolved that night. If this was the case, and the meeting was planned in advance, it could explain why West was insistent that Thelma be back at the café by 2 AM and why she was keen to stay away. It could also account for the fact that the actress chose to have Ernest Peters drop her at the front instead of accompanying her to the side door as he normally did.

Unfortunately, by insisting that she walk herself to the door, Thelma accidentally ensured that a major clue was lost. Peters testified that the front of the building was dark, but he could not see the windows in the apartment above. If those lights were on, he would certainly have noticed as he walked her up the stairs at the side of the building, thereby giving jurors reason to doubt West's assurances that he was in bed, asleep.

From everything we know about the last weeks and months of Thelma's life, it would appear that gamblers were determined to have their tables installed at the Sidewalk Café. Roland West may have been pressuring Thelma to go along with the plans, as demonstrated by the beating she had suffered in the café—apparently by his hand—several days before her death. If West was prepared to let gamblers into the café, they would not have considered him a problem, but Thelma most certainly was. The woman was not going to back down; she was a hindrance to operations and very forthright in her opinions.

Even so, it is possible that the gangsters did not come to the apartment with any intentions of killing her. But if the debate became heated and Thelma passed out—either as a result of being gagged, in a fainting spell brought on by her anxiety, or some combination of the two—then it would have presented an ideal opportunity to be rid of the woman once and for all.

The gangsters would have had cars with them, most likely parked at the back of the building where they could not be seen, and one possibility is that the unconscious actress was bundled out of the building, driven up to the garage, and then placed in her car. They were in luck with the ferocity of the wind that night, as the engine could be started without attracting the attention of Charles Harry Smith sleeping upstairs. The garage doors were then closed, and the perpetrators made their way back down the hill.

Because the autopsy showed carbon monoxide in her blood, there is no doubt that Thelma was still alive when she was taken to the garage and inhaled the poisonous gas once there. However, during the investigation it was discovered that blood had been found on numerous parts of the car, including the seat, steering wheel, door, and running board. These droplets were analyzed and found to also contain carbon monoxide. This discovery meant that Thelma must have bled onto the various car parts after she inhaled the fumes from her car and not before. It suggests that after the gangsters had gone, Thelma regained consciousness just long enough to try to get out of the car. As she did so, droplets of blood from her nose were deposited around the vehicle. However, she was in no state to make an escape, so she instead slumped over before finally, tragically passing away.

Roland West told the coroner that he believed Thelma had tried to get out of the car that evening. This part of the story was the only thing he seemed to dwell on. Perhaps this was because he had hoped Thelma never regained consciousness and died without knowing what was going on. The discovery that she did wake up and seemed to suffer during her death was something that certainly seemed to weigh on his mind.

No matter how Thelma arrived at the garage, one thing is certain: she passed away under the influence of the poisonous gas. It would not have taken her long to die in the confines of her garage with the doors closed. During the investigation, police experts visited the building and Detective Joe Whitehead (no relation to Mae) closed the doors and started the car engine. Within ninety seconds he was pounding on the door to come out, such was the level of carbon monoxide billowing into the enclosed space. "I was almost fainting. Gases filled the garage almost immediately," he said. Detectives hypothesized that it would have taken approximately two minutes for Thelma to pass away from the fumes.

It is quite a mystery as to what Roland West's part was in all this. He could have been an innocent bystander, or he may have been a willing participant, eager to be rid of his girlfriend just as much as the mobsters were. Most likely, he was a subordinate partner in the gangsters' attempts to place their gambling tables in the restaurant and had participated in that and the disposal of Thelma out of fear—fear for a loss of his business and the threatened loss of his own life. After all, if they were so willing to rid themselves of Thelma, he would have known he too was in danger of being disposed of.

This fear of retribution is echoed by Rudy Schafer Jr.'s remarks to historian Benny Drinnon, who said that his stepmother, Alberta—Jewel Carmen's sister and the cashier at the Sidewalk Café—would never talk about what had happened at the restaurant during the lead-up to Thelma's death. The only thing the woman would say was that she and others were told by some "bad guys" that if they disclosed anything they knew, not only would they be killed, but they "would suffer a long and painful death." Whoever wanted to frighten Alberta did a good job, as she would go into a panic every time she was asked about Thelma's death, and to her dying day she would never say a word about the events of 1935.

If gangsters threatened other members of staff, then there is no doubt they would have also threatened West to keep him quiet. He certainly spent a lot of time trying to get everyone to quietly drop the inquiry—which of course they eventually did—and as early as December 20 he was quoted as saying that everything was becoming exaggerated and that her death was "tragic and ineffably simple." Why was he convinced that it was all so easy, when everything pointed to the fact that it was anything but? And why was he often confused when it came to simple elements of his story, such as whether the dog was whining on that cold December night? Quite possibly because West had been the chief witness of her demise and had been threatened into silence as a result.

After the headlines surrounding Thelma's death died down, most of her scenes in *The Bohemian Girl* were reshot, though she can still be seen in a small musical number. Her last short with Patsy Kelly, *An All American Toothache*, was released in 1936 and proved to be one of the funniest films the pair had ever worked on, though some critics found it hard to laugh at the antics knowing that Thelma had now passed away.

The loss of the talented comedienne was a tragic event in cinematic history. Her short life was over, and the mystery of her death would never officially be solved.

POSTSCRIPT

*I*n the months after she discovered Thelma's body, Mae Whitehead was frequently bothered by newspaper reporters and became worried that they might be trying to blame her for her employer's death. She was a single mother taking care of her son, and it took her a little while before she was able to find work again. Eventually, however, she found employment as a personal assistant for the likes of ZaSu Pitts, Patsy Kelly, and Helen Ainsworth. To avoid any more publicity, she began using her maiden name and for a time moved in with her parents so she could care for her ailing mother. Described by her granddaughter as "religious, caring and a hard worker," Mae lived a long life, passing away in 1989 at age eighty-four.

Alice Edwards Todd never spoke publicly about her daughter after the initial statements she released shortly after Thelma's death. Losing her husband, son, and daughter during the course of twenty-five years weighed hard on her mind, and she never truly recovered. Thelma's death seemed to trouble her the most, perhaps because it was so full of mystery. Despite her public insistence that it must have been an accident, we will never know if she truly accepted this or actually still believed her initial feeling that her daughter had been murdered.

Alice disposed of most of Thelma's belongings and on February 10, 1936, left Los Angeles, telling reporters that she was moving out of California because the movie industry held such sad memories for her. Back in Massachusetts, Alice moved into 22 Bowdoin Street, where members of the Todd family had lived for years, and spent her remaining days quietly, both in Lawrence and at the family lake house, where she felt at peace.

Alice passed away December 18, 1969, almost thirty-four years to the day after her famous daughter. In death, her hair was styled by Thelma's former school friend Edna Hamel, and then Alice was buried with her daughter's ashes beside her. Up until the moment she passed, the devastated mother had kept Thelma's remains in her home, along with a beautiful photograph of her daughter.

In his lifetime, Roland West was never officially accused of having a hand in his lover's death, though over the years rumors to that effect did spring up, and questions were asked about his involvement. In spite of that, he continued to run the Sidewalk Café, which he officially named Thelma Todd's Inn/Joya's. In fact, he wasted no time in letting everyone know it was still open for business, placing notices in the press that ran just four days after the discovery of Thelma's body. In the statement (signed by manager Rudy Schafer), he thanked friends and fans for their support before vowing to carry on "as Miss Todd would have liked it," by remaining in business. West then saw to it that the establishment was prominently advertised in the *Los Angeles Times* throughout January 1936. Over the years, rumors abounded that West's gambling parties in the Tower Room continued—possibly under mob rule—though these stories have never been backed up with hard evidence.

Thelma's death proved to be good for business, as it turned out, and the building was often visited by curious fans wanting to dine and be photographed in the place where it all had happened. But there was a downside too: Roland began to complain that he received many letters from cranks, some sharing their theories of the death and others threatening harm to him and the business. One such letter was posted from Detroit on Christmas Eve 1935, less than two weeks after Thelma's death.

"Thelma Todd's death will never be solved," it said. "And the rest who were at the party had better KEEP THERE [*sic*] TRAP SHUT or something else will happen." The letter was passed immediately to the FBI, and it is probably no coincidence that shortly afterward West decided to hire a bodyguard. The man, named Raymond Babus, also acted as a personal chef and traveled around the States with his boss for some years after Thelma's death.

The café was never far from controversy, and in June 1936 it made headlines again when actress Lila McComas dined there shortly before taking off at high speed and crashing her car into a vegetable truck, killing herself in the process. Then in August of the same year it was mentioned again when seventeen-year-old Katie Turman dined there before promptly disappearing. West himself became involved in more scandal when he was mentioned in an investigation involving the tax payments of his old friend Joseph M. Schenck. He survived everything thrown at him, but the negative limelight was not something he appreciated.

In 1937, Roland decided to hire entertainment for the café and contracted Queenie's Honky Tonk, a floor show that included actress Queenie Shannon and comedian Michael Slade. West was so impressed with Queenie that he offered her the position of café manager, which she surprisingly accepted even though she had just been offered a screen contract. The woman took over Thelma's role at the front of the house, trained bartenders, and acted as a mistress of ceremonies during entertainment evenings. She prided herself on finding girls in their teens to become her "personality waitresses," dressing them up in costumes that left little to the imagination and teaching them how to wait tables. West and Queenie were rumored to be romantically involved, and the two went on trips around the United States to find new and exciting recipes for the café. The relationship did not last, however, and West accused her of squandering and wasting all of the money he had given to her. By the time he passed away, she would be left just one dollar in his will.

His estranged marriage to Jewel Carmen continued to stumble on, because of her reluctance to grant him a divorce without a payoff. This led West to make a surprising claim—that they had never been legally married anyway—so a furious Carmen enlisted heavyweight lawyer Jerry Giesler, who then fought for her financial interests. The matter was eventually settled in November 1940, when West agreed to pay Carmen $50,000 cash and made a promise that he would not contest the divorce suit. In later years she fell out of the spotlight, and she passed away in 1984.

In the mid-1940s West married actress Lola Lane, and around this time he renamed the café Chez Roland. However, West was not in the best of health, and he moved to Florida in the late 1940s, dividing his time between there and the apartment above the café. During one trip back to Los Angeles in the summer of 1949, West went to a party at Joseph M. Schenck's house, only to find himself in the company of Pat De Cicco. What they spoke about during their time together was never disclosed.

In 1951, West's health had deteriorated so much that he made the decision to put the café up for sale, and ads appeared in the *Los Angeles Times* between September and December of that year. The café was described as fabulous, a 12,500-square-foot space, fully equipped and complete with four penthouse apartments. "Owner too ill to operate," read the ad, explaining that West had slashed the price from $250,000 to the bargain price of just $100,000. However, the former director never got to see a sale being made, as on March 31, 1952, just months after the advertisements ran, he passed away during a visit to Santa Monica. His funeral was just fifteen minutes long and included his wife and a handful of friends from his silent film days.

Life for residents of Castellammare continued, though in time the glamour of a home at the beach was overshadowed by mudslides. By 1958, various streets had dropped as much as ten feet since 1941 and two feet in just the past year. Three residencies were vacated on orders of the L.A. Department of Building and Safety, and recommendations were brought forward for at least four roads to be closed.

In April 1965, residents started to complain that land in the vicinity of Revello Drive was slowly but surely moving. Some gathered as many possessions as they could and left their homes as quickly as possible.

Others did not, and in the early hours of Saturday, June 5, they awoke to the devastating realization that they'd waited too long. During the next day, houses literally traveled down the hillside, gardens collapsed into the streets below, and at least three homes and eight apartments were destroyed. Various roads and cliff-side staircases remain buried to this day, though the threat of slides seems to have eased somewhat in recent years.

For decades after Roland West's death, the building that once housed the Sidewalk Café was used by a film production company. It remained virtually untouched by time, still housing the refrigerator once used by restaurant staff, as well as the sliding doors in Thelma's room and the front doors with the Joya's name attached. Even the actress's own dining table stayed inside until an estate sale in 2015. The building has now been sold and its future is uncertain, though Thelma's fans and historians hope that it will be preserved for many years to come.

Pat De Cicco was never far from controversy in the years after his ex-wife's death. After the discovery of the body and the subsequent questioning, girlfriend Margaret Lindsay developed health problems. She had been due to act in a murder mystery film but pulled out and did comedy instead. Her relationship with De Cicco cooled.

The following summer, still describing himself as a theatrical agent, De Cicco ran into trouble with the Riviera Country Club, which claimed he owed them $61.59. He refused to pay, and after the club made fifteen attempts to obtain the money, he was finally arrested almost a year later and taken to court in July 1937. Another arrest came because of a traffic violation in November 1936, and then in February 1937, De Cicco punched an investment broker on the chin during a night out at the Clover Club in Hollywood. The broker claimed that the attack was unprovoked—that he had been minding his own business—and announced his intention to sue De Cicco to the tune of $25,000.

By July 1938, Thelma's ex claimed to be broke, and he was called into court after refusing to pay $148.50 worth of health and beauty treatments for his dog. Saying he had just four dollars to his name and no job, property, or bank account, De Cicco made the fatal mistake of arriving at the building in a car worth $3,750. It was promptly confiscated.

Several years later he joined the US Army and then married heiress Gloria Vanderbilt. However, this was not the end of his bad-boy image— in fact, in many ways it was just the beginning. In March 1942, the couple were living at the Drake Hotel in New York when De Cicco was accused of punching a hotel employee who refused to give him a pot to make spaghetti. He was arrested but later acquitted after claiming he merely pushed the clerk after being called a rude name.

Author Ernest Hemingway and De Cicco both frequented the same New York gym at the time, and when Hemingway heard about the altercation, he immediately challenged him to an amateur boxing match. De Cicco declined. Gloria Vanderbilt tried to laugh off the incident at the hotel, but cracks appeared in the marriage. The two separated and eventually divorced. She went on to write a book, *Black Knight, White Knight*, which is partly about her volatile ex-husband.

By the late 1940s, De Cicco was manager of United Artists Theaters. He busied himself with arranging the redecoration of establishments such as the Hollywood Egyptian Theatre and the California Theatre, where he associated himself with producer Samuel Goldwyn. This went some way toward cleaning up his reputation, and he even managed to get his photograph in the *Los Angeles Times*, holding a small girl and pointing toward a decorated Christmas tree.

De Cicco's wild-boy image was never far from the surface, however. He was frequently seen squiring young women around Hollywood, including tobacco heiress Doris Duke and tennis player Gertrude "Gorgeous Gussy" Moran. He eventually married actress Mary Jo Tarola— nearly twenty years his junior—in December 1952, though the two divorced eight years later.

In recent years, a rumor has been put forward that Pat De Cicco may have had a hand in the death of actor Ted Healy, who died in 1937 after three men beat him up. This has never been substantiated and is probably not true, but in light of his past endeavors, the stories linking

Healy and De Cicco are unlikely to fade. In his later years, the former agent, producer, theater manager, and mafia wannabe lived fairly quietly, spending much of his time in Spain and garnering little mention in the press. He eventually passed away in October 1978.

Mobster Tony Cornero decided to take his gambling plans offshore, and in the years after Thelma's death, he set about buying and renovating a ship. This was the *Rex*, and on May 1, 1938, he had it towed from Long Beach and anchored several miles from Santa Monica Pier. Every day taxi boats would take gamblers out to the ship, and Tony earned a tidy fortune from the operation. Tom Cavett—the same investigator who told the public of gambling interests at the Sidewalk Café—was later thought to have been kidnapped by Frank Cornero when he asked to be taken out to the *Rex* to investigate the ship. Instead Cavett was given an extended guided tour of Santa Monica bay by the Cornero brother and eventually returned, absolutely furious.

Cornero was involved on and off in the gaming ship business for a number of years, and in 1948 he became the victim of a murder attempt, when someone knocked on his door, announcing he had a package. He survived the attack but was evasive with police about who could have been responsible, acting as if he were in deep pain every time he was asked a question.

Finally Cornero decided that gambling in California was more trouble than it was worth and headed back to Nevada. There he maneuvered through various loopholes to begin work on the famed Stardust Hotel and Casino. Several weeks later he made a trip to the Desert Inn, where he became involved in an altercation with a member of staff. Minutes later he collapsed and died, apparently of a massive heart attack, though strangely no autopsy was ever performed. Rumors quickly circulated that he could have been murdered, the victim of yet another mob hit.

Stories related to Thelma's death have grown since 1935, with rumors of hushed-up involvements being particularly rife. A popular theory is that Roland West admitted to locking his lover in the garage to teach her a lesson when she returned to the café after 2 AM. The next day he was apparently horror-stricken on discovering she had died after turning on the engine, and therefore pretended he had not seen her since she left for the Trocadero party.

In the pages of this book, I have tried very hard to break down each piece of evidence and every shred of information and to pose questions on how the death could (or could not) have happened. It is my hope that my theory of how Thelma passed away will provoke more discussions and theories in the years to come. In the same way, I hope my account of what happened in her life will encourage a renewed interest in the career of a remarkably talented woman.

Thelma never wanted to be a star; she wanted to be an actress who excelled at her craft. Sadly, she never reached the heights of Hollywood superstardom, and as she edged her way toward age thirty, she knew her time was limited. The creation of the Sidewalk Café was her sanctuary, her ticket out of the business as soon as she was deemed too old to be a vamp or a slapstick comedienne. She stood in that building and welcomed friends old and new to her domain. She retreated to the café and to West when the pressures of the world outside became too much. Above all, she hoped that despite everything going on in her life, she could remain safe within its thick walls.

In the end, neither the café nor her lover West did anything to save Thelma from her fate, and in many ways, these two things and the people attracted to them were the very unmaking of her. "I'm too thoroughly New England to get away from the fundamentals of life," she once said. "Things are so extreme here. I can't quite get Hollywood. People here have no sense of values. They don't know how to live. Everything is done for effect. There's no sincerity—no balance."

NOTES

Preface: The Body in the Garage

All direct information and quotes in the preface come from the official coroner's inquest, which began on December 18, 1935, except the quote from Alice Todd, describing her daughter as being murdered. This quote was mentioned in many newspapers in the days and weeks after Thelma Todd's death, including: "Mother of Thelma Todd Thinks Death Accidental," *Independent* (Helena, MT), December 31, 1935; "Mother Hints Theory of Todd Murder," *Oakland Tribune*, December 30, 1935; "Mother Called in Todd Quiz," *El Paso Herald-Post*, December 30, 1935; and "Fresh Trail Found in Enquiry," *Los Angeles Times*, December 30, 1935.
The transcript from the inquest is available for purchase from Celebrity Collectables' Celebrity Archive, www.celebritycollectables.com.

1. Lawrence's Lucky Girl

Immigration information regarding Alice Edwards and John Todd: 1910 Federal Census database, Ancestry.com; also "John S. Todd Meets Death in New York," *Lawrence Telegram*, July 30, 1926.
The marriage between John Todd and Alice Edwards: Various records on Ancestry.com. Also "Hymen Held Sway in Lawrence," *Boston Globe*, June 21, 1900; Marriage Announcements, *Lowell Sun*, June 22, 1900.
"always a very happy, healthy child": Ann Marsters, "Thelma Todd's Life Story," chapter 1, *Boston Evening American*, December 19, 1935.
"I was fortunate": Catherine Hunter, "Blonde Menace," *Screen Play*, February 1932.
Details of the death of William Todd: Reported in two death certificates, handwritten and typed, from Vermont, Death Records, 1909–2008, and Massachusetts, Death Records, 1841–1915, Ancestry.com. Also "Boy Killed in Vermont," *Lawrence Daily Eagle*, August 26, 1910; "Boy Whirled Around Shaft," *Lawrence Daily Eagle*, August 27, 1910.

"bright and winsome," and memories of the Saunders School teachers: "Boy Whirled
    Around Shaft," *Lawrence Daily Eagle.*
William "was crushed beyond recognition": Hunter, "Blonde Menace."
"I can remember": Gladys Hall, "It's Tragic to Be Beautiful," *Movie Mirror*, March 1932.
Locals blaming John for William's death: Edna Hamel, interview by James Brubaker, circa
    1980s, relayed to the author in April 2012.
"bloomers and middies": Quote from a neighbor from "The Life Story of Thelma Todd,"
    Boston Evening American, circa 1931, Lawrence History Center, Lawrence, MA. A
    similar quote was repeated by her uncle in Marsters, "Thelma Todd's Life Story,"
    chapter 1.
Details of John as an alderman: William Donati, *The Life and Death of Thelma Todd*
    (Jefferson, NC: McFarland, 2012), 6; "John S. Todd Meets Death," *Lawrence
    Telegram.*
Thelma regarding boys as friends and brothers: David Ingram, "Thelma Todd Life Story,"
    chapter 1, *Boston Daily Record*, circa May–June 1932, Lawrence History Center.
"I hate people who are not natural": "Life Story of Thelma Todd," *Boston Evening American.*
Thelma as modest and old-fashioned: Ann Marsters, "Thelma Todd's Life Story," chapter 3,
    Boston Evening American, December 21, 1935.
"She was a regular girl": "Popular Girl," *Boston Post*, December 18, 1935.
"I'd kill a man": Hall, "Tragic to Be Beautiful."
Car race attended by Thelma and her friend: Dan Thomas's column, *Lowell Sun*, December
    14, 1933.
School newspaper: *Lawrence High School Bulletin*, circa 1923, Lawrence History Center.
"It was her father's greatest pleasure": Marsters, "Thelma Todd's Life Story," chapter 1.
Lavender and Old Lace: Ann Marsters, "Thelma Todd's Life Story," chapter 2, *Boston
    Evening American*, December 20, 1935.
Thelma's scorn of movie stars: Ibid.
"Prophecy of the Class of 1923": "Lawrence Classmates Knew Thelma as Leader," *Boston
    Globe*, December 19, 1935.
Mr. and Mrs. Fredericks: Thelma told this at least twice, in Marsters, "Thelma Todd's Life
    Story," chapter 2; and Ingram, "Thelma Todd Life Story," chapter 1.
Fur Fashion Review of 1924: "Local Girls in Fur Fashion Review at the Empire Theater,"
    Lawrence Telegram, April 15, 1924.
The Life of St. Genevieve: The story of Thelma's involvement was told in several newspapers,
    including Ann Hall, North West Notebook, *Boston Globe*, July 19, 1998; and
    obituaries for Rosario Contarino, unknown newspapers, January 10 and October 17,
    1988, Lawrence History Center.
Thelma's job woes: Marsters, "Thelma Todd's Life Story," chapter 2; "Too Pretty to Work
    Where People Could See Her," *American Weekly*, April 1926.
"I didn't hire her": "Too Beautiful for Job in Shoe Store," *Boston Post*, December 18, 1935.
John Todd's physical abuse: Hamel, interview by Brubaker.
"They are the most interesting": Frederick Russell, "They Nicknamed Her 'Hot Toddy,'"
    Film Pictorial, April 15, 1933.
Other details of Thelma's teaching career: "Kin in Lawrence Mourn Actress," *Boston Globe*,
    December 17, 1935.
"I wasn't scared": Ingram, "Thelma Todd Life Story," chapter 2.

Lowell Normal School's new rules: "Brilliant Career of Beautiful Thelma Todd," *Lawrence Evening Tribune*, December 17, 1935.

2. Bright Young Things

"She would just laugh": Ann Marsters, "Thelma Todd's Life Story," chapter 2, *Boston Evening American*, December 20, 1935.

"[It's] all very well": Alice L. Tildesley, "Why Beauty Contest Winners Are Failures," *Oakland Tribune*, November 1, 1931.

"Beauty alone cannot achieve victories": Thelma Todd, "How I Was Groomed for Stardom," *Film Weekly*, June 30, 1933.

Paramount School: Details appear in various magazines and newspapers, including "1st Players School," *Variety*, July 22, 1925; "School to Train Movie Actors Is Started by Lasky," *Charleston Gazette*, April 12, 1925; untitled article, *Lowell Sun*, August 11, 1925; "School Ma'am a Hit on Screen," *Lowell Sun*, September 17, 1925; untitled article, *Lowell Sun*, October 13, 1925; Agnes Smith, "Waiting for the Starlight," *Photoplay*, December 1925; and L. C. Moen, "Paramount School Graduates First Junior Stars," *Motion Picture News*, March 13, 1926.

"The studio told me": Tildesley, "Why Beauty Contest Winners."

"There was more noise and cheering": David Ingram, "Thelma Todd Life Story," chapter 4, *Boston Daily Record*, circa May–June 1932, Lawrence History Center, Lawrence, MA.

"a golden dream of beauty": "Bay State Beauty to Sing at Park," *Fitchburg Sentinel*, July 6, 1925.

"highest honor paid a woman": "Elected Head of Elk's Group," *Boston Globe*, June 16, 1925.

"Live a gay life": Ann Marsters, "Thelma Todd's Life Story," chapter 9, *Boston Evening American*, December 28, 1935.

Normal School surprise party: Social Chat, *Lowell Sun*, June 23, 1925.

Whalom Park event: "Bay State Beauty," *Fitchburg Sentinel*; ad for the event and "Beauty Prize Winner Sings at Whalom Park Tonight," *Fitchburg Sentinel*, July 8, 1925; "1500 See Beauty Contest Winner," *Fitchburg Sentinel*, July 9, 1925.

Boston shoe modeling job: Untitled article, *Lowell Sun*, July 3, 1925; also "Miss Galloway Is Shoe Show Model," *Lowell Sun*, July 8, 1925.

Thelma had to "run off": Edna Hamel, interview by James Brubaker, circa 1980s, relayed to the author in April 2012.

"It was a long time before I overcame": "Film Colony Is Absurdly Reviled," *Huntingdon Daily News*, August 30, 1929.

"I think I'm going to like it more": Ann Marsters, "Thelma Todd's Life Story," chapter 4, *Boston Evening American*, December 22, 1935.

3. The Paramount School

"petted and chaperoned boys and girls": Marjory Adams, "They May Be Movie Stars— Who Knows?," *Boston Globe*, February 7, 1926.

"She is on the spot": Thelma Todd, "How I Was Groomed for Stardom," *Film Weekly*, June 30, 1933.

"I suppose I was young and foolish": Ibid.

"They thought me quite terrible": Alice L. Tildesley, "Why Beauty Contest Winners Are Failures," *Oakland Tribune*, November 1, 1931.

"And I'm not relying on beauty": Ibid.

"We were looked after like kids": Todd, "Groomed for Stardom."

"My wildest dissipation was to go out dancing": Dorothy Lubou, "Movie Men Are So Crude," *Motion Picture*, June 1929.

"I don't think the school helped us": Ibid.

Thelma was "deeply engrossed" in her work: Untitled article, *Lowell Sun*, August 11, 1925.

"[She] is a real beauty": Agnes Smith, "Waiting for the Starlight," *Photoplay*, December 1925.

"Curiously enough": L. C. Moen, "Paramount School Graduates First Junior Stars," *Motion Picture News*, March 13, 1926.

"crowning glory": "Extra-ordinary!," *Los Angeles Times*, December 27, 1925.

Dorothy Nourse's memory of eating three steaks a day: Adams, "They May Be Movie Stars."

149 pounds and "terribly broad": Myrtle Gebhart, "An Eye Full," *Picture Play*, March 1929.

"It made me furiously mad": Ibid. Thelma also spoke about Dix on numerous other occasions, including in Elsi Que, "Blond and Fancy-Free," *Picture Play*, April 1931.

Diet tips: Thelma Todd, letter sent via the Famous Players–Lasky studio, Astoria, Long Island, n.d., Lawrence History Center, Lawrence, MA.

"I should like to play women with character": Adams, "They May Be Movie Stars."

"I do honestly feel that I have learned": Todd, "Groomed for Stardom."

"as if we were monkeys": Ibid.

"the substitute team": Smith, "Waiting for the Starlight."

"It's going to be pretty tough": Ibid.

"I've seen a lot of studio jealousy": Todd, "Groomed for Stardom."

Thelma's interview with Marjory Adams: Adams, "They May Be Movie Stars."

"the answer to the cry for new faces": Moen, "Paramount School Graduates."

"These youngsters are utterly without magnetism": Review of *Fascinating Youth*, *Picture Play*, June 1926.

"It can stand on its own feet": Moen, "Paramount School Graduates."

Film Daily review of *Fascinating Youth*: Reviews, *Film Daily*, March 14, 1926.

4. Fascinating Youth

Rumors of engagements: "Thelma Todd Named in Screen Romance but Her Parents Don't Believe It," *Lowell Sun*, March 20, 1926.

"I will never be conceited": "Triumphal Tour Is Made by Thelma Todd in Pierce Arrow," *Lawrence Eagle Tribune*, May 21, 1926, in "Thelma Todd Celebration Program," Lawrence History Center, Lawrence, MA.

Appearances in Boston and Lawrence for *Fascinating Youth*: "Thelma Todd Bows Before Home Folks," *Lawrence Telegram*, May 17, 1926; "Thelma Todd and Greg Blackton in Argentine Tango at Palace Thursday," *Lawrence Eagle Tribune*, May 19, 1926, in "Thelma Todd Celebration Program," Lawrence History Center; "Triumphal Tour," *Lawrence Eagle Tribune*; "Paramount School Graduates in Film at Metropolitan,"

Boston Globe, May 16, 1926; "Miss Todd to Address WNAC Woman's Club,"
    Lawrence Telegram, May 19, 1926; "To Speak Tomorrow at WNAC Woman's Club,"
    Boston Daily Globe, May 19, 1926.

John Todd's death: "Miss Thelma Todd's Father Loses Life," *Lowell Sun*, July 30, 1926;
    "John S. Todd Meets Death in New York," *Lawrence Telegram*, July 30, 1926;
    "Tributes to John S. Todd," *Lawrence Telegram*, August 3, 1926.

"My father died": Thelma Todd, "How I Was Groomed for Stardom," *Film Weekly*, June
    30, 1933.

"I am still very much a Lawrence girl": Marjory Adams, "They May Be Movie Stars—Who
    Knows?," *Boston Globe*, February 7, 1926.

Lasky's idea for another film: "Youngsters Gather Together," *Los Angeles Times*, September
    22, 1926; "Paramount 'Graduates,'" *Los Angeles Times*, November 14, 1926.

God Gave Me Twenty Cents and *The Popular Sin*: Reviews, *Motion Picture News*, December
    4, 1926, and *Picture Play*, April 1927.

"The fine, soft texture of a baby's": "Beauty Plus Personality," *Hutchinson News*, November
    19, 1926.

Rubber Heels, supposed romance with Robert Andrews: "Romance in School," *Picture Play*,
    May 1927.

"I never in all my life expected": Adams, "They May Be Movie Stars."

"She is a mighty clever girl": Marjory Adams, "Miss Todd Now Has a Chair of Her Own,"
    Boston Globe, February 20, 1927.

Rubber Heels publicity and reviews: *Appleton Post-Crescent*, June 13, 1927; *Film Daily*, July
    10, 1927; *Photoplay*, September 1927; *Motion Picture News*, July 15, 1927.

"I had always felt so cramped": Myrtle Gebhart, "An Eye Full," *Picture Play*, March 1929.

Thelma's move to Hollywood: "Contract Players Leave," *Film Daily*, March 6, 1927;
    "Thelma Todd Goes West," *Film Daily*, April 17, 1927.

"As the train carried me farther": Gebhart, "An Eye Full."

5. Welcome to Hollywood

"stimulated me instead of enervating me": Myrtle Gebhart, "An Eye Full," Picture Play,
    March 1929.

"She is the one who is entitled": "Thelma Todd Discusses Her Work in the Moving
    Pictures," *Lawrence Evening Tribune*, August 22, 1929.

"It has been a life-saver": Thelma Todd, letter to Irish fan Mr. Cloney, October 30, 1931,
    collection of Benny Drinnon.

"There was nothing up here": Frederick Russell, "They Nicknamed Her 'Hot Toddy,'" *Film
    Pictorial*, April 15, 1933.

Movie camera as the enemy: Larry Swindell, *The Last Hero: A Biography of Gary Cooper*
    (London: Robson, 1981).

Grace Kingsley column about Thelma's hair: *Los Angeles Times*, May 7, 1927.

"Gradually I began to come out of my shell": Gebhart, "An Eye Full."

"black velvet, a slow smile and dignity": Cal York, Gossip of All the Studios, *Photoplay*,
    August 1927.

"she was a shadowy figure": Gebhart, "An Eye Full."

Premiere of *Man Power*: Advertisement for the event, *Los Angeles Times*, July 22, 1927.

The Gay Defender: "Former School Marm Wins Role," *Los Angeles Times*, August 26, 1927; "Richard Dix Screen Row Terminated," *Los Angeles Times*, September 1, 1927; "Legendary Bandit Is Picturized," *Los Angeles Times*, December 31, 1927; Review of *The Gay Defender*, *Film Daily*, January 1, 1928.

"I am an actor now": Alma Whitaker, "Ten Years Hence," *Photoplay*, January 1928.

"Dix has sideburns and a mustache": Review of *The Gay Defender*, *Variety*, December 28, 1927.

"who does the most improbable feats": Review of *The Gay Defender*, *Film Daily*, January 1, 1928.

"California has given me the youth": Gebhart, "An Eye Full."

"Their attitude lacks": Dorothy Lubou, "Movie Men Are So Crude," *Motion Picture*, June 1929.

"Girls out here have cheapened themselves": Ibid.

Thelma's comments on the casting couch, the crudeness of men: Ibid.; Llewellyn Carroll, "What Hollywood Did to a New England Schoolmarm," *Photoplay*, February 1932.

Hell's Angels information in this and later chapters appears in many different magazines and newspapers, including: Ralph Wilk, A Little from "Lots," *Film Daily*, November 8, 1927; "Nine of U.A. Scheduled Listed by Lichtman," *Film Daily*, May 1, 1928; "Hell's Angels New United Artists Caddo Release," *Motion Picture News*, December 9, 1927; "Both Sound and Color in 'Hell's Angels,'" *Motion Picture News*, August 4, 1928; "2 Million Feet of 'Hell's Angels' to Be Cut to 12,000," *Motion Picture News*, May 25, 1929; untitled article, *Motion Picture News*, June 29, 1929; "United Artists to Release 19 in 1928–1929," *Exhibitors Herald and Moving Picture World*, July 14, 1928; "Hughes to Use Sound," *Exhibitors Herald and Moving Picture World*, July 21, 1928; "Hell's Angels Has Both Color, Sound," *Exhibitors Herald and Moving Picture World*, July 28, 1928; "Ben Lyon Finishes with 'Hell's Angels,'" *Exhibitors Herald and Moving Picture World*, August 11, 1928; Last Minute News, *Motion Picture Classic*, October 1928.

Thelma's car accident: "Thelma Todd Hurt as Truck Smashes Auto," *Los Angeles Times*, November 4, 1927; "Thelma Todd Injured," *Lowell Sun*, November 18, 1927.

Abie's Irish Rose appearance: "Cohens Invited to Be at Depot," *Los Angeles Times*, November 5, 1927; "Real Cohens Go to Greet Stage Pair," *Los Angeles Times*, November 6, 1927; untitled photo, *Motion Picture News*, December 9, 1927.

The Traveling Salesman: Grace Kingsley's column, *Los Angeles Times*, November 10, 1927; "Dix Hurt While Acting in Desert," *Los Angeles Times*, November 15, 1927; "Good Omen," *Charleston Daily Mail*, November 13, 1927; "Thelma Todd Opposite Dix," *Film Daily*, October 12, 1927; "Dix Unit on Location," *Film Daily*, November 9, 1927.

"I have lots of luck": Ralph Wilk, A Little from "Lots," *Film Daily*, January 20, 1928.

"First National is dickering": "Seeks Thelma," *Film Daily*, January 24, 1928.

Further information about First National: Benjamin B. Hampton, *A History of the Movies* (New York: Covici Friede, 1931).

"Miss Pickford paid more": Advertisement for *Daddy Long Legs*, *Picture Play*, June 1919.

Contract with First National: Copy of agreement between Thelma and First National, February 16, 1928, and letter, June 7, 1928, both in Warner Bros. Archive, University of Southern California School of Cinematic Arts, Los Angeles, CA. Also Grace Kingsley's column, *Los Angeles Times*, February 24, 1928; "Thelma Todd Signed by First National," *Lowell Sun*, March 19, 1928.

6. What's Your Dream?

Cinema managers on *Vamping Venus*: Reviews, *Exhibitors Herald and Moving Picture World*, November 3, 1928.

"one of the finest performances": Review of *The Noose*, *Los Angeles Times*, March 26, 1928.

"A mighty fine production": Reviews, *Film Daily*, January 15, 1928.

"Thelma Todd, who is one of my favorites": Donald Beaton, As They Appeal to a Youth, *Film Spectator*, May 26, 1928.

Café Montmartre: Martin Turnbull, "Café Montmartre—Where Hollywood Nightclubbing Started," *Garden of Allah* blog, March 2, 2012, https://martinturnbull.wordpress .com/2012/03/02/cafe-montmartre-where-hollywood-nightclubbing-started/.

"I guess a certain amount of success": Dorothy Lubou, "Movie Men Are So Crude," *Motion Picture*, June 1929.

"break up the monotony": "Thelma Todd Discusses Her Work in the Moving Pictures," *Lawrence Evening Tribune*, August 22, 1929.

"Sometimes you get so nervous": Ibid.

Thelma's party for Otto Kahn: Myra Nye, Society of Cinemaland, *Los Angeles Times*, April 1, 1928.

"I venture the suggestion": Benjamin B. Hampton, *A History of the Movies* (New York: Covici Friede, 1931).

"This Al Jolson picture": Delight Evans' Reviews, *Screenland*, January 1928.

"Old reliables wobble": "Old Reliables Wobble, New Names on Wing as Sound Alters Star Values," *Motion Picture News*, March 15, 1930.

"He stepped off the oblivion end": "Success," *Motion Picture Herald*, April 21, 1934.

Lasky and Mayer on the sound process: "How They View 1930 Outlook," *Motion Picture News*, January 4, 1930.

"I think Thelma would do well": "Thelma Todd Passes Test for Talking Movies—'Perfect' Voice," unknown newspaper, circa December 1928, Lawrence History Center, Lawrence, MA.

"we naturally use good diction": Alice L. Tildesley, "Why Beauty Contest Winners Are Failures," *Oakland Tribune*, November 1, 1931.

"Something refused to let me fear": Elsi Que, "Blond and Fancy-Free," *Picture Play*, April 1931.

"I think the answer lies": Thelma Todd, "How I Was Groomed for Stardom," *Film Weekly*, June 30, 1933.

More false engagement rumors: "Among the 'Victims,'" *Boston Globe*, August 25, 1928; "Screen Actress Denies She'll Wed," *Los Angeles Times*, August 27, 1928; "Betrothal Rumors Denied by Actress," *Los Angeles Times*, September 18, 1928; "Todd Ford Actress Engagement," *Motion Picture News*, September 1, 1928.

"Jimmy is a boy from my home town": Lubou, "Movie Men."

"If you don't get thin": Martin Martin, Chatter from Hollywood, *Screenland*, July 1928.

"I began to get ambitious": Lubou, "Movie Men."

Problems with tonsils and fainting: Fainting spells were described by Thelma's mother during an interview with Edwin Schallert, "Thelma Todd's Mother Discloses Own Story," *Los Angeles Times*, December 20, 1935. They were also mentioned in "Actor and Actress Undergo Operation," *Los Angeles Times*, October 24, 1928.

The Crash and *The Haunted House* reviews: *Film Spectator*, December 15, 1928; *Exhibitors Herald and Moving Picture World*, December 29, 1928; *Motion Picture*, December 1928; *Motion Picture Almanac 1929* (Chicago: Quigley, 1929), 199; *Exhibitors Herald-World*, January 5, 1929.

"by saying nothing, smiling at everyone": "The Life Story of Thelma Todd," *Boston Evening American*, circa 1931, Lawrence History Center. A similar quote also appeared in David Ingram, "Thelma Todd Life Story," chapter 8, *Boston Daily Record*, circa May–June 1932, Lawrence History Center.

Naughty Baby reviews: *Motion Picture*, February 1929; *Film Daily*, January 20, 1929; *Motion Picture News*, February 9, 1929.

7. There's No Place Like Home

Thelma becoming a freelance player: On a Lot of the Lots, *Exhibitors Herald-World*, January 5, 1929.

Reviews of *The House of Horror*: *Motion Picture News*, March 2, 1929; *Photoplay*, May 1929.

"hodgepodge mystery story": Reviews, *Photoplay*, June 1929.

"[She] manages to look both beautiful": Review of *Seven Footprints to Satan*, *Photoplay*, February 1929.

Café Montmartre celebration: Grace Kingsley's column, *Los Angeles Times*, January 22, 1929; "Montmartre's Revue," *Los Angeles Times*, January 23, 1929.

Careers: The film was announced in "Thelma Todd Busy," *Los Angeles Times*, March 3, 1929. Other items about the movie appeared in Grace Kingsley's column, *Los Angeles Times*, March 15, 1929; and untitled article, March 22, 1929. Reviews appear in *Picture Play*, September 1929 and October 1929.

"a rotten story of a diplomatic chief": Reviews, *Exhibitors Herald-World*, September 7, 1929.

"quite nicely . . . even to the extent": Norbert Lusk, The Screen in Review, *Picture Play*, September 1929.

"the sweetest and most charming woman": Thelma Todd, letter to Billie Dove, 1929, Benny Drinnon's blog, http://benny-drinnon.blogspot.co.uk/2013/12/autograph-thelma-todd-letters.html.

Thelma signs with Hal Roach: Ralph Wilk, A Little from "Lots," *Film Daily*, April 25, 1929; untitled article, *Los Angeles Times*, April 8, 1929; Grace Kingsley's column, *Los Angeles Times*, April 25, 1929; "Talkie Voice to Go on Records," *Milwaukee Sentinel*, May 11, 1929.

"I didn't know what a good time I was missing": Bob Moak, "Hollywood Draws the Line," *Picture Play*, September 1929.

"They were fond of Thelma Todd": Question from Benny Drinnon to Stan Laurel's daughter, Lois, which appeared on the Laurel & Hardy official website, 2002, www.laurel-and-hardy.com/dyk/asklois-2002.html.

"The talkies are much more different": "Thelma Recalls Day Jim Carney Took Her Nickel," *Lawrence Telegram*, August 22, 1929.

Unaccustomed as We Are and *Hurdy Gurdy*: Reviews, *Motion Picture News*, June 29 and July 13, 1929, and *Picture Play*, September 1929; Patrick J. Picking, notes on *Hurdy*

Gurdy, Picking's personal website, accessed June 1, 2015, www.picking.com /hurdygurdy.html.

"a really wonderful man": "Thelma Todd Discusses Her Work in the Moving Pictures," *Lawrence Evening Tribune,* August 22, 1929.

"Instead of progressing": Ibid.

Thelma's thoughts on beauty contests: Dan Thomas, "How Thelma Became a New Woman," *Independent* (Helena, MT), October 11, 1931; Alice L. Tildesley, "Why Beauty Contest Winners Are Failures," *Oakland Tribune,* November 1, 1931.

Fancy costume ball: Myra Nye, Society of Cinemaland, *Los Angeles Times,* May 5, 1929.

Trial Marriage premiere: "Favorites Aid Talent Quest," *Los Angeles Times,* May 10, 1929.

"interesting story" and "good cast": Reviews, *Film Daily,* April 28, 1929.

KHJ radio show: "Film Hour on KHJ Antennae," *Los Angeles Times,* June 29, 1929.

Fashion show for the Elks wives: Myra Nye, Society of Cinemaland, *Los Angeles Times,* July 7, 1929.

"an outstanding example": "Thelma Todd Example of New Type of Leading Women," *Hollywood Filmograph,* July 27, 1929.

"[That is] the greatest feeling in the world": "Day Jim Carney Took Her Nickel," *Lawrence Telegram.*

"It is only to the very few": Ann Marsters, "Thelma Todd's Life Story," chapter 9, *Boston Evening American,* December 28, 1935.

"I found that the gossip": "Einstein Missed by Crowd While Film Star Is Mobbed," *Glasgow Daily Record,* June 20, 1933. Thelma also spoke about the gossip of teachers in Kinoman, "U.S. Film Star in Glasgow," *Glasgow Evening Times,* June 20, 1933.

"fine but you can't keep it up": "Einstein Missed by Crowd," *Glasgow Daily Record.* Thelma also gave her thoughts on teaching in Kinoman, "U.S. Film Star in Glasgow." Thelma's thoughts about going to places she used to know in Lawrence were discussed during the various publicity appearances she gave toward the end of her visit. They were also reported in "Day Jim Carney Took Her Nickel," *Lawrence Telegram*; and "Thelma Todd Discusses Her Work," *Lawrence Evening Tribune.*

Young boy requests Thelma's pet seal: "Day Jim Carney Took Her Nickel," *Lawrence Telegram.*

"I thought of your faith in me": Ibid.

8. Queen of Slapstick

Harvey Priester's sister and family: "Mrs. Priester's Funeral Rites Will Be Today," *Los Angeles Times,* March 7, 1929; "The Grand Old Lady of Mining," *Los Angeles Times,* August 31, 1969.

"wild and wicked": Grace Kingsley, Romping Through Hollywood, *Los Angeles Times,* February 9, 1930.

"apparently dangerously devoid": Myra Nye, Society of Cinemaland, *Los Angeles Times,* February 9, 1930.

Party at Harry Langdon's house: Grace Kingsley, Romping Through Hollywood, *Los Angeles Times,* April 6, 1930.

"Character work is hard work": "Thelma Todd Discusses Her Work in the Moving Pictures," *Lawrence Evening Tribune,* August 22, 1929.

"I don't belong in this business": Alice L. Tildesley, "Why Beauty Contest Winners Are Failures," *Oakland Tribune*, November 1, 1931.

"The laughs are plenty": Reviews, *Motion Picture News*, March 29, 1930.

"He's too much a playboy": Catherine Hunter, "Blonde Menace," *Screen Play*, February 1932.

"It can be done of course": Elsi Que, "Blond and Fancy-Free," *Picture Play*, April 1931.

"Miss Todd is looking her very best": Reviews, *Hollywood Filmograph*, July 12, 1930.

Dolores Del Rio marriage: "Dolores Del Rio to Marry Cedric Gibbons," *Boston Globe*, August 5, 1930.

Divorce of Lina Basquette: Reported around the United States, including "Marley Wins Divorce from Lina Basquette," *Los Angeles Times*, September 11, 1930; "Marley Granted Divorce from Lina Basquette," *Charleston Gazette*, September 11, 1930; and "Husband Divorces Lina Basquette," *Boston Globe*, September 11, 1930.

Lina Basquette's memories of Thelma: William Donati, *The Life and Death of Thelma Todd* (Jefferson, NC: McFarland, 2012), 43.

"favorite occupation has always been": Thelma Todd, untitled clipping, *Saturday Stardust*, n.d., George Eells Papers, Arizona State University Libraries Special Collections, Tempe, AZ.

"Women never trust women": Gladys Hall, "It's Tragic to Be Beautiful," *Movie Mirror*, March 1932.

"A thoroughly disagreeable person": Review of *Aloha*, *Los Angeles Times*, March 9, 1931.

Her Man reviews: *Film Daily*, September 21, 1930; *Exhibitors Herald-World*, October 4, 1930. NOTE: *Exhibitors Herald-World* incorporated a variety of reviews previously printed in New York newspapers.

Follow Thru reviews: *Los Angeles Times*, September 5, 1930; *Exhibitors Herald-World*, September 13 and September 20, 1930; *Film Weekly*, September 14, 1930; *Talking Screen*, October 1930; *New Movie Magazine*, December 1930.

Reviews of Hal Roach shorts: *Exhibitors Herald-World*, November 8 and 15 and December 27, 1930; *Motion Picture News*, October 4 and December 13, 1930; *Picture Play*, May 1931 and June 1931.

The Dominoes: *Los Angeles Times* reported on the club on many occasions, including "Social Club Conducts Business Only," September 21, 1930; and Alma Whitaker, Sugar and Spice, October 5, 1930. Information about the 1930 revel was found in those articles and also "Miss Master of Ceremonies," *Picture Play*, January 1931.

Film Welfare League: "Halloween Celebration," *Los Angeles Times*, October 29, 1930.

Summer Olympic Games celebration: "Olympian Visitors' Names All Greek to Announcer," *Los Angeles Times*, February 9, 1931; "Rehearsal of Pageant Announced," *Los Angeles Times*, February 14, 1931; "Spectacle Set for Tomorrow," *Los Angeles Times*, February 15, 1931; "Coronation Pageant to Be Tonight," *Los Angeles Times*, February 16, 1931.

Chickens Come Home review: Reviews, *Photoplay*, August 1931.

"Two tried and true troupers": Short Subjects of the Month, *Photoplay*, June 1931.

"especially effective": Review of *Love Fever*, *Exhibitors Herald-World*, November 15, 1930.

"the cleverest of the new line": Review of *Love Fever*, *Exhibitors Herald-World*, November 1, 1930.

"Don't go": Muriel Babcock, "Hollywood's Going Highbrow!," *Silver Screen*, August 1931.

"When I am invited to parties": Hall, "Tragic to Be Beautiful."

Teaming of Thelma and ZaSu: Ralph Wilk, Hollywood Flashes, *Film Daily*, March 4, 1931; advertisement for the Pitts/Todd shorts, *Film Daily*, June 26, 1931; Personalities A-View, *Los Angeles Times*, July 5, 1931.

Ivan Lebedeff: Harry Lang, "He Is the Real Thing," *Photoplay*, November 1931.

"I had a few qualms": Hunter, "Blonde Menace."

"I want a home": Ibid.

9. Alison Loyd Meets a Married Man

Roland West: Descriptions of his life and career appear in various newspaper reports, including the *Los Angeles Times* articles "Quits Grocery for Producing," January 10, 1926; "Wests Return from Extended Cruise," January 22, 1933; "Roland West, Veteran Film Director, Dies," April 1, 1952; and "Final Tribute Paid Director Roland West," April 3, 1952.

Jewel Carmen: Description of her life and career appear in various newspaper reports, including the *Los Angeles Times* articles "Jewel Carmen Returns," April 24, 1918; "Jewel Carmen Wins," July 11, 1919; "Jewel Carmen Carries On," April 11, 1926; "Alimony Given to Ex-Actress," December 21, 1939; and "Suit Settled by Ex-Actress," November 29, 1940. Also William Donati, *The Life and Death of Thelma Todd* (Jefferson, NC: McFarland, 2012), 48ff.; Billy Doyle, "Jewel Carmen: Shaded in Scandal," *Classic Images*, May 1999, www.classicimages.com/1999/may99/carmen .html (page no longer available).

"to take the taint of comedy away": Let's Talk About Hollywood, *Modern Screen*, December 1931.

"It is an attempt to change her personality": Dan Thomas, "How Thelma Became a New Woman," *Independent* (Helena, MT), October 11, 1931.

"I've yet to be entirely pleased": Elsi Que, "Blond and Fancy-Free," *Picture Play*, April 1931.

"Everyone has always thought of Thelma Todd": Thomas, "New Woman."

"I'll have to change her name to Susie Zilch": Let's Talk About Hollywood, *Modern Screen*, December 1931.

Name change problems: "Corsair Holds Much Action and Romance," *Los Angeles Times*, December 20, 1931; advertisement for *Corsair*, *Los Angeles Times*, December 22 and 24, 1931; Looking Them Over, *Movie Classic*, October 1931; "Thelma Todd Changing from Comedy to Dramatic Roles, Also Changes Name," *Frederick Post*, August 5, 1931; Thomas, "New Woman"; untitled article, *Photoplay*, October 1931.

"kind of odd guy": Quote from William Bakewell, filed in George Eells Papers, Arizona State University Libraries Special Collections, Tempe, AZ.

"a sinister, sneaky kind of guy": Rudy Schafer Jr., correspondence with Benny Drinnon, collection of Benny Drinnon.

"I believe in divorce": Alice L. Tildesley, "Why Beauty Contest Winners Are Failures," *Oakland Tribune*, November 1, 1931.

Thelma "was rumored to have been quite fond": Llewellyn Carroll, "What Hollywood Did to a New England Schoolmarm," *Photoplay*, February 1932.

"a real Hollywood Mystery Romance": Let's Talk About Hollywood, *Modern Screen*, December 1931.

"It just didn't work out": Gladys Hall, "It's Tragic to Be Beautiful," *Movie Mirror*, March 1932.

"One who's about ten years older": Catherine Hunter, "Blonde Menace," *Screen Play*, February 1932.

10. I Love You, I Love You Not

"I will take the necessary legal steps": Dan Thomas, "How Thelma Became a New Woman," *Independent* (Helena, MT), October 11, 1931.

Mae Whitehead: Mae's granddaughter Robyn Osborne, interview by the author, September 6, 2012.

Social events of Thelma and ZaSu: Grace Kingsley, Heard in Hollywood, *Los Angeles Times*, September 21, 1931; Cal York, Monthly Broadcast from Hollywood, *Photoplay*, December 1931.

"has many laughs": Review of *The Pajama Party*, *Film Daily*, October 18, 1931.

Monkey Business reviews: *Los Angeles Times*, September 21, 1931; *Silver Screen*, January 1932.

New Dominoes clubhouse: Margaret Nye, Society of Cinemaland, *Los Angeles Times*, September 27, 1931; Grace Kingsley, "Hi-ho-ing with the Dominoes," *Los Angeles Times*, October 18, 1931.

"Some of the roles are not too pleasing": Thelma Todd, letter to Irish fan Mr. Cloney, October 30, 1931, collection of Benny Drinnon.

Corsair reviews: *Film Daily*, November 22, 1931; *Silver Screen*, February 1932; *Screenland*, February 1932.

New Dominoes revue and radio play: Today's Radio High Lights, *Los Angeles Times*, February 27, 1932; News of the Cafes, *Los Angeles Times*, March 2, 1932; Grace Kingsley, Hobnobbing in Movieland, *Los Angeles Times*, March 13, 1932.

The Big Timer reviews: *Modern Screen*, June 1932; *Motion Picture Herald*, March 26 and April 16, 1932; *Hollywood Filmograph*, March 19, 1932.

Horse Feathers review: Norbert Lusk, "Marx Brothers Score Real Hit," *Los Angeles Times*, August 21, 1932.

"a tepid farce": Review of *This Is the Night*, *Picture Play*, July 1932.

"sophisticated and highly spiced": Review of *This Is the Night*, *Photoplay*, June 1932.

May Company appearance: Advertisement, *Los Angeles Times*, May 1, 1932; Marian Manners, Requested Recipes, *Los Angeles Times*, May 2, 1932.

"Black Outs a la New Yorker": Untitled article, *Modern Screen*, June 1932.

"I have annoying habits": Gladys Hall, "It's Tragic to Be Beautiful," *Movie Mirror*, March 1932.

"Something he had bought and paid for": Ibid.

"Naturally we were thrown together a bit": A. L. Wooldridge, "Is Ronald in Love?," *Picture Play*, April 1932.

"[I'm] just like any normal girl": Catherine Hunter, "Blonde Menace," *Screen Play*, February 1932.

"Hollywood marriages are not that successful": David Ingram, "Thelma Todd Life Story," chapter 10, *Boston Daily Record*, circa May–June 1932, Lawrence History Center, Lawrence, MA.

Pat De Cicco: Michelle Morgan, *Marilyn Monroe: Private and Confidential* (New York: Skyhorse, 2012), 130–131.

"He was insanely jealous": Hunter, "Blonde Menace."

Dancing with other men at Hillcrest Country Club: Grace Kingsley's column, *Los Angeles Times*, July 24, 1932.

Olympic International Ball: "Screen Star Hostesses for Grand Ball Chosen," *Los Angeles Times*, July 27, 1932; "Celebrities of Films to Play Hosts," *Los Angeles Times*, August 3, 1932.

Fire at the Brown Derby: Unknown newspaper, August 28, 1932, Benny Drinnon's blog, http://benny-drinnon.blogspot.co.uk/2014/07/newspaper-article-thelma-todd-fire-at.html.

Speak Easily review: *Photoplay*, September 1932.

Klondike reviews: *Film Daily*, September 24, 1932; *Photoplay*, November 1932; *Educational Screen*, December 1932; *Hollywood Filmograph*, September 17, 1932.

Call Her Savage fight scene: Dorothy Manners, Looking Them Over, *Movie Classic*, January 1933; Grace Kingsley's column, *Los Angeles Times*, October 12, 1932; "Clara Bow Back on Screen," *Los Angeles Times*, December 2, 1932; Cal York, Monthly Broadcast from Hollywood, *Photoplay*, December 1932.

Thelma's peritonitis: "Thelma Todd Seriously Ill," *Lowell Sun*, October 14, 1932; "Thelma Todd Recovers from Major Operation," *Moorhead Daily News*, October 15, 1932; "Thelma Todd Past Crisis," *Pittsburgh Press*, October 15, 1932; "Film Star Is Said Recovering," *Sandusky Star Journal*, October 18, 1932; "Actress Paid Last Honor," *Los Angeles Times*, November 7, 1932; and Jim Brubaker, correspondence with the author, April 2012.

Something of a "shotgun" affair: Hal Roach, interview by Jim Brubaker, circa 1980s, relayed to the author in April 2012.

"as wise to the ways of these openings": Dan Thomas's column, *Lowell Sun*, January 23, 1933.

"[My mother] is a companion": Elsi Que, "Blond and Fancy-Free," *Picture Play*, April 1931.

Car accident and hospital stay: "Thelma Todd Injured," *Los Angeles Times*, January 23, 1933; Hobnobbing in Hollywood, *Los Angeles Times*, February 6, 1933; "Thelma Todd Hurt in Crash," *San Antonio Light*, January 24, 1933; "Injuries of Thelma Todd Serious," *Lowell Sun*, January 24, 1933.

Plans for a film in London: "Thelma Todd," *Los Angeles Times*, April 22, 1933; Thelma's travel records, from UK, Incoming Passenger Lists, 1878–1960, Ancestry.com.

Thelma's comments to the press in Chicago: "Thelma Todd to Wed Again but She Doesn't Say Who," *Milwaukee Sentinel*, April 28, 1933.

Rumors of Thelma's impending divorce: "Thelma Todd and Her Husband Will Split," *Hollywood Reporter*, May 3, 1933.

11. London Calling

Thelma's love for London: "They Shine in Other Ways," *Daily Mirror*, August 20, 1934; "Thelma Todd Looks Ahead," *Film Pictorial*, August 17, 1935.

"a bit of a thrill": Thelma Todd, "Thelma Todd Didn't Know She Was a Real Countess," unknown source, n.d., George Eells Papers, Arizona State University Libraries Special Collections, Tempe, AZ.

Studio electrician on American actresses: What the Fans Think, *Picture Play*, November 1934.

"I've never had such a thrill": Nora Laing, "Thelma Todd Looks Ahead," *Film Pictorial*, August 17, 1935.

Thelma's night out at the Café de Paris: "Morton Downey—the Famous American, Radio, Film and Recording Star. Filmed at Cafe de Paris, London," British Pathé video, July 17, 1933, 2:33, www.britishpathe.com/video/morton-downey/.

Dennis Banks, Jerry Horwin, and Dorchester Hotel robbery: Rambling Reporter, *Hollywood Reporter*, June 1 and June 15, 1933.

Ida Lupino on Thelma's health issues: William Donati, *The Life and Death of Thelma Todd* (Jefferson, NC: McFarland, 2012), 76–77.

Thelma's interest in Einstein: Hal Roach publicity material, 1931, collection of Craig Calman.

Thelma's reaction to Glasgow mob: "Einstein Missed by Crowd While Film Star Is Mobbed," *Glasgow Daily Record*, June 20, 1933.

"I'm really sorry": "American Film Star Mobbed," *Aberdeen Journal*, June 20, 1933.

"gather her carefully arranged bouquets": "Brief Fame," *Glasgow Herald*, June 21, 1933.

"Thelma speaks at first-hand": Kinoman, "U.S. Film Star in Glasgow," *Glasgow Evening Times*, June 20, 1933.

"thrilling instances": "Einstein Missed by Crowd," *Glasgow Daily Record*.

"When Thelma Todd and her husband": Untitled article, *Photoplay*, July 1933.

"You would be too": "No Divorce for Thelma," *Lowell Sun*, July 6, 1933.

"In Hollywood one has as much privacy": Ibid.

"With so many being discussed": "Thelma, Off by Air, Denies Divorce Talk," *Boston Daily Globe*, July 6, 1933.

"Is that the best kiss": "No Public Necking for Actress," *Los Angeles Times*, July 10, 1933.

Thelma's wedding anniversary: "No Divorce for Thelma," *Lowell Sun*.

"fails to click": Review of *Cheating Blondes*, *Film Daily*, May 20, 1933.

"Miss Todd is as pictorial as ever": Review of *Cheating Blondes*, *Variety*, May 23, 1933.

12. Marriage Does Interfere with a Career

"swell to me": Dena Reed, "Spice of the Show," *Picture Play*, May 1935.

"I never fell in my life": Gladys Hall, "'Tis the Likes of the Kelly You'll Be After Liking Now," *Motion Picture*, January 1937.

"Those first days," "blue, busted and disgusted," and "Get off, Kelly": Sara Hamilton, "How Thelma Todd Is Haunting Patsy Kelly," unknown magazine, n.d., author's collection.

"may creep gradually on": Thelma Todd, "How I Was Groomed for Stardom," *Film Weekly*, June 30, 1933.

Patsy Kelly's crash: "Girl in Malin Auto to Live," *Los Angeles Times*, August 11, 1933; "Patsy Kelly to Leave Hospital," *Los Angeles Times*, August 19, 1933; "Patsy Is Recovering Fast," *Hollywood Filmograph*, August 19, 1933.

"It did things to me": Dena Reed, "Spice of the Show."

"She was a smart girl": "'Tis the Likes of the Kelly," *Motion Picture*.

Thelma throwing plates at the new publicity director: Jeanette Meehan, "Thelma Todd 'Behind the Movie Screen' Story: Actress Loved Hollywood, Its Glamour and Fame," syndicated nationally, including in *Syracuse Herald*, December 28, 1935.

"overcome the handicaps of such trite material": Review of *I'll Be Suing You*, *Variety*, October 30, 1934.

"lowdown nonsense": Review of *Sing Sister Sing*, *Variety*, November 20, 1934.

Changes to Thelma's will: Thelma Todd, will dated September 19, 1933, available for purchase from Celebrity Collectables' Celebrity Archive, www.celebritycollectables .com.

"sulk for a while": "Marriage Does Interfere with a Career," RKO publicity department, circa 1933, George Eells Papers, Arizona State University Libraries Special Collections, Tempe, AZ.

You Made Me Love You reviews: *Daily Mirror*, November 24, 1933; *Los Angeles Times*, December 8 and December 17, 1933; *Hollywood Filmograph*, December 9, 1933; *Yorkshire Post*, January 2, 1934.

Hal Roach Studios banquet: "Hal Roach Dined by More Than 500," *Film Daily*, December 9, 1933; Hobnobbing in Hollywood, *Los Angeles Times*, December 9, 1933; Tip Poff, That Certain Party, *Los Angeles Times*, December 10, 1933.

RKO contract: "Thelma Todd Signed to Long Term Contract by RKO-Radio Pictures," *Hollywood Filmograph*, December 2, 1933; "Thelma Todd Gets Long Term Contract," *Lowell Sun*, December 9, 1933.

Thelma's divorce: Details appeared in many newspapers, including "Thelma Todd Seeks Divorce," *Lowell Sun*, February 23, 1934; untitled article, *Oshkosh Northwestern*, February 24, 1934; "Actress Asks Her Freedom," *Los Angeles Times*, February 24, 1934; "Screen Blond Nods, Divorced," *Los Angeles Times*, March 3, 1934; "Thelma Todd Gets Divorced from Agent-Husband," *Charleston Gazette*, March 3, 1934; "Thelma Todd Wins Divorce," *New York Times*, March 3, 1934; and "Thelma Todd Says Yes, Wins Divorce," *Oakland Tribune*, March 2, 1934.

"pleasure loving and temperamental": "Di Cicco [*sic*] Ridicules Theory of Foul Play," *Los Angeles Evening Herald and Express*, December 19, 1935.

"All this talk": "Hotel Left by Di Cicco [*sic*]," *Los Angeles Times*, December 20, 1935.

13. Castellammare

Castellammare development: Details appeared in newspapers at various times, including in the *Los Angeles Times* articles "Community Development: Beach Tract to Rank with Best," November 23, 1924; "Pattern Coast Area on Italy," October 11, 1925; "Pedestrian Span Nears Completion," June 6, 1926; "Warm Weather Boosts Seaside Property Sales," May 15, 1927; "Film Notables Plan Dwellings," October 30, 1927; and Peg o' Los Angeles, July 29, 1928.

Carl Curtis's death: "Full List of Pupils Expected," *Los Angeles Times*, August 28, 1932; "School Owner Takes Own Life," *Los Angeles Times*, December 15, 1932; "Curtis Memory Wins Laudation," *Los Angeles Times*, January 22, 1933.

The café "had the finest and best equipment": Roland West, testimony during the coroner's inquest, the transcript of which is available for purchase from Celebrity Collectables' Celebrity Archive, www.celebritycollectables.com.

"bosom friend": "Hat Is Mystery in Mrs. West's Story," *Los Angeles Evening Herald and Express*, December 19, 1935.

"We write our own stories": Frederick Russell, "They Nicknamed Her 'Hot Toddy,'" *Film Pictorial*, April 15, 1933.

"Comedy teaches one to act": Ibid.

"Whoever hears of them now?": Nora Laing, "Thelma Todd Looks Ahead," *Film Pictorial*, August 17, 1935.

"their hopes shattered": Thelma Todd, "How I Was Groomed for Stardom," *Film Weekly*, June 30, 1933.

"My pal's dead": Grace Kingsley, Romping Through Hollywood, *Los Angeles Times*, April 6, 1930.

"I like to keep my finger on the pulse": Laing, "Thelma Todd Looks Ahead."

"I always did like to cook": "Film Folk Mourn Thelma Todd, Beauty Winner Who Made Good," *Lawrence Evening Tribune*, December 18, 1935.

"When the studios no longer want me": Laing, "Thelma Todd Looks Ahead."

"I might have to accept a pair of shoes": "Shadows of Four Darken Probe," *Xenia Evening Gazette*, January 3, 1936.

The chef's temper tantrums: Rudy Schafer Jr., correspondence with Benny Drinnon, collection of Benny Drinnon.

Family visit: "Brilliant Career of Beautiful Thelma Todd," *Lawrence Evening Tribune*, December 17, 1935; "Kin in Lawrence Mourn Actress," *Boston Globe*, December 17, 1935.

Court troubles: "Something New—Reps Sue Each Other," *Hollywood Reporter*, February 13, 1934; "Agents Settle Fight," *Hollywood Reporter*, February 16, 1934; "Thelma Todd and Ex-Mate Sued for Rent, *Los Angeles Times*, October 6, 1934.

"It was nice of you to have air-mailed": Letter to Lee Heidorn, November 6, 1934, Benny Drinnon's blog, http://benny-drinnon.blogspot.co.uk/2013/12/thelma-todd-letter .html.

"This picture is a sort of farce": Molly Marsh, "Thelma Todd Hollywood Cocktail," *Milwaukee Journal*, November 18, 1934.

14. All Good Things

"[I] snuck away on the yacht": Letter to unidentified person, n.d., Benny Drinnon's blog, http://benny-drinnon.blogspot.co.uk/2013/12/autograph-thelma-todd-letters.html.

"tall dark gentleman": Malcolm H. Oettinger, "Recipe for an Elegant Evening," *Picture Play*, February 1935.

Letters from the Ace: "Mystery Extortionist Threatens Miss Todd," *Los Angeles Times*, March 6, 1935; untitled article, *Manitowoc Herald Times*, March 7, 1935; "Letter Threats Investigated," *Reno Evening Gazette*, March 7, 1935; "Extortion Threats Rare in Hollywood," *Daily Boston Globe*, March 8, 1935; and many pages of the FBI files, collection of Benny Drinnon.

"suitably worried": "Mystery Extortionist," *Los Angeles Times*. Also untitled article, *Manitowoc Herald Times*, March 7, 1935; "Threatened," *New Castle News*, March 8, 1935.

"This Thelma Todd matter": "Letter Threats," *Reno Evening Gazette*.

"very upset by the whole matter": "New Alarm in Todd Case," *Los Angeles Times*, March 7, 1935.

Harry Carr's comments: "The Lancer—Kidnap Threats," *Los Angeles Times*, August 24, 1935.

Thelma's sandwich tips: Thelma Todd, "Hints on Fine Art of Sandwiches," *Adelaide News*, March 23, 1935.

Eileen Sedgwick party: Tip Poff, That Certain Party, *Los Angeles Times*, May 19, 1935.

"Will be waiting for signal": This and copies of other extortion letters were in FBI files.

California Pacific International Exposition: "Hollywood's Elect to Help Greet Foreign Visitors at Opening of World's Fair," *Los Angeles Times*, May 26, 1935; "Screen Stars Attend Fair," *Los Angeles Times*, June 2, 1935.

Thelma travels to Hollywood Boulevard: Untitled clipping, *New York Evening Journal*, December 26, 1935, George Eells Papers, Arizona State University Libraries Special Collections, Tempe, AZ.

Thelma's perfume collection: Untitled article, *Photoplay*, December 1934.

Thelma's house is burgled: "Burglars Escape with Thelma Todd £3000 Wardrobe," *Syracuse Herald*, June 28, 1935; "Thelma Todd Residence Plundered by Burglars," *Los Angeles Times*, June 28, 1935.

Thelma "has a lovely flat": An Explorer, "Eating with the Stars," *Perth Western Mail*, March 28, 1935.

"it will be tough on you": FBI files.

West puts bars on the windows: Roland West, testimony during the coroner's inquest, the transcript of which is available for purchase from Celebrity Collectables' Celebrity Archive, www.celebritycollectables.com.

"Thelma Todd has a bit and no more": Review of *After the Dance*, *Independent Exhibitors Film Bulletin*, August 21, 1935.

"Nancy Carroll has little to do": Review of *After the Dance*, *Variety*, August 21, 1935.

Glass in Thelma's food: Mae's granddaughter Robyn Osborne, interview by the author, September 6, 2012.

Fan letter received from Newton Avenue: FBI files.

"Oh, I'm so relieved": "Man Seized in Todd Case," *Los Angeles Times*, August 19, 1935.

The Bohemian Girl: Oliver Hardy, letter to his wife, Myrtle, November 25, 1935, sold by Bonhams auction house in November 2013 and viewable at www.bonhams.com /auctions/21427/lot/13/; Sam W. B. Cohn, memo to Joe Rivkin, in Craig Calman, *100 Years of Brodies with Hal Roach* (Albany, GA: BearManor Media, 2014), 187–188.

Lee Heidorn's memories: Michael G. Ankerich, "Dove Tails—Lee Lunches with Thelma Todd and Visits Jean Harlow on the Set," *Close-Ups and Long Shots* (blog), February 24, 2012, https://michaelgankerich.wordpress.com/2012/02/24/dove-tails-lee -lunches-with-thelma-todd-and-visits-jean-harlow-on-the-set/.

Thelma's destruction of later threatening letters: FBI files.

"protect Schimanski": "Seized as Writer of Extortion Notes," *New York Times*, November 8, 1935.

Arrest of Edward Schiffert, handwriting analysis, and letters from psychiatrists: FBI files.

Thanksgiving ritual, and memories of Reverend Proppe: "Notables Bow Heads," *Los Angeles Times*, December 20, 1935.

Generosity toward Mae Whitehead's baby son: Granddaughter Robyn Osborne, interview by the author.

Fan who asked to be Thelma's chauffeur: Llewellyn Carroll, "What Hollywood Did to a New England Schoolmarm," *Photoplay*, February 1932.

"You see, there is no place in Hollywood": Nora Laing, "Thelma Todd Looks Ahead," *Film Pictorial*, August 17, 1935.

"I'm going to have some new ideas": "Film Folk Mourn Thelma Todd, Beauty Winner Who Made Good," *Lawrence Evening Tribune*, December 18, 1935.

"She was greatly upset": "Kin in Lawrence Mourn Actress," *Boston Globe*, December 17, 1935.

Rudy Schafer Jr.'s memories of the gambling room: Rudy Schafer Jr., correspondence with Benny Drinnon, collection of Benny Drinnon.

Other gambling room details: "Gamblers' War Cause of Killing," *Independent* (Helena, MT), December 20, 1935; untitled clippings, *New York Evening Journal*, December 19, 1935, and *New York Daily News*, December 18, 1935, both in George Eells Papers.

"aroused hostility": "Miss Todd Reported Seen Long After 'Death Hour,'" *Los Angeles Times*, December 19, 1935. Also described in untitled clipping, *New York Daily News*, December 18, 1935, George Eells Papers; "Hearing Opens Tomorrow in Mystery," *Los Angeles Evening Herald and Express*, December 19, 1935; and "Gamblers' War," *Independent* (Helena, MT).

15. The Gangsters

This chapter draws from various photographs and articles related to Tony Cornero, including the following *Los Angeles Times* pieces: "Three Seized in Campaign to Keep Reported Gangsters in Southland," November 18, 1931;"Clara Bow Sued Again," December 3, 1931; "Eight Held Guilty of Gambling," January 6, 1933; "Plea Made for Divorce by Cornero," May 31, 1934; "Cruelty Tale Gives Divorce to Cornero," June 23, 1934; Albert F. Nathan, "What's Become of the Rum-Runners," September 16, 1934; "New Pirate Arrest Near," August 8, 1935; "Gaming Ship Halts Play," October 29, 1935; "Cornero Hit by Tax Lien," November 28, 1935;"Sea Gaming Plan Fought," May 2, 1938; "Ban Put on Gambling Ship with Aid of Court Order," May 27, 1938; advertisement "There is only one Rex," May 8, 1939; "State Sues Cornero for $496,000 Penalties," October 26, 1939; "500 Crowd Chapel for Tony Cornero Funeral," August 5, 1955; L.A. Scene: The City Then and Now, June 27, 1994; "Ruler of an L.A. Gambling Empire Had a Softer Side," April 11, 2012.

Sources from other papers include: Alan Balboni, "Tony Cornero," *Las Vegas Review-Journal*, February 7, 1999; "Gives Self Up," *New Castle News*, November 7, 1929; "Gangster Keeps Promise to Give Coast Officer Machine Gun," *Salt Lake Tribune*, December 24, 1929; "Clara Bow and Rex Bell Sued," *Galveston Daily News*, December 3, 1931; untitled article, *Nevada State Journal*, March 3, 1932; "Four Killed in Accidents," *Nevada State Journal*, July 15, 1941; "Probe Opens as Gambler Tony Cornero Stricken," *Nevada State Journal*, August 2, 1955; "Frank Cornero and Sister Guilty, Dry-Law Violation," *Bakersfield Californian*, December 2, 1933; "Cornero Better; to Try to Identify First Suspect," *Bakersfield Californian*, February 11, 1948; "Tony Cornero's Widow Arrested," *Bakersfield Californian*, January 17, 1956; "New Hotel Work Starts at Vegas," *Reno Evening Gazette*, May 14, 1931; "Three Are Dead in Nevada Crashes," *Reno Evening Gazette*, July 14, 1941; "Meadow Burns in Clark County," *Reno Evening Gazette*, February 9, 1943; "Gambling Ship Ban Demanded," *Reno Evening Gazette*, June 13, 1946; untitled article, *Hayward Review*, August 10, 1946; "Ship Not Used for Purpose Licensed, Government Says," *Corona Daily Independent*, September 17, 1946; "Howser Aide Replies to Charge," *Oakland Tribune*, October 4, 1946; "Pacific Coast Gambler Shot," *Charleston Daily Mail*,

February 10, 1948; "Tony Cornero Not in L.B. Gambling," *Long Beach Independent,*
April 23, 1948; "Admiral Outsmarts Nevada with Casino," *Syracuse Herald American,*
July 24, 1955; "Gambler Tony Cornero Dies; Brother to Take Over Hotel," *Oxnard
Press Courier,* August 1, 1955; "Louis Cornero to Manage Hotel," *Humboldt Standard,*
August 2, 1955.

Also Ernest Marquez, *Noir Afloat: Tony Cornero and the Notorious Gambling Ships of
Southern California* (Santa Monica, CA: Angel City, 2011).

Charles "Lucky" Luciano and gangsters in general: "Gang Slayer Suspect Kills Self with
Gas," *Jefferson City Sunday News and Tribune,* October 27, 1935; "Termed Successors
to Schultz," *Greenville Record-Argus,* October 29, 1935; "Gangsters Refuse to Talk,
Probe of Slayings Blanked," *Huntingdon Daily News,* November 7, 1935; "Held in
Shooting of 3 Pedestrians," *New York Times,* September 1, 1933; "Federal Men List
Racket 'Big Shots' in Tax Drive Here," *New York Times,* May 20, 1935; "Usury Racket
Stirred Gang War," *New York Times,* October 25, 1935; "Criminals' Tricks Spur
Law Reform," *New York Times,* December 1, 1935; "Mussing Up Ordering in Gang
Chase," *Los Angeles Times,* October 30, 1935.

"the finest thing in the entire state": "New Hotel Work Starts at Vegas," *Reno Evening
Gazette.*

Sidewalk Café's similarity to the Meadows: See photo of the Meadows at This Week in
Gaming History, Museum of Gaming History, April 27, 2014, www
.museumofgaminghistory.org/mogh.php?p=history&sd=1398571200.

Ransom handoff at Thelma Todd's café: Matt Weinstock, "Little Known Tale of State's Top
Ransom," *Los Angeles Times,* December 17, 1963.

"the defiance that lawless elements have": "Gambling Ship Ban Demanded," *Reno Evening
Gazette.*

Rex's "law enforcement room": Comments made by Governor Earl Warren, mentioned in
ibid.

"She told me she was opposed to gambling": "Actress Deeply Troubled, but Gay, Says
Attorney," *Los Angeles Times,* December 25, 1935.

16. A Change Is Coming

Elements of this chapter draw from the official coroner's inquest report, the transcript of
which is available for purchase from Celebrity Collectables' Celebrity Archive, www
.celebritycollectables.com.

Billing order in Thelma's contract: Sam W. B. Cohn, Western Union telegram to Joe
Rivkin, December 6, 1935, collection of Craig Calman.

Other positive career developments: Reported in several newspapers, including "Story of
Todd Row Scouted by West," *Los Angeles Evening Herald and Express,* December 28,
1935.

"I wish I could get back to Elstree": "Thelma Todd Dead in Car After 3 am Party," *Daily
Express* (UK), December 17, 1935.

"Always I must be the other woman": Elsi Que, "Blond and Fancy-Free," *Picture Play,* April
1931.

"Why doesn't Hollywood give Thelma Todd": Letters, *Picture Play,* May 1935.

"I'll tell you why": Ibid., August 1935.

Shopping trip with ZaSu Pitts, and comments to Helen Ainsworth: "Miss Todd's Evil
    Fate Fear Told Grand Jury," *Los Angeles Times*, December 25, 1935; "West Ready to
    Disclose Todd 'Guest,'" *Los Angeles Times*, December 28, 1935; "ZaSu Pitts Called by
    Todd Case Jury," *New York Times*, December 25, 1935.
"We were all so silly together": Don Gallery, interview by the author, 2012.
Fight in the café: Untitled clipping, *New York Daily News*, December 27, 1935, George
    Eells Papers, Arizona State University Libraries Special Collections, Tempe, AZ;
    "Actress Reported Severely Beaten Just Before Death," *Bismarck Tribune*, December
    27, 1935; "Report Man Gave Beating to Thelma Todd," *Fitchburg Sentinel*, December
    27, 1935; "Puzzle Stays—Grand Jury Unable to Solve Thelma Todd Mystery,"
    Southeast Missourian, December 28, 1935; "Fight Linked to Death of Miss Todd," *Los
    Angeles Times*, December 27, 1935.
Thelma crying with her mother: Several newspapers, including untitled clipping, *New York
    American*, December 30, 1935, George Eells Papers.

17. Farewell

Elements of this chapter draw from the official coroner's inquest report, the transcript of
    which is available for purchase from Celebrity Collectables' Celebrity Archive, www
    .celebritycollectables.com.
"I was struck by her charm": Unidentified clipping, n.d., George Eells Papers, Arizona State
    University Libraries Special Collections, Tempe, AZ.
De Cicco turning up at the party: "West Ready to Disclose Todd 'Guest,'" *Los Angeles
    Times*, December 28, 1935; "Todd Death Night Phone Call Traced," *Los Angeles
    Times*, December 29, 1935; "Thelma Todd Wanted Death," *Nottingham Evening Post*,
    January 3, 1936. Quotes from Pat also appear in "Thelma Todd Feared Gang's Bullets,
    Claim," *La Crosse Tribune and Leader Press*, December 18, 1935; and "Dramatic
    Testimony at Thelma Todd Inquest," *Los Angeles Evening Herald and Express*,
    December 28, 1935.
"Pat learned that Miss Todd": Untitled clipping, *New York American*, December 24, 1935,
    George Eells Papers.
Margaret Lindsay's memories of the party: Ibid.
"I'm in the midst of the most marvelous romance": This statement and details on the
    search for the man in question were repeated many times during the investigation and
    reported in dozens of newspapers, including "Todd Death Probe Not to Be Dropped
    by LA Officials," *Nevada State Journal*, January 2, 1936; "Seek Clues to 'Last Love' of
    Actress," *Los Angeles Evening Herald and Express*, December 28, 1935; and "Thelma
    Todd's Romance with San Francisco Man Revealed," *Los Angeles Examiner*, December
    24, 1935.
"When she came back": "Tiff Precedes Actress' Death," *San Antonio Express*, December 18,
    1935.
Roland West's memories of the Grauman call: Testimony during the coroner's inquest.
"[The Sidewalk Café] closed about 2 o'clock": "Host at Trocadero Party Says Actress
    Cheerful," *Los Angeles Times*, December 17, 1935.
"Don't let Hollywood change you": "Tiff Precedes Actress' Death," *San Antonio Express*.
"The irony": "Film Actor Tells 'Last Dance' with Actress at Café," *Los Angeles Evening
    Herald and Express*, December 19, 1935.

Ernest Peters' memories of the trip back to the café: All taken from testimony during the coroner's inquest.

18. The Discovery

This chapter draws from photographs of the crime scene found on eBay and other Internet sites and in the collection of Jill Kaiser Adams, as well as testimony given by various people during the inquest, including Captain Bruce F. Clark, Dr. A. F. Wagner, Robert "Bob" Anderson, Harvey Priester, and Russel Monroe. The transcript from the inquest is available for purchase from Celebrity Collectables' Celebrity Archive, www .celebritycollectables.com.

Details of the car engine choking off: Car salesman Robert H. Cooper told the coroner's inquest about the car having dirty spark plugs during the investigation. Also "Jury Calls Witnesses for Todd Death Probe," *Los Angeles Evening Herald and Express*, December 19, 1935.

Autopsy findings: Taken from the official coroner's inquest report, as well as "Coroner Says Collapse Preceded Star's Death," *Los Angeles Times*, December 18, 1935.

"She ascribed it to the condition of her heart": "Actress' Faint in Surf Told by Wife of West," *Los Angeles Times*, December 18, 1935.

"She was in perfect health": "Hunt 2 Missing Witnesses in Film Star Case," *Los Angeles Evening Post-Record*, circa December 19, 1935.

"Either Miss Todd": "Surprises Mark Todd Death Case," *Berkeley Daily Gazette*, December 31, 1935.

De Cicco thinking the inquest had already been held: "Ex-Husband Flies East," *Los Angeles Times*, December 18, 1935.

De Cicco interviewed in New York: "Hotel Left by Di Cicco [sic]," *Los Angeles Times*, December 20, 1935; "Di Cicco [sic] Ridicules Theory of Foul Play," *Los Angeles Evening Herald and Express*, December 19, 1935.

De Cicco's comments to the grand jury: "Todd Inquiry May Be Closed," *Edwardsville Intelligencer*, December 28, 1935; "Ex-Husband Scouts Todd Suicide Hints," *Los Angeles Evening Herald and Express*, December 28, 1935.

"Thelma passed away": "Kin in Lawrence Mourn Actress," *Boston Globe*, December 17, 1935.

"She was such a fine girl": Ibid.

"Thought I'd be handing": "Brilliant Career of Beautiful Thelma Todd," *Lawrence Evening Tribune*, December 17, 1935.

"She has so much to live for": "Death Parts Film Team: Patsy Kelly Collapses," *Los Angeles Times*, December 17, 1935; "Patsy Kelly Collapses," *Lawrence Evening Tribune*, December 17, 1935.

Charley Chase's sadness: Craig Calman, *100 Years of Brodies with Hal Roach* (Albany, GA: BearManor Media, 2014), 189.

"shocked beyond words": "Death Parts Film Team," *Los Angeles Times*.

19. Death According to West

Roland West's version of events was gleaned from the official coroner's inquest report. I also referred to bartender Robert "Bob" Anderson's answers. The transcript from the

inquest is available for purchase from Celebrity Collectables' Celebrity Archive, www
.celebritycollectables.com.

"or answer the contrary at your peril": Coroner's summons of jurors, collection of Tegan
Summer.

West's different versions of the dog story: Coroner's inquest transcript, as well as "Body of
Thelma Todd Found in Death Riddle," *Los Angeles Times*, December 17, 1935; "Thelma
Todd Death Probe Continues," *Circleville (OH) Herald*, December 17, 1935; "Thelma
Todd Movie Actress Found Dead in Auto," *Bismarck Tribune*, December 17, 1935.

The inaudible engine: "Todd Death Tests Made," *Los Angeles Times*, December 23, 1935.

C. Harry Smith's memories: "Tragedy Garage Sleeper Tells of His Movements," *Los Angeles
Times*, December 20, 1935.

20. The Case Is Closed

"All right, that is all the evidence we have": The closing comments of the coroner's inquest,
the transcript of which is available for purchase from Celebrity Collectables' Celebrity
Archive, www.celebritycollectables.com.

"I'm so sorry she was called so early": "Pathos Treads Path Past Bier of Thelma," *Los Angeles
Evening Herald and Express*, December 19, 1935.

"She would never let a whole day pass": Edwin Schallert, "Thelma Todd's Mother Discloses
Own Story," *Los Angeles Times*, December 20, 1935.

Thelma's funeral: "Star Was in Fear of Threats of Kidnapping," *Lawrence Evening Tribune*,
December 18, 1935; "New Mystery Injected into Thelma Todd's Death," *Port Arthur
News*, December 19, 1935; "Thousands Rich and Poor Pay Last Tribute to Thelma
Todd," *Los Angeles Evening Herald and Express*, December 19, 1935.

"In her going, I have lost": "Notables Bow Heads," *Los Angeles Times*, December 20, 1935.

"Now Mrs. Todd": Letter to Alice Todd, in the FBI files, collection of Benny Drinnon.

"Information was furnished": Letter in FBI files.

"strange and unusual things": "Mrs. Todd Quizzed on Thelma's Life," *Los Angeles Evening
Herald and Express*, December 30, 1935.

Jurors' revolt: "Thelma Todd Quiz Stirs Up Revolt in Jury's Ranks," *Logansport Pharos-
Tribune*, January 9, 1936.

"unbearable": "Death Probe Disgusts Thelma Todd's Mother," *San Antonio Express*, January
7, 1936. Alice Todd's thoughts also appear in "Actress Mother in Rage Against Los
Angeles Jury Quiz," *Salt Lake Tribune*, January 7, 1936.

"Obviously a crackpot": "Los Angeles Police Pass Up Ogden Tip on Actress' Slayer," *Salt
Lake Tribune*, March 28, 1936; "Thelma Todd Death Clue Reported by Ogden Police
Chief," *Berkeley Daily Gazette*, March 27, 1936; "Todd Death Quiz Revives," *Los
Angeles Times*, March 28, 1936.

21. The Mysterious Sightings

Phone call to Martha Ford: Details appeared in various newspapers around the country,
including "Thelma Todd Dead; Found in Garage," *New York Times*, December 17,
1935. Her story also appears in testimony during the coroner's inquest, the transcript
of which is available for purchase from Celebrity Collectables' Celebrity Archive,
www.celebritycollectables.com.

Other sightings: Stories of the cigar store sighting appeared in various newspapers, including untitled clipping, *New York Evening Journal*, December 24, 1935, George Eells Papers, Arizona State University Libraries Special Collections, Tempe, AZ; also "West Ready to Disclose Todd 'Guest,'" *Los Angeles Times*, December 28, 1935. The Christmas tree story was reported in many newspapers around the country, including "Quiz Witnesses Get Threats," *El Paso Herald-Post*, December 24, 1935. Various other sightings were reported widely, including in "The Strange Death of Thelma Todd," *Liberty Magazine*, n.d., George Eells Papers.

"I was evasive": The story given by Jewel Carmen was reported in many newspapers, including untitled clippings, *Herald Tribune*, December 19, 1935, and *New York Evening Journal*, December 19, 1935, both in George Eells Papers.

Further updates and stories on the mysterious sighting were in "Grand Jury Seeks Murder Proof in Probe of Thelma Todd's Death," *Racine (WI) Journal-Times*, December 23, 1935; "West Ready to Disclose Todd 'Guest,'" *Los Angeles Times*; and "Maid Tells of Last Hours with Thelma Todd," *Los Angeles Evening Herald and Express*, December 19, 1935.

The anonymous letter: "Kidnap Threat Adds to Todd Death Riddle," *Syracuse Herald*, December 20, 1935. Also, a copy of the letter itself was sent to me by Benny Drinnon.

Thelma's investments and arguments with West: "Movie Writer Is Summoned in Todd Case," *Ogden Standard Examiner*, December 31, 1935; "Fresh Trail Found in Enquiry," *Los Angeles Times*, December 30, 1935; "West Is Recalled to Witness Stand," *North Adams Transcript*, December 31, 1935.

"No one could row with Thelma": "Story of Todd Row Scouted by West," *Los Angeles Evening Herald and Express*, December 28, 1935.

22. The Theories

Grand jurors' visit to the café: Details can be found in various newspapers, including "Grand Jury Divides on Miss Todd's Death," *New York Times*, January 4, 1936; "Thelma Todd Jury Split in Opinions," *Montreal Gazette*, January 4, 1936; "Shadows of Four Darken Probe," *Xenia Evening Gazette*, January 3, 1936; and "Todd Suicide Key Charged," *Los Angeles Times*, January 4, 1936.

Thelma breaking the window: Roland West, testimony during the coroner's inquest, the transcript of which is available for purchase from Celebrity Collectables' Celebrity Archive, www.celebritycollectables.com.

Carbon monoxide warnings: One such warning was posted in "Monoxide Danger Grows with Winter's Approach," *Los Angeles Times*, November 1, 1931.

"too many people are woefully ignorant": "Gas Poison Perils Told," *Los Angeles Times*, January 31, 1936.

"the smartest dumb blonde": Obituary for Dorothy Gulliver, *Independent* (UK), June 13, 2001.

"I have a Cadillac": David Ingram, "Thelma Todd Life Story," chapter 10, *Boston Daily Record*, circa May–June 1932, Lawrence History Center, Lawrence, MA.

"It is apparent Miss Todd did not die accidentally": "Suicide or Murder Theory Supported Before Grand Jury," *Xenia Evening Gazette*, January 3, 1936.

"individual with the strength of any man": West, testimony during the coroner's inquest.

Schafer and Priester on the possibility of suicide: Comments come from the official
    coroner's inquest report.
Patsy Kelly on the possibility of suicide: "Thelma No Suicide Says Patsy Kelly," *Boston
    Evening American*, December 26, 1935.
ZaSu Pitts's memories and Mae Whitehead's concerns: Don Gallery, interview by the
    author, 2012; Mae's granddaughter Robyn Osborne, interview by the author,
    September 6, 2012.
Memories from retired police officers: Various members of the police force were interviewed
    by Jim Brubaker during the 1980s. Detectives' suspicions of murder at the time of the
    investigation appeared in many newspapers, including "Kidnap Note Hints Movie
    Star Slain," *Newark Advocate*, December 20, 1935; "New Evidence Indicates Murder
    of Thelma Todd," *Salt Lake Tribune*, December 20, 1935; "Says Actress May Have
    Been Slain," *Winnipeg Free Press*, December 20, 1935; "Seek Love Clues in Thelma
    Todd Death Probe," *Los Angeles Evening Herald and Express*, December 21, 1935;
    and "Mrs. Todd Quizzed on Thelma's Life," *Los Angeles Evening Herald and Express*,
    December 30, 1935.
Gagging/unconsciousness theories: "Jury to Air Miss Todd Café Deal," *Los Angeles Times*,
    December 26, 1935; "Triple Todd Clues; Hunt Man, Girl, Car," *Boston Evening
    American*, December 26, 1935; "Hearing Opens Tomorrow in Mystery," *Los Angeles
    Evening Herald and Express*, December 19, 1935; "Mrs. Todd Quizzed on Thelma's
    Life," *Los Angeles Evening Herald and Express*, December 30, 1935; "Todd Mystery
    Guest Sought," *Woodland Daily Democrat*, December 20, 1935; "Hunt 2 Missing
    Witnesses in Film Star Case," *Los Angeles Evening Post-Record*, circa December 19,
    1935; untitled clipping, *New York American*, December 26, 1935, George Eells
    Papers, Arizona State University Libraries Special Collections, Tempe, AZ; "Reports
    Miss Todd Bruised on Throat," *New York Times*, December 26, 1935.
"The swelling could be attributed": Katy King, interview by the author, February 23, 2015.
Waiter kidnap threats: "Kidnap Note Hints Movie Star Slain," *Newark Advocate*, December
    20, 1935; "Kidnap Threat Adds to Todd Death Riddle," *Syracuse Herald*, December
    20, 1935; "Witness in Todd Probe Threatened," *Oakland Tribune*, December 20,
    1935; "Seek Love Clues," *Los Angeles Evening Herald and Express*; "Push Two Inquiries
    in the Todd Death," *New York Times*, December 20, 1935.

23. The Death of Thelma Todd

Blood in and around the car: "Thelma Todd Blood Clue Found in Car," *Boston Evening
    American*, December 21, 1935; "Todd Riddle Clarified by Key Figures," *Los Angeles
    Times*, December 21, 1935; "Blood Stains in Thelma Todd's Car," *Sunday Post* (UK),
    December 22, 1935.
Detectives starting the car: "Los Angeles Grand Jury Finds New Clues in Todd Tragedy,"
    Salt Lake Tribune, January 8, 1936; "Todd Death Tests Made," *Los Angeles Times*,
    December 23, 1935.
Alberta Schafer's fears: Rudy Schafer Jr., correspondence with Benny Drinnon, collection of
    Benny Drinnon.
"tragic and ineffably simple": "West Would Drop Enquiry," *Los Angeles Times*, December
    20, 1935.

Postscript

"religious, caring and a hard worker": Mae's granddaughter Robyn Osborne, interview by the author, September 6, 2012.

"as Miss Todd would have liked it": Rudy Schafer, announcement from on behalf of Thelma Todd's Inn, *Los Angeles Times*, December 20, 1935.

"Thelma Todd's death will never be solved": Letter from a crank, in the FBI files, collection of Benny Drinnon.

Raymond Babus and the threats against Roland West: "Movie Producer to Arrive Here on 60 Foot Yacht," *St. Petersburg Times*, December 1, 1937; "Todd Suicide Key Charged," *Los Angeles Times*, January 4, 1936.

Lila McComas's death: "Crash Fatal to Actress," *Los Angeles Times*, June 14, 1936.

Katie Turman's disappearance: "Santa Monica Police Seeking Two Lost Girls," *Los Angeles Times*, August 29, 1936.

Queenie Shannon: Nona Parker, "Movie Greats Are No Thrill," *St. Petersburg Times*, December 5, 1937; "Noted Brothers," *Los Angeles Times*, June 23, 1937; "Bulk of Roland West's Estate Left to Widow," *Los Angeles Times*, May 13, 1952.

West and Jewel Carmen divorce: "Alimony Given to Ex-Actress," *Los Angeles Times*, December 21, 1939; "Suit Settled by Ex-Actress," *Los Angeles Times*, November 29, 1940.

West and De Cicco at same party: Airi in Hollywood, *Clatskanie Chief*, September 2, 1949.

"Owner too ill to operate": Classifieds, *Los Angeles Times*, September 2 and 9, October 7, and December 16, 1951.

Roland West's death and funeral: "Roland West, Veteran Film Director, Dies," *Los Angeles Times*, April 1, 1952; "Final Tribute Paid Director Roland West," *Los Angeles Times*, April 3, 1952; "Bulk of Roland West's Estate," *Los Angeles Times*.

Mudslides at Castellammare: Details come from various sources, including the *Los Angeles Times* articles "$1,250,000 Allocated for Slide Area," April 24, 1958; and Charles E. Davis Jr., "Landslides Destroy Costly Homes in Pacific Palisades," June 6, 1965.

De Cicco and Gloria Vanderbilt: "Pat Di Cicco [*sic*], Heiress' Husband, in Hotel Row," *Los Angeles Times*, March 19, 1942; "Pat Di Cicco [*sic*] Cleared in Row over Pot to Cook Chicken," *Los Angeles Times*, March 27, 1942; "Poor Little Rich Girl Has Last Word," *Boston Sunday Advertiser Pictorial Review*, November 25, 1942.

United Artists Theaters: "Theater Jobs Cost $300,000," *Los Angeles Times*, November 27, 1949; "Goldwyn Will Play Santa at Theater Tree," *Los Angeles Times*, December 14, 1949.

Further information about De Cicco: "Punching Victim Sues Di Cicco [*sic*]," *Los Angeles Times*, February 24, 1937; "Screen Agent Sought on Traffic Charge," *Los Angeles Times*, February 27, 1937; "Pat De Cicco Given Release," *Los Angeles Times*, June 8, 1937; "Transfer of 12 Fox Theaters Arranged," *Los Angeles Times*, January 31, 1950; "Former Husband of Thelma Todd Broke," *Lewiston Sun*, July 15, 1938; untitled article, *Boston Sunday Advertiser Pictorial Review*, November 15, 1942.

Tony Cornero: All sources of information related to Cornero can be found in chapter 15, "The Gangsters."

Theory that West locked Thelma in the garage: Marvin J. Wolf and Katherine Mader, "Thelma Todd's Death Solved!," *Los Angeles Magazine*, December 1987.

"I'm too thoroughly New England": Dorothy Lubou, "Movie Men Are So Crude," *Motion Picture*, June 1929.

NOTE: *Many vintage magazine articles are available from an extraordinary website called the Media History Digital Library. This remarkable nonprofit organization is looking for donations and sponsors so they can continue making public domain magazines available to researchers and the general public. To find out more and support their cause, please visit their website: http://mediahistoryproject.org/.*

SELECTED BIBLIOGRAPHY

Ankerich, Michael G. *Dangerous Curves Atop Hollywood Heels*. Albany, GA: BearManor Media, 2011.

———. *Mae Murray: The Girl with the Bee-Stung Lips*. Lexington: University Press of Kentucky, 2013.

Bankhead, Tallulah. *My Autobiography*. Jackson: University Press of Mississippi, 2004.

Betts, Ernest. *Daily Express Film Book*. London: Daily Express, 1935.

Blum, Daniel. *A Pictorial History of the Silent Screen*. London: Spring Books, 1953.

Burk, Margaret Tante. *Are the Stars Out Tonight? The Story of the Famous Ambassador and Cocoanut Grove, "Hollywood's Hotel."* Los Angeles: Round Table West, 1980.

Calman, Craig. *100 Years of Brodies with Hal Roach*. Albany, GA: BearManor Media, 2014.

Cowie, Peter. *Louise Brooks: Lulu Forever*. Edited by Eva Prinz. New York: Rizzoli, 2006.

Davis, Lon. *Silent Lives: 100 Biographies of the Silent Film Era*. Albany, GA: BearManor Media, 2008.

Donati, William. *The Life and Death of Thelma Todd*. Jefferson, NC: McFarland, 2012.

Edmonds, Andy. *Hot Toddy: The True Story of Hollywood's Most Sensational Murder*. London: Macdonald, 1989.

Eyman, Scott. *Mary Pickford: From Here to Hollywood*. New York: Donald I. Fine, 1990.

Fiell, Charlotte, and Emmanuelle Dirix, eds. *Fashion Sourcebook 1920s*. London: Fiell Publishing, 2011.

———. *1930s Fashion: The Definitive Sourcebook*. London: Goodman/Fiell, 2012.

Fitzgerald, F. Scott. *The Great Gatsby*. London: Penguin Modern Classics, 2000.

Giroux, Robert. *A Deed of Death: The Story Behind the Unsolved Murder of Hollywood Director William Desmond Taylor*. New York: Knopf, 1990.

Golden, Eve. *John Gilbert: The Last of the Silent Film Stars*. Lexington: University Press of Kentucky, 2013.

———. *Platinum Girl: The Life and Legends of Jean Harlow*. New York: Abbeville Press, 1991.

———. *Vamp: The Rise and Fall of Theda Bara*. New York: Emprise Publishing, 1998.

Hampton, Benjamin B. *A History of the Movies*. New York: Covici Friede, 1931.

Harter, Chuck, and Michael J. Hayde. *Little Elf: A Celebration of Harry Langdon*. Albany, GA: BearManor Media, 2012.

Hayde, Michael J. *Chaplin's Vintage Year: The History of the Mutual-Chaplin Specials*. Albany, GA: BearManor Media, 2013.

Kanin, Garson. *Hollywood*. New York: Viking, 1974.

Kazan, Elia. *Elia Kazan: A Life*. New York: Knopf, 1988.

Kirby, Richard. *Desperately Seeking Marie Prevost*. Albany, GA: BearManor Media, 2014.

Kirkpatrick, Sidney D. *A Cast of Killers*. New York: E. P. Dutton, 1986.

Kobal, John. *People Will Talk*. London: Aurum, 1986.

Leider, Emily W. *Dark Lover: The Life and Death of Rudolph Valentino*. London: Faber and Faber, 2004.

Lobenthal, Joel. *Tallulah! The Life and Times of a Leading Lady*. London: Aurum, 2005.

Mackrell, Judith. *Flappers: Six Women of a Dangerous Generation*. London: Macmillan, 2013.

Mann, William J. *Kate: The Woman Who Was Hepburn*. London: Faber and Faber, 2006.

Marquez, Ernest. *Noir Afloat: Tony Cornero and the Notorious Gambling Ships of Southern California*. Santa Monica, CA: Angel City, 2011.

Massa, Steve. *Lame Brains and Lunatics: The Good, the Bad, and the Forgotten of Silent Comedy*. Albany, GA: BearManor Media, 2013.

Matzen, Robert. *Fireball: Carole Lombard and the Mystery of Flight 3*. Pittsburgh: GoodKnight Books, 2014.

McPherson, Edward. *Buster Keaton: Tempest in a Flat Hat*. London: Faber and Faber, 2004.

Merritt, Greg. *Room 1219: The Life of Fatty Arbuckle, the Mysterious Death of Virginia Rappe, and the Scandal That Changed Hollywood*. Chicago: Chicago Review Press, 2013.

Merton, Paul. *Silent Comedy*. London: Random House, 2007.

Miller, Patsy Ruth. *My Hollywood: When Both of Us Were Young*. Albany, GA: BearManor Media, 2012.

Morgan, Michelle. *The Mammoth Book of Hollywood Scandals*. London: Robinson, 2013.

———. *Marilyn Monroe: Private and Confidential*. New York: Skyhorse, 2012.

Munthe, Axel. *The Story of San Michele*. London: John Murray, 1937.

O'Brien, Scott. *Ruth Chatterton: Actress, Aviator, Author*. Albany, GA: BearManor Media, 2013.

Paris, Barry. *Louise Brooks: A Biography*. London: Mandarin Paperbacks, 1990.

Pickford, Mary. *Sunshine and Shadow*. London: William Heinemann, 1956.

Poulsen, Ellen. *The Case Against Lucky Luciano: New York's Most Sensational Vice Trial*. New York: Clinton Cook, 2007.

Powell, Hickman. *Lucky Luciano: The Man Who Organized Crime in America*. New York: Barricade, 2000.

Rice, Christina. *Ann Dvorak: Hollywood's Forgotten Rebel*. Lexington: University Press of Kentucky, 2013.

Rooney, Darrell, and Mark A. Vieira. *Harlow in Hollywood: The Blonde Bombshell in the Glamour Capital, 1928–1937*. Santa Monica, CA: Angel City, 2011.

Rydzewski, Steve. *For Art's Sake: The Biography & Filmography of Ben Turpin*. Albany, GA: BearManor Media, 2013.

Schessler, Ken. *This Is Hollywood: An Unusual Movieland Guide.* 11th ed. Redlands, CA: Ken Schessler, 1993.

Schickel, Richard, and George Perry. *Bette Davis: Larger Than Life.* Philadelphia: Running Press, 2009.

Schmidt, Christel, ed. *Mary Pickford: Queen of the Movies.* Lexington: University Press of Kentucky, 2012.

Schroeder, Barbara, and Clark Fogg. *Beverly Hills Confidential: A Century of Stars, Scandals and Murders.* Santa Monica, CA: Angel City, 2012.

S.D., Trav. *Chain of Fools: Silent Comedy and Its Legacies from Nickelodeons to YouTube.* Albany, GA: BearManor Media, 2013.

Shearer, Stephen Michael. *Gloria Swanson: The Ultimate Star.* New York: Thomas Dunne, 2013.

Stenn, David. *Bombshell: The Life and Death of Jean Harlow.* New York: Doubleday, 1993.

———. *Clara Bow: Runnin' Wild.* London: Ebury, 1989.

Stoliar, Steve. *Raised Eyebrows: My Years Inside Groucho's House.* Albany, GA: BearManor Media, 2011.

Stumpf, Charles. *ZaSu Pitts: The Life and Career.* Jefferson, NC: McFarland, 2009.

Swindell, Larry. *The Last Hero: A Biography of Gary Cooper.* London: Robson, 1981.

———. *Screwball: The Life of Carole Lombard.* New York: William Morrow, 1975.

Tornabene, Lyn. *Long Live the King: A Biography of Clark Gable.* New York: Pocket Books, 1976.

Torrence, Bruce. *Hollywood: The First 100 Years.* Hollywood: Hollywood Chamber of Commerce and Fiske Enterprises, 1979.

Vanderbilt, Gloria. *Black Knight, White Knight.* New York: Knopf, 1987.

Webb, Michael, ed. *Hollywood: Legend and Reality.* London: Pavilion, 1986.

Wilkerson, Tichi, and Marcia Borie. *The Hollywood Reporter: The Golden Years.* New York: Coward-McCann, 1984.

Wills, David, and Stephen Schmidt. *Hollywood in Kodachrome.* New York: It Books, 2013.

Wolf, Marvin J., and Katherine Mader. *Fallen Angels: Chronicles of L.A. Crime and Mystery.* New York: Ballantine, 1986.

Yallop, David. *The Day the Laughter Stopped.* London: Corgi Books, 1991.

INDEX